The Rise of Christianity in Northern Europe, 300–1000

Cassell Religious Studies

This series is an open forum for a variety of approaches to the study of theology and religion. It is also 'open' in the sense that it encourages work which explores the relationship between religion and neighbouring disciplines.

Published titles in this series:

God's Place in the World: Sacred Space and the Sacred Place in Judaism
   by Seth Kunin

The Meaning of Lives: Biography, Autobiography and the Spiritual Quest
   by Richard A. Hutch

Mormon Identities in Transition edited by Douglas J. Davies

Forthcoming titles in the series:

Early Christian Historiography: Narratives of Retribution by G.W. Trompf

Messianic Judaism by Dan Cohn-Sherbok

The Rise of Christianity in Northern Europe, 300–1000

Carole M. Cusack

CASSELL

London and New York

Cassell
Wellington House, 125 Strand, London WC2R 0BB
370 Lexington Avenue, New York, NY 10017-6550

First published in hardback as *Conversion Among the Germanic Peoples* in 1998
Reprinted in paperback in 1999

British Library Cataloguing in Publication Data
A catalogue record for this book is available from the British Library.

ISBN 0 304 70155 6 (hardback)
 0 304 70735 X (paperback)

Library of Congress Cataloging-in-Publication Data
Cusack, Carole M., 1962–
     The rise of Christianity in Northern Europe, 300–1000/Carole M. Cusack.
      p. cm.
     Includes bibliographical references and index.
     ISBN 0-304-70155-6 (hardcover): 0-304-70735-X (paperback)
     1. Christianity and other religions—Germanic. 2. Germanic
peoples—Religion. 3. Germanic peoples—Missions. 4. Conversion—
Case studies. 5. Europe—Church history. 6. Europe—Church
history—600–1500. I. Title.
BR128.G4C88 1998
274.3′02–dc21   97–45096
                                                                CIP

Typeset by BookEns Ltd, Royston, Herts.
Printed and bound in Great Britain by Bookcraft (Bath) Ltd,
Midsomer Norton, Somerset.

Contents

Preface   vi

Acknowledgements   viii

Abbreviations   x

1 The nature of conversion   1

2 Christianity and the Germanic peoples in late antiquity   30

3 The Franks: Arianism and Catholicism   63

4 The Anglo-Saxons: reclaiming the lost province   88

5 Anglo-Saxon missions to the continent   119

6 Christianity in the North   135

7 The conversion of Iceland   158

8 Conclusion   173

Bibliography   181

Index   207

Preface

This book began in 1986 as a study of those aspects of Germanic pre-Christian religion which were incorporated into Christianity after the conversion. Rather than focusing on the conversion itself, the modification of Christianity by the converted group was examined. However, after two years of part-time candidature studying for a doctorate, my interests had changed, and the encounter between the representatives of Christianity and the priests and leaders of the Germanic kingdoms had assumed paramount importance. It seemed that the indigenization of Christianity by the Germanic peoples was a direct result of this encounter. Also, the period of history examined had changed. The original plan concentrated on the Anglo-Saxons: the book as it now stands has become a survey of the experience of conversion for the Germanic peoples from the third to the eleventh centuries.

This book is a study of the process of conversion among the Germanic peoples in the late antique and early medieval periods. The intent is twofold: to examine previous scholarship on conversion and to develop a model of conversion appropriate to the Germanic peoples; and to produce a comparative study of six Germanic conversions.

Chapter 1 reviews the existing models of conversion developed by scholars in a number of fields, principally psychology, anthropology and religious studies. All these models have flaws and biases which make them inapplicable to mass conversions in the pre-modern era; the most common problem being a view of conversion as a purely individual, interior experience. They do, however, offer cross-disciplinary possibilities which have yet to be fully realized by historians. This book develops an alternative model which explores the cognitive and social structures of pre-Christian Germanic society; highlights the roles and motivations of agents of mission and traditional secular and religious leaders; validates the spiritual dimension of corporate decision-making in religious transition; and celebrates the indigenization of Christianity by the mission-field cultures.

Chapters 2 to 7 are case studies which apply this model to the conversions of the Goths, Franks, Anglo-Saxons, continental Saxons, Scandinavians, and Icelanders. Despite the geographical and temporal variation, a striking similarity is found. A virtually identical set of elements was present in all these conversions. These included a proto-feudal social organization consisting of a sacral king maintained by a band of retainers, casual and incidental contacts with Christianity preceding the arrival of agents of conversion who carry with them the threat of political domination. The decision for the new faith is therefore made in circumstances where the survival of the traditional culture is in doubt. The Christianity which results from such corporate decisions incorporates elements of the old religion, due to defensive adaptation on the part of the traditional culture, which may be conscious or unconscious. The reciprocal nature of the interaction becomes apparent; the group is converted but Christianity also changes.

Finally, Chapter 8 presents in summary form the insights from the case studies.

Acknowledgements

This book is a revised version of my 1995 doctoral thesis at the University of Sydney. I wish to thank Emeritus Professor Eric J. Sharpe for nine years of patient and occasionally inspired supervision, and for advising me to read Chesterton whenever I was tired or discouraged. This book could not have been written without him. The School of Studies in Religion at the University of Sydney provided me with congenial colleagues, the opportunity to teach courses relevant to my research since 1985, and a group of fellow-travellers in the School's Postgraduate Seminar. Professor Garry W. Trompf and Dr Tony Swain require special thanks for friendship and support over a long time.

The material in Chapter 1 has previously appeared twice: in a very rough form as 'Methodological Problems in the Study of Mission and Conversion', in C. Cusack and J. Wooding (eds), *Progress, What Progress?*, Sydney University Postgraduate Representative Association, 1992, pp. 108–17; and in a more refined form as 'Towards a General Theory of Conversion', in Lynette Olson (ed.), *Religious Change, Conversion and Culture*, Sydney Studies in Society and Culture, no. 12, 1996, pp. 1–21.

Chapter 2 benefited from the extensive knowledge of Late Antiquity of my colleague Ruth Lewin, and the participants of the Australian Association for the Study of Religion Conference, 3–6 October 1991, who heard an earlier draft of the chapter and offered their comments. My postgraduate student Daniel Bray provided the references on Indo-European sacral kingship, and allowed me to read his 1994 Fourth Year Honours paper 'Sacral Kingship in Indo-European Religion'.

Chapter 3 owes much to Jonathan Barlow of the Department of History, University of Queensland, who allowed me to read draft chapters of his 1993 doctoral thesis 'The Success of the Franks: Regional Continuity in Northern Gaul in Late Antiquity', which he completed in the Department of History, University of Sydney. In February 1992 Jonathan and I participated in a workshop co-ordinated by Dr Lynette Olson of Sydney's History Department, on 'Religious Change' at the XVIth Australian and New Zealand Association for Medieval and Renaissance Studies (ANZAMRS) Conference, University of Melbourne, which decisively influenced the shape and content of the final draft of Chapter 3.

Jonathan Wooding, my co-teacher for ten years of the Adult Matriculation Course 'The Germanic World to 1000 CE', is the chief influence on Chapter 4. Students from that course, including Sheleyah Niven, Mark Simmonds, Madeleine Rigby, Janet Kahl and Don Barrett, produced essays which entertained me and often contained material I had overlooked. An early draft of this chapter entitled 'The Role of the Interpreter in the Conversion of the Anglo-Saxons: Missionary's Mouthpiece or Doctrinal Diplomat?' was presented at the XIVth ANZAMRS Conference, University of Sydney, February 1988, where the criticisms of Audrey Meaney were especially helpful.

For Chapter 6 I would like to thank Ruth Odlander and Ken Jørgensen, who provided me with translations from Danish, Swedish and Norwegian secondary sources. Avril Vorsay deserves thanks for providing me with translations from French and German secondary sources.

Chapter 7 benefited from many conversations with Louise Trott, whose doctorate on women and magic in the Icelandic sagas had many points of interest for me. Professor Eric J. Sharpe introduced me to the subject of the conversion of Iceland in 1982 in a Religious Studies Second Year Honours course, 'The Sociology of Germanic Religion', and we have had many interesting conversations since. I also remember with fondness the late Professor Harold Leslie Rogers of the English Department, University of Sydney, who taught me Old Icelandic in 1986.

Many friends assisted me during the production of my doctoral thesis and the revision which resulted in this book. Special thanks are due to Andrew Gollan for Latin translations at short notice and great friendship; to Danny Yee for editing and intellectual discipline; Guy Tranter for proofreading and symphony concerts; Matthew Charet and Mark Byrne for support and friendship at work; my family — John, Maree, Julie, Kate and John Patrick; my oldest friend Andrea; and Michael Usher, Tangerine and Leo for support and friendship at home.

Abbreviations

AASR	Australian Association for the Study of Religion
AB	Analecta Bollandiana
ANZAMRS	Australian and New Zealand Association for Medieval and Renaissance Studies
A-SE	Anglo-Saxon England
BAR	British Archaeological Reports
CH	Church History
CSSH	Comparative Studies in Society and History
GRBS	Greek Roman and Byzantine Studies
JIS	Journal of Indo-European Studies
JMH	Journal of Medieval History
JRA	Journal of Religion in Africa
JRH	Journal of Religious History
JRS	Journal of Roman Studies
JTS	Journal of Theological Studies
MA	Medieval Archaeology
MGH	Monumenta Germaniae Historica
MGH:AA	Auctorum Antiquissimorum
MGH:E	Epistolarum
MGH:S	Scriptorum
MGH:SRG	Scriptores Rerum Germanicarum in Usum Scholarum
MGH:SRM	Scriptorum Rerum Merovingicarum
M&H	Medievalia et Humanistica
MS	Medieval Scandinavia
NMS	Nottingham Medieval Studies
NP-NF	Nicene and Post-Nicene Fathers
P&P	Past and Present
PL	Patrologiae Latinae
RBPH	Revue Belge de Philologie et d'Histoire

1   The nature of conversion

One finds broad disagreements about the factors behind conversion. ... This range of opinion can be explained ... by the fact that the term *conversion* has led researchers to believe that everything under that name in different contexts refers to the same phenomenon.

Nils G. Holm[1]

Introduction

The history of the conversion to Christianity of the Germanic peoples has been examined in a number of fine books and articles. E.A. Thompson's *The Visigoths in the Time of Ulfila*, Henry Mayr-Harting's *The Coming of Christianity to Anglo-Saxon England*, Dag Strömbäck's *The Conversion of Iceland* and Georg Sverdrup's *Da Norge ble Kristnet* have all made an impressive contribution to understanding this particular process among these particular peoples. James C. Russell's recent *The Germanization of Early Medieval Christianity* also proposes a model of 'religious interaction between folk-religious societies and universal religions'[2] which locates the conversion of the Germanic peoples in the context of other 'colonial' Christian expansions. Russell's model is indebted to anthropological and post-colonial thought, and heralds a new era in late antique and early medieval religious studies. The focus is as much on how the Germans inculturated Christianity as it is on how Christianity transformed them. However, the book concludes with the death of Boniface in 754, and therefore is not an effective general survey, as it excludes the conversions of Scandinavia and Iceland. Therefore this book aims to provide a general survey of the conversion to Christianity of the Germanic peoples. In the first chapter a framework for the interpretation of the conversion experience for the Germanic peoples is proposed, and then successive chapters examine the conversions of the Goths, the Franks, the Anglo-Saxons, the Continental Saxons, the Scandinavians and the Icelanders in the light of that framework.

The phenomenon of conversion to Christianity may be approached from many differing viewpoints: as history of missions; as a sociological process;

as a personal journey from unbelief to faith; and as an aspect of the political and territorial expansion which has advanced the power of certain hegemonic cultures throughout the last two thousand years. There are as many viewpoints as there are viewers. Each of these perspectives may be illuminating, but difficulties result in attempting to discern the fundamental nature of conversion amid the plethora of methodologies.

Eric J. Sharpe has said that the missionary historian should ideally be to some extent a social, political and economic historian; a geographer, ethnologist and historian of religions; as well as a Christian historian in the more usual sense.[3] This daunting list of skills reveals the complexity of studying religious phenomena. There can be no argument with the basic contention of Sharpe's argument regarding the writing of history: that a chronicle as a factual record of the past, if such a thing can exist, is only part of the picture. The historian inevitably enters into the broader business of historiography, where opinions about societies and about the construction of the past are also at issue. History involves the interpretation of material as well as mere cataloguing, and interpretation is a subjective activity. The regulation of this subjectivity is one of the perennial challenges of history.

Sociological approaches to conversion

Until the edifice of Christianity was challenged thoroughly in the mid-nineteenth century, histories of conversion tended to speak of the triumph of the Holy Spirit and the progress of salvation. Along with the questioning of the truth of Christianity, the nineteenth century saw the development of the idea of history as a science, with methods derived from those of the physical sciences, which rely on observation of evidence and demonstration of proof.[4] Naturally, this social-scientific form of history was not without its own biases, but it did effectively discourage the more hagiographical style of missiological history. Throughout the twentieth century missiological writings have become increasingly secularized. Sharpe notes that this has not necessarily affected the quality of much of the work in question, and indeed has produced a greater depth of perception in many cases:

> not all missionary historians are Christians; and those who are, are not identical Christians. Theological assessments are legion. At the risk of sounding overly dogmatic, I would state my own opinion that unless the 'sociological factors' have been understood – thoroughly understood, on a basis of all the available evidence – the superimposition of the will of God upon the record may remain arbitrary.[5]

Sociological factors have enjoyed increasing attention since the late nineteenth century, following the work of Emile Durkheim and Max Weber. Both these scholars sought social explanations for religious phenomena. The attractions of such an empirical approach are immediately obvious: grappling with the truth-claims of Christianity or attempting to analyse theological propositions are difficult activities, because of their insubstantiality (in empirical terms); whereas physical manifestations of religious belief in the life of the community of believers are observable realities.

The sociologist proposes social explanations of events such as conversion to Christianity by a society. O'Dea's description of the conversion of the Scandinavians exemplifies this approach:

> the conversion of the Nordic peoples to Christianity coincided with the attainment of national unity and a vast process of expansion. Christian kingship, consecrated by ecclesiastical rites and given the sacred charisma of Church approval, was an element aiding the development of such a unity. Christianity supported and in fact partially inspired these efforts of unification.[6]

The societal changes coinciding with the acceptance of Christianity are documented, but the internal transformation of individuals is neglected, or deemed inaccessible. It is quite easy to explain the adoption of a new religion in terms of social phenomena. Factors such as the relation of the economic conditions of the society to the form of religion developed,[7] the cultural prestige that the new religion has in the eyes of the prospective adherents,[8] the social processes involved in the formation of the self,[9] and the charisma of the missionary and his status in the society in question,[10] are advanced by the sociologist to illuminate the events leading to the acceptance of a new faith.

The value of such an approach is indisputable, and its insights into events such as mass conversions (and mass movements in religion in general) are sometimes startling.[11] However, the sociological approach has limitations. The internal experience of the individual convert is lost, for example. The most obvious difficulty with the application of the sociological method to religious phenomena is that its relentlessly materialist reductionism ignores the supernatural focus of most religion.[12] Durkheim considered the concept of a deity to be a society's projection of its ideal self. This view can lead to the trivialization of religious phenomena and the neglect of the profound experiential dimensions of religion, which are seen by many believers to be the essence of being religious. A secondary problem is the inaccessibility of much sociological terminology, as evidenced by Peter Berger's definition of conversion:

in other words, 'conversion' (that is, individual 'transference' into another world) is always possible in principle. This possibility increases with the degree of instability or discontinuity of the plausibility structure in question. ... Conversely, the individual who wishes to convert, and (more importantly) to 'stay converted', must engineer his social life in accordance with this purpose. Thus he must disassociate himself from those individuals or groups that constituted the plausibility structure of his past religious reality ...[13]

Berger is describing an essentially familiar experience in terminology so forbidding as to render the subject incomprehensible.

Ultimately sociological approaches, as with any exclusive methodological position, are unable to provide a comprehensive exposition of conversion in all its complexity. Recent scholarship has become increasingly eclectic, proposing models and frameworks informed by a multiplicity of disciplines.[14]

Psychological approaches to conversion

If sociology may be accused of giving too shallow and too external a picture of conversion, certain scholars who developed their methods under the influence of the 'psychology of religion' school, originating with William James' ground-breaking study *The Varieties of Religious Experience*, are culpable of doing precisely the opposite. Arthur Darby Nock, whose great work *Conversion* remains impressive sixty years after publication, concentrated on a definition of 'conversion' as an essentially individual, experiential phenomenon. He distinguished between 'adhesion', which was acceptance of a religious position to a degree but which required no absolute allegiance, and 'conversion', of which his famous definition, owing much to James, is: 'by conversion we mean the reorienting of the soul of an individual, his deliberate turning from indifference or from an earlier form of piety to another, a turning which implies a consciousness that a great change is involved, that the old was wrong and the new is right'.[15]

Nock's definition does two things: makes conversion a phenomenon which involves moral judgements; and locates that phenomenon within the psyche of the individual. The mass focus of the sociologists is totally absent; only an individual can be converted. Nock was concerned to demonstrate the appropriateness of his definition, and to justify the progress of Christianity within its terms. He believed he could identify 'elements in the mind of the time'[16] which explained the success of Christianity as a missionary religion. Speculation on the contents of the mind of any other person or era is a perilous activity, and this statement of principle led Nock to conclude that in the ancient world no religion (apart from Christianity and Judaism) required conversion, because they did not worship deities which required absolute allegiance. Mithraism, for Nock, did not own its faithful in the way the Judeo-Christian religious complex did.[17]

Nock analysed the religious appeal of the mystery cults, which were popular in the late Roman period along with Christianity, in some detail. That these cults were popular and had a profound spiritual effect on the lives of the devotees is demonstrated by spiritual autobiographies such as Apuleius' *The Golden Ass*, which describes the author's devotion to Isis, and the change that this experience wrought in his life. Nock identified three major aspects of these cults: they had elaborate pictures of the universe, which particularly involved astrology; they were fundamentally concerned with immortality and its acquisition through ritual and knowledge; and they displayed great curiosity about supernatural phenomena. In short, the mystery cults offered knowledge about otherwise unknown things and their appeal was essentially gnostic.

In terms of conversion as Nock defines it, these cults were closer to the Judeo-Christian norm than other forms of pre-Christian religion; devotees of Isis, Sarapis, Cybele and other oriental deities were required to make substantial changes to their lives (Propertius' poems about his mistress Cynthia's devotions to Isis show this).[18] Nock also considers conversion to various philosophical systems of the ancient world, and concluded that: 'any philosophy of the time set up a standard of values different from those of the world outside and could serve as a stimulus to a stern life, and therefore be something like conversion when it came to a man living carelessly'.[19] He notes that the term used for conversion to philosophy was *epistrophe*, which Plato used in the sense of a turning round of the soul[20] and which was later used by Christians to speak of conversion. *Conversio* has the same meaning in Latin, of turning from carelessness to true piety. In the ancient world some philosophers even appealed to their students in terms of faith, exhorting them to believe.

Nock saw a direct relationship between this attitude and that of Christianity, asserting that: 'In the last struggle Christian dogma was in conflict not with the free Greek spirit, but with other dogma and with fossilized tradition. The philosophy which addressed itself to the world at large was a dogmatic philosophy seeking to save souls.'[21] It must be suspected here that Nock is seeking to present the spirit of Plato and that of Christianity as essentially in harmony. There is historical precedent for this view, but it is not applicable to all varieties of Christianity. Christianity differs from the philosophical schools and the mystery cults in that it demands absolute allegiance, the Christian God is a 'jealous God'. The conversion experience of Paul, who turned from persecution of Christians to evangelism and eventual martyrdom, would appear to be Nock's paradigm.

So far Nock's analysis of the phenomenon of conversion is confined to the inner state of the individual, who chooses to belong to a new faith because of a personal spiritual conviction. Chapter XII, 'The Spread of Christianity as a Social Phenomenon' attempts to deal with a broader picture. Nock considered how the Christians appeared to the society in which they lived, and made the point that the image of Christianity was negative, that it was the mob who wanted Christians thrown to the lions. However, Nock does not adequately account for the mass conversions which took place in the late antique and early medieval periods, perhaps because he cannot: such a mass movement, in terms of his definition, could not be an instance of conversion.

The same theoretical problems are encountered in the work of a near-contemporary scholar, A. C. Underwood. His study *Conversion: Christian and Non-Christian* is subtitled 'A Comparative and Psychological Study', and commenced with an admission that most research up to that point (1925) had been Protestant and Evangelical in orientation, and a claim that his study corrected this deficiency. However Underwood has an *agendum* of his own: his book is an avowed exploration of the fundamental identity of religious experience, and his approach is openly psychological. The authorities he cites to establish a definition of conversion (for example, Starbuck and James) all stress suddenness and moral–personal integration as features of the conversion experience,[22] and Underwood's own definition of conversion is 'the unification of the unhappy soul by its obtaining a stronger grip on religious realities'.[23]

Underwood traced this form of individual conversion through the Old Testament and classical Christianity, then through Hinduism, Buddhism, Islam, and finally the philosophical schools of Greece and Rome. In dealing with Islam, Underwood revealed the same distaste for mass movements as Nock. He referred to the widespread apostasy after the death of Muhammad, and pointed out that subsequent 'conversion of millions of non-Arabs was the work, not of apostles, but of generals. With the rise of Sufism, however, we get a return to greater inwardness in religion.'[24] Underwood's discussion of the mystery cults took a similar direction, and stressed the power of ritual to create profound emotional and spiritual agitation. This is difficult to reconcile with Christian baptism, where the ritual act is supposed to follow the spiritual experience. The final sections of *Conversion: Christian and Non-Christian* deal with a purely psychological theory of conversion and the comparative aspects of the phenomenon. Here Underwood made an important point: while conversion is a human fact, and found in all religions, its incidence is largely affected by the traditions and expectations of the group and of the period.[25]

This observation contained the kernel of the problem with the inward-looking and individualistic definition of conversion. All studies of religious experience conducted from a comparative viewpoint have the problem that it is not really possible to separate the experience which is being described from its social, religious and cultural context. Rudolf Otto in *The Idea of the Holy*[26] attempted to prove that there was one common religious experience found in all world religions. His basic experience most closely resembled that of the Old Testament theophany, filtered through German Romanticism,[27] and was not really appropriate to the religious experience found in Eastern religions.

A further problem which emerged from his study is that the comparison of religious experiences is really the comparison of the accounts given by the experiencers, and these accounts are inevitably dependent on their cultural and religious presuppositions and on how much they are prepared to reveal. This does not solve the question of whether the experience is the same; indeed it widens the scope of the argument. This position was essentially adopted by R. C. Zaehner in *Mysticism: Sacred and Profane*, in which he proposed that there were three types of religious experience: nature mysticism, monistic mysticism and theistic mysticism. This debate reached its apogee with the work of Steven Katz,[28] who argued that the isolation of pure experience was impossible and that the cultural frameworks of the experiencers must *ipso facto* constitute the experience.

The relevance of this debate concerning mystical experience to the discussion of conversion is obvious: to posit that there is an essential conversion experience, and that all authentic conversions involve that interior change narrows the scope of the term severely. If conversion requires this internal experience, then all those societies which converted for other reasons (political, social, the desire to have the protection of a more powerful deity, and so on), with limited or no understanding of the doctrines of the new faith, and grew slowly into piety throughout the generations, were never truly converted, never received the true faith.

That even the champions of individual, personal and psychological conversion were aware of the problems here is revealed by Underwood's caution that:

> it is ... important to point out that the significance of what has been said is not exhausted by saying that the convert imposes on his experience the doctrinal themes of the faith in which he finds unification. The doctrinal system also controls to a large extent his expectations, and for this reason he tends to discover in his conversion what he has been led to expect to find.[29]

In other words, the conversion experience is not really the authenticated constant for which Underwood has argued. It is culturally conditioned and easily manipulated, and may be a misleading standard for a model of conversion. Perhaps mass conversions may be authentic in some sense too.

Contemporary Christian approaches to conversion

Much missiological writing of the second half of the twentieth century is still by Christians, many of them missionaries working in the field, and concerned to resolve dilemmas they have personally encountered. The next two sections of this chapter tend also to overlap, as many Christian theorists of conversion are influenced by anthropological models. Among committed Christian writers, however, the interior view of conversion often persists. In missionary writing from the 1950s it is possible to discern the emergence of a variety of trends in missionary activity and writing about missionary activity. These trends may be broadly classified into the 'ecumenical' and the 'evangelical'. The evangelical pattern has continued to conform strongly to the traditional eschatological understanding of mission and individual salvation: the ecumenical view has adapted to social and political change.

The 1960s were a decade of great social instability and rapid change, necessitating a new attitude as the traditional centre and periphery of the Empire and the colonies disintegrated. In response to this:

> the West became ever more conscious of its faults, mistakes and shortcomings. Where the West did not realize this of its own accord, the Third World was only too ready to point it out. . . . Western colonialism, civilisation and attitudes of superiority came under fire, as did 'Western Religion'. This resulted in the West, and Western Christian churches, adopting an apologetic attitude.[30]

Concepts in mission such as 'witness' began to be replaced by the notion of 'dialogue', in which the non-Christian religions were accorded status and the encounter between Christianity and such faiths was perceived as a meeting of equals. The emphasis also shifted from active to passive modes of mission, where Christian presence was stressed rather than active intervention.

The assemblies of the World Council of Churches since that of Uppsala in 1968 have favoured a positive evaluation of the world and of the process of secularization, stressing that the Church is part of the world and must respond to it. The conservative Evangelical wing responded to such liberalism by issuing the Frankfurt Declaration in 1970, which identified seven basic elements of mission:

> (i) the basis of mission is to be founded only in the command of the risen Christ; (ii) the main purpose of mission is the glorification of God, not humanization; (iii) there is no salvation apart from Jesus Christ; (iv) eternal salvation is attained through preaching, conversion and baptism; (v) the concrete and visible task of mission is to establish a church as the new people of God; (vi) the offer of salvation is for all men, but the adherents of non-Christian religions only share

in that salvation through faith, conversion and baptism; (vii) the Church is engaged in mission until Christ comes again.[31]

It is clear that the supporters of this position can offer the scholar few insights in the development of a historically and culturally sophisticated approach to conversion. The Frankfurt Declaration asserts the continued relevance of traditional theological understandings of conversion, but does not engage with the vexed question of the relationship between Christianity and culture. Among ecumenical Christians, attempts to develop a theory of mission and conversion have fared better.

One major breakthrough this century is the recognition by Christian writers that any preaching of a new faith involves cross-cultural communication.[32] It must also be remembered that culture is inextricably tied to language, and that language differences are a major barrier to cross-cultural communication.[33] Obvious as this seems, it was not generally acknowledged in earlier missionary efforts.[34] The issue is one of missionaries needing to be aware of their cultural presuppositions, and needing to be attuned to the culture of their audience. Friedrich Dierks observed that the meaning of a message is not determined by the sender, but by the receiver:

> at this point an important rule of communication is applicable, namely that the meaning of a message does not reside in the words in which the message is couched, but in receptors and their world-view. When a missionary proclaims the Christian message, he should realise that he cannot really transfer the meaning of his message to its receptors; rather, it is they who apply the meaning themselves.[35]

This recognition has been enthusiastically taken up by some, who emphasize the example of St Paul and his willingness to adapt his message to different audiences. It is also congruent with the attempt of the West to abandon its more stridently colonial habits: as Hillman observed, the fact that Christianity has become an integral part of Western cultures 'does not mean that those have become Christian cultures. ... No particular set of cultural patterns and social structures is in itself specifically Christian.'[36] This rehabilitation of mission-field cultures has produced many interesting insights into the ways in which the Christian message has become obscured by cultural accretions which are mistakenly perceived as essential to the faith.

One particularly fascinating example of this is Friedrich Dierks' encounter with an African theologian, Gabriel Setiloane, author of *The Image of God among the Sotho-Tswana*. Dierks presents this meeting in the context of an article about the interference of 'world-view' in cross-cultural communication. He wrote:

I asked him whether the concept of God as he had described it was a personal one, so that one could speak of God and apply to God the personal pronoun 'you', as one usually does with human beings, or whether his concept of God was that of an impersonal power. Setiloane replied that the question of whether God was personal or impersonal originated in a typically Western world-view which was foreign to the Sotho-Tswana. He then defended the opinion that the image of God should not be bound to a dualistic Western thought-pattern where God must be either personal or impersonal. God's personhood is a concept which could also be conceived of in non-dualistic African thought-forms where a personal God and an impersonal divine power are not mutually exclusive concepts.[37]

Setiloane's challenge is a profound one. Western Christianity has absorbed Western thought-forms, many of which distort the Christian message. Western thought is dualistic,[38] as Setiloane claims. It also is excessively 'spiritualized', seeing the physical dimension as inherently negative; it has internalized highly complex intellectual structures which are foreign to other cultures; and it is biased in favour of the individual.[39] This last bias is present, as has been demonstrated, in Western views of mission and conversion.

Several others in the field of mission have emphasized the similarity between the function of the missionary and that of the anthropologist,[40] and have suggested ethno-theological sensitivity[41] and the adoption of anthropologically developed roles in order to relate effectively to alien societies. The latter suggestion is remarkably useful. A missionary cannot immediately expect to be acknowledged by a society and allocated a place within it. The employment of insider and outsider roles (an insider role is one where the missionary gains acceptance as a true member of the society and an outsider role is one where the missionary accepts his/her alienness and attempts to provide services by means of this alienness) makes the development of a relationship possible. To be accepted as an insider implies full initiation into the society, not merely being well-informed or sympathetic, so insider roles are more difficult to sustain, because 'the person who wants to become a true insider needs to recognize that unless he turns away more or less completely from his own culture and people, he is bound to create serious if not insurmountable conflict'.[42] This cultural conflict often results in the community's losing faith in the missionary as a trustworthy person. Outsider roles do not require that the missionary or anthropologist abandon their own culture and are therefore easier to maintain. All of these studies are immensely useful in helping the scholar come to grips with missions throughout history. Most of the people who have developed these broadly anthropological approaches are themselves Christians. However, among others in the Church contingent this recognition of other cultures has merely set off alarms about potential identity crises for missionaries,[43] and resulted in the pitting of a biblical view of missionary activity against a culturally-aware view.[44]

What then can be concluded about Christian attempts to formulate a theory of mission and conversion which gives full recognition to the legitimacy of the mass movement and which does not rely on an exclusively Western, interior view of the role of religion in human life? It must be acknowledged that Christian doctrine can and should be separated from the cultural presuppositions of the West. Luzbetak commented:

> by 'culture' we mean the set of socially-shared ideas that a given society (or, segment of it, in the case of subcultures) has for being a success in life and for solving human problems. ... Not everything in Jewish culture was approved or tolerated by Jesus. He nevertheless was born a true Jew and could instantly be recognized as a Galilean, rejecting only what was incompatible with His divinity and His mission.[45]

This definition has a positive view of human cultures and their role in providing foundations for people's lives and acknowledges that a person's culture is an essential part of them. What follows from this is an understanding that for those cultures which do not accord great status to the individual, but have a more collective emphasis, it is inappropriate to apply versions of Christianity which focus strongly on individual, interior religious sentiment, because such a version of Christianity is alien to such a culture. The next recognition is that there is a plurality of Christianities, throughout history and across varying cultures, and that this is both inevitable and not to be regretted. It is inevitable because: 'just as socialization seems to be a necessary condition for religiosity – religion is learned – so the situational factors seem to be intervening variables which modify learned beliefs and practices'.[46]

Anthropological approaches to conversion

The most influential recent theory of conversion is that proposed by Robin Horton, an Africanist, in the 1970s. Horton's seminal article, 'African Conversion', reviewed John Peel's book *Aladura,* in which Peel advanced an essentially sociological explanation of the conversion process among the Yoruba. Horton expressed doubts about Peel's failure to distinguish between this-worldly and other-worldly religions, and his untested assumption that certain peoples or groups have a greater tendency to be rational than others. He commented:

> one final criticism of *Aladura* concerns the phenomenon of conversion ... he

makes a serious slip when he talks of Christianity as if it were one cult coming in alongside the existing cults. ... For one salient feature of Christian proselytization in Yorubaland has surely been the identification of the Christian God with the indigenous supreme being Olorun, and the presentation of Christianity as the 'true' way of contacting this being.[47]

Horton isolated three main elements in African cultures which facilitated conversion to Christianity and Islam. First, there was the intellectual background: those concepts current in a given society which may be harmonized with, or said to anticipate, Christian concepts. Here he focused on concepts of a supreme being who may be equated with the Christian God. Horton's second element is the recognition that the requirements of the microcosm differ from those of the macrocosm. Here he focused on the differences between local spirits and the supreme being, linking these to the encounter of tribal societies with colonizing powers. The final element of African culture which facilitated conversion was, for Horton, the specialized roles of secular and religious leaders within tribal society.

Some critics of Horton have seen Horton's focus on the supreme being within the 'intellectual background' as a limitation: while conceding that the Horton theory 'correct[s] some of the *lacunae* in sociological theories of change', Lesley Stevens noted that Horton's ideas did not seem to fit the conversion of other African peoples, specifically the Haya.[48] This claim that the Haya elude the Horton paradigm casts some doubt on its universal applicability. Yet the issue of the role of the Supreme Being in conversion to Christianity in Africa is more problematic than this criticism might suggest.

The Supreme Being has been a contentious concept in comparative religious studies, because of its links with the possible validation of the truth-claims of particular religions. Theories of the origin of religion are as varied as totemism, animism and Freud's psychoanalytic theory.[49] They are all classifiable as evolutionary or Edenic, where the evolutionary model posits that religious concepts were originally simple and became complex, and the Edenic model posits that truth and complexity were originally present and that religious ideas have since become corrupted.[50]

In the tangled political context of post-colonialism, the search for authentic aboriginal concepts is fraught with difficulties. Horton's unquestioning acceptance that Olorun is an indigenous Supreme Being, rather than an imported or hybrid deity resulting from centuries of casual and deliberate contact between Africans and Europeans in trading and missionary activities, seems naïve in the light of other studies.[51] The criticisms of ahistoricity which have been levelled at Horton are therefore deserved.[52]

Horton's meditations on the Supreme Being also led him to speculate on the reasons why Christianity has had little success in converting members of the 'mystical religions of the East'.[53] He mistakenly regards this as the result of a tension between this-worldly and other-worldly religious *foci*, and fails to understand the difference between a strongly-defined concept of deity and the attenuated concepts found in India and China.[54]

Horton's second element, which is linked to his ideas about the Supreme Being, but can be separated from them, is the difference between the religious requirements of the local microcosm and those of the wider macrocosm. He argued that:

> If thousands of people find themselves outside the microcosm, and if even those left inside see the boundaries weakening if not actually dissolving, they can only interpret these changes by assuming that the lesser spirits (underpinners of the microcosm) are in retreat, and that the supreme being (underpinner of the macrocosm) is taking over direct control of the everyday world.[55]

This then resulted in a lack of attention to the lesser spirits and an increased interest in the activities of the hitherto-distant Supreme Being, which encouraged conversion to monotheistic religions, which are for Africans representative of the macrocosm. This shift of focus towards the Supreme Being is a parallel process to the impact of colonial powers on society generally.

The third element Horton isolated is the specialized role of rulers and religious leaders. His speculations here are especially interesting. His argument is that the more involved a person is in the old cosmology, the more likely they are to be involved in the transition to the new:

> although the philosophers fill a thoroughly traditional role, the very nature of their involvement with the old cosmology makes it likely that they will be more acutely aware of the interpretative challenge of ... change than anyone else ... they may become deeply involved with the new developments in cosmology and ritual, and may even take the lead in formulating such developments.[56]

Rulers, Horton argued, also have a role to play in the religious transition, because they have the greatest exposure to the new culture and must rapidly adjust in order to maintain status among their people. He asserted that although these individuals have a greater stake in the old situation, they are likely to be in the forefront of the development of new concepts for the community: 'the rulers, then, were no desperate "men of two worlds", dodging back and forth between incompatible cosmologies'.[57]

Again, Horton undermined the effectiveness of this point by concentrating on the attitude of rulers to the Supreme Being and on the idea that the intellectual basis for the acceptance of Christianity was already present in African communities. He argued that:

> They lived in the light of a single world view, which, in its essentials, was that of their rural subjects. However, since their involvement with the wider world was significantly greater than that of their subjects, they laid correspondingly greater emphasis on the cult of the supreme being.[58]

The really valuable point here is the expansion of the world which often occurs when a culture becomes exposed to Christianity, and the close relationship between the developing understanding of Christianity and the developing understanding of the outside world.

Scholars focusing on cultures in transition and the modern colonial experience have favoured Horton's approach. Yet more profound insights may be found elsewhere. Garry Trompf, apparently without knowledge of Horton, has proposed that the encounter of the 'mythic' *mentalité* with the historical consciousness results in new theologies and myths which attempt to resolve the shocking discontinuities. Melanesian cargo cult myths are used to illustrate this thesis, and his conclusion is politically more incisive than that of Horton:

> of prime importance is understanding that these attempts are usually responses by primal people to finding their culture infiltrated by imperialists who are immeasurably more militarily and technologically powerful. Their efforts are also an index to the still more sobering reality that almost every corner of the earth has at last been opened up to the behemoth of internationalism and that time has been standardized through newspaper culture and history-oriented propaganda (whether sacred or secular, papal or Marxist).[59]

Whereas the Horton thesis implicitly granted a positive role to colonial powers in bringing about the shift from a purely local viewpoint to a more inclusive perspective, Trompf has exposed the destructive effects of colonial contact upon the material life of primal cultures and upon their intellectual heritage. His approach is aware of the ethical minefield that missionary and colonial encounters with primal cultures has become.

Trompf's argument is also fascinating because he attempts to identify such a transition in the development of Gnostic theologies in the early Christian period, demonstrating that the colonial paradigm may be useful in illuminating the more distant past. Though his conclusions differ radically from Horton's, he too becomes embroiled in the debate about the theological presuppositions of mission-field cultures which facilitate their acceptance of Christianity. In an article which attempted to isolate the characteristics of the 'perennial religion' (and which, incidentally, analysed the strengths and weaknesses of this-worldly and other-worldly religious *foci*), Trompf triumphantly charted the victory of this-worldly primal concepts over other-worldly Christian ideas. Perennial religion is characterized by a concern for the physical well-being of the individual and the tribe, an ideal of warriorhood, and a continued relationship with departed ancestors. Key terms in this world view include power, fertility, light and darkness.[60] Salvation in this context is this-worldly, and Trompf argues that the introduction of more developed concepts 'seems like calling for emergency measures after complicating matters in the first place'.[61] The mission-field culture has to develop its own theology in order to 'domesticate' Christianity, which results in the kind of dislocations previously discussed.

The issue of whether the reaction to the world's expansion is positive or negative could be debated at length; Trompf has argued that it is negative. Schreuder and Oddie, discussing the Indian case, noted that social mobility as a result of Christianity and the expanding horizon is often viewed positively:

> another reason given for the spread of these Christian movements is the association of the mission with modernisation and with increased economic and other benefits, such as modern Western education, new job opportunities (especially through the mission networks) ... allied with this line of argument is the contention ... that Christianity was attractive because it provided a means of social mobility and of participation in modern sectors of the economy.[62]

What is agreed upon by all is the potential for radical change in the encounter of faiths and cultures.

Conversion, Christianization and religious change

Anthropological and sociological theory concerns itself with the external, observable features of societies rather than with the interior processes of individuals. From this perspective the difficulties experienced by Underwood, Nock and James in analysing mass conversions do not arise. The debate is opened up sufficiently to permit the question 'is "conversion" a useful term?' Its origins in the notion of the 'turning-around' of a soul have been discussed, and it appears to be firmly anchored in the personal and individual sphere of activity.

'Christianization' has become the preferred term among many scholars who focus on the process of the spreading of Christianity. Mass conversions, where large numbers become Christians and evidence of their inner state is limited, invite the use of this term. J. W. Pickett's influential work on India suggests a threefold analysis of mass acceptance of Christianity, focusing on human social units acting as units, on the programme of education subsequent to the group's religious change, and on the role of indigenous leaders in maintaining the group and propagating the new faith. His case studies indicated that: the group deciding for Christ ordinarily is composed of one caste, and often includes all members of that caste in one, or more than one, village.[63] He argues that up until the 1880s missionaries in India generally sought converts from the higher castes, while mass movements were a lower caste phenomenon where the group sought out the missionaries. The issue of social mobility is covered, with the observation that Christianity overtly offered a better life spiritually, so the analogous seeking of a better life materially was comprehensible.

Ensuring that the baptized group remained Christian was largely achieved through education and, where this was effective, native-born clergy and leaders soon emerged. Pickett commented:

> where converts have received little instruction prior to baptism, but have been successfully incorporated into churches providing regular and frequent opportunities for worship and oversight by faithful ministers, they have become established as Christians ... where they have been well instructed prior to baptism, but for any reason have not been organised into churches ... they have not become established in Christian faith.[64]

This may seem obvious now, but it was a revelation in Pickett's era. It is also illuminating for the spread of Christianity in the late antique and early medieval periods.

Pickett stressed that the converting group must be protected from social dislocation and suggested that mass movements which preserve 'the integration of the individual in his group',[65] guard against this. Mass movements also reduce the likelihood of Westernization by preserving the social group identity. He identified some weak links in the process, such as the neglect of personal piety, but concluded that the mass movement is an authentic means of becoming Christian.

Recent works such as Susan Bayly's *Saints, Goddesses and Kings* continue the debate on mass movements, in Bayly's case with an overtly sociological *agendum*. Her study of conversion in India, like Pickett's, focused on a community of converts and the way in which it fits into the wider society. She challenged the traditional, interior view of conversion from the start:

> It has sometimes been implied that the coming of the major 'conversion' religions must obliterate all pre-existing beliefs and social ties amongst its new affiliates. .... This study seeks to ... [ask] what religious conversion really meant in South India over the last three centuries. What kinds of meetings and interactions occurred when practitioners of the so-called world religions

encountered the values and cultural norms which already prevailed in South India?[66]

This suggests the use of terminology such as 'religious transition' or 'religious change', rather than 'conversion' or 'Christianization'. In this book the three terms will be used interchangeably, as it seems that to attempt to define any one exclusively from the other two is excessively pedantic and severely limits the possibilities inherent in the study of religions. In this context, the models developed in Lewis Rambo's *Understanding Religious Conversion* are particularly helpful.

Rambo's book is an example of the interaction between specifically Christian models of conversion and anthropological models of conversion. Rambo's own experience as a Christian minister has influenced his thinking, but he also drew upon anthropologists like Horton and sociologists like John Lofland and Rodney Stark,[67] to produce a model of conversion which is remarkably elastic and inclusive. He is adamant that it is 'not yet a complete theory; it is a beginning framework only'[68] and his model is holistic, concentrating on cultural, societal, personal and religious factors which may facilitate conversion. The greatest strength of Rambo's book is its analysis of conversion as a process rather than an event, and a process which may be viewed from many different angles. He presents a sequential stage model of conversion in the chapter 'Models and Methods', arguing that:

> a stage model is appropriate in that conversion is a process of change over time, generally exhibiting a sequence of processes, although there is sometimes a spiraling effect – a going back and forth between stages. A stage may be seen as a particular element or period during that process of change. Each stage has a cluster of themes, patterns, and processes that characterize it.[69]

The stages developed are context, crisis, quest, encounter, interaction, commitment and consequences, and Rambo has designed diagrams which enable the model to be presented with any one of these stages at the centre. This means that the model is flexible, and that when one particular factor dominated the conversion experience of an individual or group, that factor can be central in the interpretation of the experience. Similarly, if one particular stage appears to be absent in an instance of conversion, the other stages may carry greater weight for the scholar. The problems inherent in Rambo's framework derive from its strengths: the fluidity and elasticity of the sequential stage model sometimes seem to be applicable to too many possible changes and transitions, which weakens the apprehension of conversion; and Rambo's inclusion of much material on the secularization process results in a parallel weakening of his concept of religion.

Nonetheless, his insistence on the paradoxical nature of conversion and its ability to encompass contradictory elements makes his book the most important purely theoretical study of conversion to date.[70]

Medieval historians and models of conversion

Thus far the models and theories of conversion discussed have been anchored in the recent colonial context. The figure of the missionary has not been examined in detail, and case studies of conversion from the remote past, accessible to the scholar through documentary or archaeological evidence, have not been considered. Attempts to evaluate conversion in the early medieval period and the role of the medieval missionary have concentrated on the structure of medieval society, and have identified factors which facilitated the change from one religion to another. In general, the more internally-oriented and doctrinally defined versions of Christianity and associated theories of religious experience are demonstrably inappropriate to the study of Christianization in the early medieval period, principally because the people who comprised the various early medieval societies were not accustomed to regarding themselves as discrete individuals capable of personal decisions in the area of beliefs and practices.

Also at issue is the role of religion in that type of communal society, and the extent to which that role is a cognitive one for the group. So far, no definition of religion has been proposed. Some limitations on the scope of religion are required. If:

> religion is treated as cultural – that is, as a cognitive and evaluative model – then there is a conceptual relationship between religion and reality. This follows by definition. When a certain religious belief is adopted, a new reality is inherent in it. It seems obvious that it is not productive to carry this line of reasoning too far. Conversion to a religion, even by an entire community, does not necessarily mean a change in the structure of the community ...[71]

This is a valuable observation, because, in the case of early medieval conversions involving entire peoples and political units, there was frequently no or only gradual change to power structures.[72] Addison, in *The Medieval Missionary*, argued for the pivotal role of the king in the transition to Christianity in these group-oriented societies (what has come to be known as the 'top-down' model of conversion). He analysed cases of conversion and the role played by rulers, and concluded that there were three possible scenarios:

1) independent rulers, recently converted and free from external pressure,

exerting influence over their own countrymen; 2) monarchs of Christian lands extending their protection to missionaries among weaker or dependent neighbouring peoples; and 3) Christian conquerors exercising force against alien non-Christian races.[73]

Actually, the king was of crucial importance even before the encounter with Christianity, in that he symbolized the society and often represented its connection with the supernatural world. He was therefore the natural focus for missionaries, in both a political and a religious sense.

For the late antique and early medieval Germans, society was close-knit, with the people in order of their social rank bound by ties of loyalty to the ruler. Tacitus, in the *Germania* (98CE), and other classical authors comment on the high value assigned to loyalty to the lord by the warrior aristocracy. (An extended analysis of early and medieval Germanic society will be given in Chapter 2.) These works are ideological in intent,[74] but it is possible to confirm from later sources that such an ethic existed and was profoundly influential among the Germanic peoples. The Germanic kings traced their descent from the gods, which legitimized their political position and cemented their religious importance for the people. 'Belief in descent from a god was an important ideological principle in the ordering of society among the early Germans. It gave ethnic coherence to peoples, and royal authority to the dynasty which ruled them.'[75] This supernatural element in the constitution of the authority of the Germanic kings has been commented on extensively.[76]

The techniques of the missionaries are often difficult to establish, as the vast majority of writings from the period say little or nothing about them. In general the missionaries approached the ruler, who may have maintained a Christian presence at court. The missionaries were protected by the Church, a Christian ruler, or both. Preaching, mass baptism, the establishment of churches and monasteries, the ransoming of Christian hostages and the freeing of Christian slaves were among their activities.[77] Nevertheless, the interior definition of conversion persists in late antique studies, most notably in the work of Ramsay MacMullen, whose definition is as follows:

> Let me declare Christian conversion, then, to have been that change of belief by which a person accepted the reality and supreme power of God and determined to obey Him. Whether actual, entire, and doctrinally centrist obedience resulted would depend on cases.[78]

For the Germanic peoples in the early Middle Ages, Christianity was never perceived as a thing in itself: it always came with cultural connections, such as the power of the continental Christian rulers and the legacy of the Roman Empire.[79] The Germanic rulers had strict codes which governed their responses to the missionaries. Michael Richter has argued that the success of conversion among the Anglo-Saxons is as much due to the agency of rulers as of missionaries:

> Barbarian kings cherished ideals of hospitality to strangers, including strangers of a different religious persuasion. It can be argued that for an ultimately successful mission the attitude of the Kentish royalty towards the missionaries from Italy was just as crucial for their success as the determination of the missionaries to evangelise.[80]

Richter also proposes that in some cases the missionaries were assisted by 'agents of conversion',[81] laity who contributed to the spread of Christianity. Horton's intellectualist theory has not been neglected by medievalists,[82] and Eric Sharpe's comments on the prepared soil in Germanic culture on to which Christian concepts of salvation fell are (without apparent knowledge of Horton) very Hortonesque:

> religiously, however, the Germanic mind was very far indeed from being a *tabula rasa* on which the first words of salvation were to be written by the Christian Church. The presentation of Christ as the cosmic victor and the symbolism in which that act of salvation was depicted fell into prepared soil. . . . They understood the drama, the mythos of salvation; and they understood the power of the risen and ascended Christ. . . . To this end they took and re-shaped their ancient symbols and their ancient concepts, conscious that they were now part of a greater Empire, but conscious equally of their own distinctive heritage.[83]

Sharpe's reference to an Empire highlights another crucial factor in 'top-down' conversions: the element of political force. Rulers frequently accepted Christianity due to pressure from external powers, as in the conversion of Pomerania in the twelfth century.[84] The identification of the new faith with political power and wider horizons made the choice easier.

Alongside the 'top-down' model is the 'bottom-up' model, which works in reverse. Pagan groups conquered Christian territories and the subjugated populations became servants and slaves, bringing Christian influence into the conquerors' households.[85] In frontier societies traders introduced Christian items and Christian beliefs casually into pagan communities; Christian princesses married pagan kings to cement alliances; and Christian and pagan served side by side in the army.[86] It may be doubted that bottom-up conversion was ever in itself sufficient to win over a hostile society, but it has been demonstrated that the creation of a receptive environment for Christian ideas often aided top-down conversions.[87]

Medievalists have also stressed the prevalence of syncretism, the intermingling of different beliefs due to long co-existence, and the failure of attempts to stamp out the old beliefs. Bayly and Sharpe have already been quoted on the danger of assuming (as with the old psychological model of conversion) that, when a religious change occurs, all that was formerly believed was forgotten. The Germanic peoples reinterpreted Christianity in the light of their culture, as do all converts.[88]

The final theorist of conversion to be considered is James C. Russell, whose *The Germanization of Early Medieval Christianity* has already been mentioned. The first half of this book is a theory of conversion developed specifically for application to the late antique and early medieval Germans. It is therefore especially significant in relation to this book. Russell is aware that throughout history Christian missionaries have been 'compelled to take a path between the twin opposing dangers of cultural alienation and religious syncretism'.[89] His theory is interesting chiefly because of its genuinely two-way application; the Germanic peoples became Christians, and Christianity (and through the Church, all medieval society) became Germanic. There are nine postulates in his model of religious transformation: that social structure influences ideological structure; that the promise of salvation appeals more to individual than collective societies; that where a desire for salvation exists within a society, that society is predisposed to adopt a universal religion; the offer of salvation coupled with a community was the greatest appeal of Christianity in the later Roman Empire; that the social structure and ideological currents of the declining empire were in many ways inherently conducive to the promise of salvation offered by Christianity; societies where there is little desire for salvation are usually more interested in the temporal benefits of religion; that Christianity was generally world-rejecting and Indo-European religion was generally world-accepting; the Germans were not desirous of salvation; and for Christianity to make inroads into Germanic culture when that culture did not desire salvation, it had to accommodate the world-accepting ethos of Germanic society.[90]

This is a sensible description of a process of religious transformation, but it falls short of being a theory in that it is clearly grounded in the encounter of two specific cultures (Christian Roman and pre-Christian Germanic) and therefore not universally applicable. Chapter 5 'Germanic Religiosity and Social Structure' is very weak, relying as it does on a 'pot-pourri of secondary sources'[91] and the comparative Indo-European hypotheses of Georges Dumezil, to the neglect of much relevant primary material from the period in question. Chapters 6 and 7, which deal with the actual conversions, are quite brief, and are more successful as historical sketches than as illustrations of the posited theory. Their brevity also imposes a selectivity on Russell which prevents his survey being definitive. Therefore, *The Germanization of Early Medieval Christianity* is best viewed as an interesting experiment which opens up avenues for further research.[92]

Conclusion

In developing a theory of conversion, both the traditional Christian and the psychological characterization of the phenomenon, which focus on internal transformations, prove incapable of explaining conversion in its multifarious forms. Factors which need to be considered include the relationship of the individual to the society (for example, family and kin-group ties); mass conversions and individual conversions (and their degree of completeness or incompleteness); theology (how is the message being presented in the light of pre-existing theological assumptions and what adaptations are being made by the receiving culture); terminology (which is particularly relevant for teaching the new faith); and finally, worship and organization.

These factors are all relevant to the encounter of cultures and religions. Political and military contexts may also determine the course of a conversion. Often the political dimensions are disturbingly simple: the non-Christian society stands to lose all (through invasion and conquest) and conversion involves political subjugation. This was the case with the Norwegian interference in Icelandic affairs at the Althing of 1000 CE, with the mission of Otto of Bamberg to Pomerania (one of the last remaining strongholds of European paganism) in the early twelfth century,[93] and with the spread of Christianity through modern colonialism.

This book examines the process of conversion among the Goths, Franks, Anglo-Saxons, Saxons, Scandinavians and Icelanders. These conversions were generally mass movements where a ruler (or governing body in the case of the Icelandic Althing) agreed to be baptized and brought his retainers with him. In developing a theory to illuminate these religious transitions, two pitfalls must be negotiated. The type of theory developed by Rambo and Russell derives much of its strength from elasticity and open-endedness. However, it also runs the risk of being overly inclusive, imprecise, and of disintegrating into a description of conversion, or a catalogue of factors likely to be present in an instance of conversion. To avoid this methodological imprecision is the first pitfall to be negotiated.

In contrast, the type of theory proposed by Horton derives its strength from its crystalline formulation, and its tendency to speak firmly of there being three crucial factors in African conversion to monotheism, which explicate the process admirably. It is important in formulating a theory of conversion not to simplify, but to be aware always of the complexity of the material involved. With these principles in mind, for the purpose of this book 'conversion' and 'Christianization' will be used interchangeably, with no special interior or spiritual meaning attached to the former term. It seems unfeasible to abandon 'conversion' entirely, and wiser to loosen its definition. Likewise, the debate over the legitimacy of mass movements is considered a non-issue, and they are viewed as authentic instances of conversion, bearing in mind Addison's conclusion: 'Group conversions are not likely to occur except where social and religious traditions make them normal and natural.'[94] This leads to the principles derived from previous theories of conversion.

Horton's narrow focus on similarities between concepts of the Supreme Being is ignored, but his broader ideas are the foundation of the approach used here: the importance of pre-existing intellectual structures; the collision of the microcosmic and the macrocosmic when Christianity (or any international or universalist belief system) is introduced to a localized culture group; and the role played by both secular and religious leaders in the transition from one religion to another. This accords well with the top-down conversion models used in the analysis of medieval conversion and can incorporate Richter's insights into the significant role played by secular 'agents of conversion' as well as the role of missionaries. In appraising the role of missionaries in conversion, it is important to assess their cross-cultural communication skills and the insider and outsider roles they adopt in order to gain acceptance into the mission-field culture.

Building on these concepts is Trompf's and Russell's assertion that the mission-field culture will contextualize Christianity to make it harmonious with their traditional perspective, and Pickett's emphasis on the importance of social cohesion and structural support in the process of Christianization. These points lead to an analysis of the development of vernacular religious literature and the training of native clergy and the immense potential for syncretistic beliefs. This is the keystone for an approach to the conversion of the late antique and early medieval Germans which can take into account all the available evidence and derive from it an understanding of the phenomenon which is both subtle and rich.

Notes

1. Nils G. Holm, 'Pentecostalism, Conversion and Charismata', *International Journal for the Psychology of Religion*, 1, (3), p. 139.
2. James C. Russell, *The Germanization of Early Medieval Christianity*, Oxford, 1994, p. 3.
3. Eric J. Sharpe, 'Reflections on Missionary Historiography', *International Bulletin of Missionary Research*, April 1989, p. 76.
4. Hugh Trevor-Roper, 'The Past and the Present: History and Sociology', *Past and Present*, 42, 1969, p. 9.
5. Sharpe, 1989, *op. cit.*, pp. 80–1.
6. Thomas O'Dea, *The Sociology of Religion*, Englewood Cliffs, NS, 1966, pp. 64–5.
7. Jan Brøgger, 'Socio-Economic Structures and the Form of Religion', *Temenos*, 13, 1977, pp. 7–30.

8. O'Dea, *op. cit.*, p. 65.
9. Thomas Luckmann, *The Invisible Religion*, New York, 1967, p 49. See also Hans Mol, *Identity and the Sacred*, New York, 1976, for an extended treatment.
10. Joachim Wach, *The Sociology of Religion*, London, 1947, p. 366.
11. For example, Joshua Starr's 'The Mass Conversion of Jews in Southern Italy (1290–1293)', *Speculum*, 21, (2), 1946, pp. 203–11, deals with a mass movement for which there is little evidence apart from official records of baptisms, legal records dealing with the disposal of property and accounts of the Inquisition's activities in Italy, and offers explanations of the behaviour of the Jewish 'converts' based on a reconstruction of the society of the time and their role in that society.
12. Robert Segal, *Religion and the Social Sciences*, Atlanta, 1989, ch. 7, 'The Social Sciences and the Truth of Religious Belief', *passim*.
13. Peter Berger, *The Sacred Canopy*, New York, 1967, pp. 50–1.
14. Prefiguring this approach, Eric J. Sharpe in 'Some Problems of Method in the Study of Religion', *Religion*, 1, 1971, speaks of the value of 'complementary (not competing) methods', p. 12.
15. A. D. Nock, *Conversion*, Oxford, 1933, p. 7.
16. *Ibid.*, p. 10.
17. This raises the issue of the status of ceremonies of initiation: many people were baptized, which is an external sign of conversion, but the corresponding internal transformation cannot be easily observed or measured.
18. See Chapter 2, Section 'Christianity in the Roman Empire'.
19. Nock, *op. cit.*, p. 173.
20. Plato, *The Republic*, ed. and trans. Desmond Lee, Harmondsworth, 1974, part XI, 'The Immortality of the Soul', pp. 440–55.
21. Nock, *op. cit.*, p. 181.
22. This approach has persisted among many Christian writers, for example F. Peter Cotterell, 'The Conversion Crux', *Missiology*, II, (2), April 1974, who stated that 'the conversion experience in mission, then, is a painful, decisive decision between two alternative ways of life, and the crux is whatever experience is critical in establishing a lasting, permanent break between the two ways', p. 185.
23. A. C. Underwood, *Conversion: Christian and Non-Christian*, London, 1925, p. 15.
24. *Ibid.*, p. 82.
25. *Ibid.*, p. 251.
26. *Das Heilige* published in German in 1917 and translated into English as *The Idea of the Holy* for Oxford University Press in 1923.
27. Philip Almond, *Mystical Experience and Religious Doctrine*, Berlin, 1982, ch. 5, 'The Mystical, the Numinous, and Metaphysics: The Theory of Rudolf Otto', pp. 92–119; in particular pp. 106, 109, and 119.
28. Steven T. Katz, 'Language, Epistemology and Mysticism', in S. Katz (ed.), *Mysticism and Philosophical Analysis*, New York, 1978, pp. 22–35.

29. Underwood, *op. cit.*, p. 257.

30. David J. Bosch, 'Crosscurrents in Modern Mission', *Missionalia*, 4, (2), August 1976, p. 56.

31. *Ibid.*, p. 72.

32. For example, 'A religious mission can be understood as being a special form of cultural transmission', Arild Hvitfeldt, 'History of Religion, Sociology and Sociology of Religion', *Temenos*, 7, 1971, p. 86; 'I personally know of missionaries who themselves traced their failure to their inability to communicate, with all the attendant frustrations', Donald S. Deer, 'The Missionary Language Learning Problem', *Missiology*, III, (1), January 1975, p. 89; and Trevor D. Verryn, 'What is Communication? Searching for a Missiological Model', *Missionalia*, II, (1), April 1983, pp. 17–25.

33. Theories about the relationship between language and culture abound, but the principal concerns of sociolinguists tend to arise from the pioneering Sapir-Whorf study of 1929, which stressed that language is not simply 'a technique of communication, [but] it is itself a way of directing the perceptions of its speakers and it provides for them habitual modes of analyzing experience into significant categories', Harry Hoijer, 'The Sapir-Whorf Hypothesis', in Ben G. Blount (ed.), *Language, Culture and Society*, Cambridge, MA, 1974, p. 120.

34. Tony Swain and Deborah Bird Rose (eds), *Aboriginal Australians and Christian Missions*, Australian Association for the Study of Religion, 1988, contains a number of essays demonstrating that this problem continued well into the twentieth century. I would draw attention to Michael Alroe's 'A Pygmalion Complex Among Missionaries: The Catholic Case in the Kimberley', pp. 30–44, and Noel Loos' 'Concern and Contempt: Church and Missionary Attitudes toward Aborigines in North Queensland in the Nineteenth Century', pp. 100–20.

35. Friedrich Dierks, 'Communication and World View', *Missionalia*, II, (2), August 1983, p. 45.

36. Eugene Hillman, 'Pluriformity in Ethics: A Modern Missionary Problem', *Missiology*, 1, (1), January 1973, p. 61.

37. Dierks, *op. cit.*, p. 49.

38. Eric J. Sharpe, in conversation, has expressed doubts about this argument, claiming that monism and idealism both exist in Western thought, in addition to dualism. This is undoubtedly correct, but I would hazard that the majority of Western people have been dualists, whether consciously or not.

39. Dierks, *op. cit.*, writes 'Africans have an inborn appreciation for existence in a group and community because such a life is for them an existential necessity. Westerners, on the other hand, experience great difficulties in belonging to a community because such a life is a limitation of their freedom and individualistic opportunities', p. 56; and Bengt Sundkler, in *The Christian Ministry in Africa*, London, 1962, points out that Africans who have moved to urban centres attempt to replicate the village community in the city, p. 55.

40. For example, Donald R. Jacobs and Jacob A. Loewen, 'Anthropologists and

Missionaries Face to Face', *Missiology*, II, (2), April 1974, pp. 161–74.

41. Louis J. Luzbetak, 'Unity in Diversity: Ethnotheological Sensitivity in Cross-Cultural Evangelism', *Missiology*, IV, (2), April 1976, pp. 207–16.

42. Jacob A. Loewen, 'Roles: Relating to an Alien Social Structure', *Missiology*, IV, (2), April 1976, p. 225.

43. David J. Hesselgrave, 'The Missionary of Tomorrow – Identity Crisis Extraordinary', *Missiology*, III, (2), April 1975, states that 'the missionary of today may be excused for concluding that it is a rather dubious distinction to be called by that title, at least for the time being. And the missionary of tomorrow may be pardoned for a certain degree of schizophrenia upon the realization that he is being trained to be what nobody will be or what everybody is already!', p. 228.

44. Klaus Nürnburger, in 'Ethical Implications of Religious and Ideological Pluralism', *Missionalia*, 13, (3), November 1985, states that 'the biblical witness is quite explicit in its view that there can be no authentic human experience in separation from the (biblical) God. Whenever people encountered this God they could not escape the ultimacy of a call out of all other loyalties .... There is a religious or devotional exclusiveness over against other ultimates. There is a metaphysical exclusiveness over against other normative systems. This exclusiveness of the biblical faith is one of its most outstanding characteristics. Intolerance, even fanaticism, has never been far from devotion to Yahweh or Christ', p. 99.

45. Luzbetak, *op. cit.*, p. 214.

46. Paavo Seppänen, 'Religious Solidarity as a Function of Social Structure and Socialization', *Temenos*, 2, 1966, p. 128.

47. Robin Horton, 'African Conversion', *Africa*, XLI, (2), 1971, p. 100.

48. Lesley Stevens, 'Religious Change in a Haya Village, Tanzania', *JRA*, XXI, (1), 1991, p. 20.

49. Garry Trompf, *In Search of Origins*, London, 1990, offers a survey of theories of the origin of religion.

50. Eric J. Sharpe, *Comparative Religion*, London, 1975, ch. 5, 'Culture and History', pp. 172–94, discusses the work of Fr Wilhelm Schmidt on 'high gods', which resulted in *Der Ursprung der Gottesidee*, 1912, and *The Origin and Growth of Religion: Facts and Theories*, 1931, among other works, in which Schmidt, a Roman Catholic priest, attempted to prove the primacy of belief in a high god, using what I have termed the 'Edenic model'.

51. Tony Swain, *A Place for Strangers*, Cambridge, 1993, rejected utterly the high god in Australian Aboriginal religion, and argued cogently and conclusively for the importation of the All-Mother (from Indonesia) and the All-Father (from Christian missionaries), two possible candidates for that role. His work presents a challenge to scholars who believe it is possible to isolate authentic native or aboriginal ideas and concepts, so vast is the labyrinth of contact, colonial or otherwise.

52. Deryck Schreuder and Geoffrey Oddie, 'What is "Conversion"? History, Christianity and Religious Change in Colonial Africa and South Asia', *JRH*, 15, (4), 1989, p. 505, citing the criticisms of Robert Elphick.

53. Horton, 1971, *op. cit.*, p. 97.
54. *Ibid.*, p. 94. Horton indicated his lack of interest in 'comparative religionists', and reveals a total lack of awareness of comparative concepts of deity, assuming that all such concepts resemble the strongly-defined Judeo-Christian-Islamic god; whereas the Eastern concepts of deity such as Brahman (Hinduism), Tien (Confucianism), Tao (Taoism) and the virtually atheistic absence of god in Theravada Buddhism are of great variety, and offer a challenge for the theorist of conversion. This book concentrates on conversion to Christianity, and does not pretend to insights into conversion to Buddhism (the great Eastern missionary faith).
55. *Ibid.*, p. 102.
56. *Ibid.*, p. 103.
57. Robin Horton, 'On the Rationality of Conversion Part II', *Africa*, 45, (4), 1975, p. 375.
58. *Ibid.*
59. Garry W. Trompf, 'Macrohistory and Acculturation: Between Myth and History in Modern Melanesian Adjustments and Ancient Gnosticism', *CSSH*, 31, (4), 1989, p. 633.
60. For example, E. J. Sharpe, *Seasons of Light and Darkness*, a study of pre-Christian religion in Britain, unpublished typescript lent to me by the author.
61. Garry W. Trompf, 'Salvation and Primal Religion', *Prudentia*, suppl. no., 1988, p. 223.
62. Schreuder and Oddie, *op. cit.*, p. 513.
63. J. W. Pickett, *Christian Mass Movements in India*, The Abingdon Press, 1933, p. 23.
64. *Ibid.*, pp. 240–1.
65. *Ibid.*, p. 331.
66. Susan Bayly, *Saints, Goddesses and Kings*, Cambridge, 1989, p. 1.
67. Rambo is particularly reliant upon John Lofland and Norman Skonovd's 'Conversion Motifs', *Journal for the Scientific Study of Religion*, 20, 1981, pp. 373–85; and John Lofland and Rodney Stark's, 'Becoming a World-Saver: A Theory of Conversion to a Deviant Perspective', *American Sociological Review*, 30, 1965, pp. 862–75.
68. Lewis Rambo, *Understanding Religious Conversion*, New Haven, CT, 1993, p. 7.
69. *Ibid.*, pp. 16–17.
70. Rambo's almost poetic concluding paragraph reads: 'Conversion is paradoxical. It is elusive. It is inclusive. It destroys and saves. Conversion is sudden and it is gradual. It is created totally by the action of God, and it is created totally by the action of humans. Conversion is personal and communal, private and public. It is both passive and active. It is a retreat from the world. It is a resolution of conflict and an empowerment to go into the world and to confront, if not create, conflict. Conversion is an event and a process. It is an ending and a beginning. It is final and open-ended. Conversion leaves us devastated – and transformed', *ibid.*, p. 176.
71. Erik Allardt, 'Approaches to the Sociology of Religion', *Temenos*, 6, 1970, p. 18.

72. Eric J. Sharpe has likened this phenomenon to a takeover of a supermarket by a new company: the structure of society remains unaltered, but the management is different. An effective example is given in Robert N. Bellah, *Beyond Belief*, New York, 1970, p. 105, where he quotes from the testimony of Ebina Danjo, a Japanese convert to Christianity in the 1860s, where in Christ Danjo finds a replacement for his human lord who had died, and a way of retaining his lifestyle under the new religion: 'I was convinced that even a Confucianist could do it'.

73. James Thayer Addison, *The Medieval Missionary*, London, 1936, p. 22.

74. Rosemary Woolf, 'The Ideal of Men Dying with their Lord in the *Germania* and in *The Battle of Maldon*', A-SE, 5, 1976, p. 64.

75. Hermann Moisl, 'Anglo-Saxon Royal Genealogies and Germanic Oral Tradition', *JMH*, 7, (3), p. 217.

76. David Dumville, 'Kingship, Genealogies and Regnal Lists', in P. H. Sawyer and I. Wood (eds), *Early Medieval Kingship*, Leeds, 1977, pp. 72–104; also Anthony Faulkes, 'Descent From the Gods', *MS*, 11, 1978–79, pp. 92–125.

77. Stephen Neill, *A History of Christian Missions*, Harmondsworth, 1964, *passim*.

78. Ramsay MacMullen, *Christianizing the Roman Empire (AD 100–400)*, New Haven, CT, 1984, p. 5.

79. Christopher Dawson, *Medieval Essays*, London, 1953, p. 55.

80. Michael Richter, 'Practical Aspects of the Conversion of the Anglo-Saxons', in Próinséas Ní Chatháin and Michael Richter (eds), *Irland und die Christenheit*, Stuttgart, 1987, p. 364.

81. *Ibid.*, p. 363.

82. See Lynette Olson, 'The Conversion of the Visigoths and the Bulgarians Compared', in Lynette Olson (ed.), *Religious Change, Conversion and Culture*, Sydney Studies in Society and Culture, 12, pp. 22–32.

83. Eric J. Sharpe, 'Salvation: Germanic and Christian', in E.J. Sharpe and J.R. Hinnells (eds), *Man and His Salvation*, Manchester, 1973, p. 261.

84. Robert Bartlett, 'The Conversion of a Pagan Society in the Middle Ages', *History*, 70, (229), 1985, p. 191.

85. See Rufinus of Aquileia's discussion of the influence of a female captive in the conversion of the Iberians, Françoise Thelamon, *Païens et Chrétiens au IVe Siècle*, Paris, 1981, pp. 97–8.

86. Aspects of bottom-up conversion are discussed in A. P. Vlasto, *The Entry of the Slavs Into Christendom*, Cambridge, 1970, *passim*; William Toth, 'The Christianization of the Magyars', *CH*, XI, 1942, p. 36 (role of Christian slaves), p. 53 (marriage of Christian Princess Gizella of Bavaria to pagan Vajk, later baptized Stephen); and M. N. Tikhomirov, 'The Origins of Christianity in Russia', *History*, 44, 1959, *passim*.

87. A recent PhD thesis by Jonathan Barlow, *The Success of the Franks*, Department of History, University of Sydney, 1993, argues for a strong Christian presence in Frankia in the late fifth century, influencing Clovis's adoption of Catholic Christianity.

88. Arnaldo Momigliano, 'Ancient Biography and the Study of Religion in the

Roman Empire', in A. Momigliano, *On Pagans, Jews, and Christians*, Wesleyan University Press, 1987, p. 177.

89. Russell, *op. cit.*, p. 11.
90. *Ibid.*, pp. 102–3.
91. Pegatha Taylor, 'Review of James C. Russell, *The Germanization of Early Medieval Christianity*', *Medievalia et Humanistica*, New Series, 23, p. 173.
92. Russell does not appear to know Horton's work, which is unfortunate as his own theory would have benefited from some of Horton's clarity of thinking and expression.
93. Bartlett, *op. cit.*, *passim*.
94. Addison, *op. cit.*, p. 71.

2 Christianity and the Germanic peoples in late antiquity

All authority in heaven and on earth has been given to me. Go, therefore, make disciples of all nations; baptise them in the name of the Father and of the Son and of the Holy Spirit, and teach them to observe all the commands I gave you. And know that I am with you always; yes, to the end of time.[1]

Christianity in the Roman Empire

The missionary journeys of Paul, chronicled in the *Acts of the Apostles*, culminated in the establishment of the Church in Rome, and Paul's imprisonment and eventual death (and that of Peter) in that city. Rome was the centre of the known world, and the establishment of Christianity there made good its claim to be a world religion. Jesus' last command, the Great Commission, was enthusiastically pursued by the early Christian Church, and through the arguments of Paul the message was preached to the Gentiles as well as the Jews. When Christianity first began winning converts in the Empire it appeared to be no more than one of many mystery religions. The Roman state cult, with deities such as Jupiter, Apollo, Ceres and Bacchus (all appropriated from the Greek Olympian cult) had long since ceased to satisfy the Roman people spiritually. Ceremonies in honour of the state cult were performed for the well-being of Rome as a political entity; for their spiritual needs a proportion of the Roman people turned to foreign cults, mostly from the Middle East and Asia Minor, and to a number of philosophical schools.

These included the cults of Phrygian Cybele, Egyptian Isis and the Persian god Mithras (popular in the Roman army), and the philosophical systems of Stoicism, Epicureanism and Pythagoreanism. These cults and philosophies entered the city of Rome from approximately 200BCE onwards, and had varying degrees of success.[2] Amid this plethora, Christianity was merely another mystery cult offering arcane knowledge and salvation through ritual initiation and sacrament.[3]

It soon became apparent that Christianity more closely resembled

Judaism, not merely because it had emerged in Jerusalem but because of certain attitudes the two religions shared, particularly the exclusive worship that their Gods demanded. The Christian doctrines of the Kingship of Christ and the Kingdom of God, emerging from the Jewish understanding of the Messiah, were of paramount importance in determining how Christians related to the secular Roman state. The Younger Pliny's letter to Trajan (early second century CE) reports that Christians will not worship the Emperor's statue and that the cult is potentially dangerous:

> I have therefore postponed any further examination and hastened to consult you. The question seems to me to be worthy of your consideration, especially in view of the number of persons endangered; for a great many individuals of every age and class, both men and women, are being brought to trial, and this is likely to continue. It is not only the towns, but villages and rural districts too which are infected with this wretched cult. I think though that it is still possible for it to be checked and directed to better ends.[4]

This letter is significant because it is written between 110 and 113CE and is thus very early; because it indicates that there was a large number of Christians of all social classes in Bithynia, a Roman province on the southern shore of the Black Sea; and because it shows that the test of asking Christians to do homage to the Roman emperors had already been developed.[5]

Many Roman writers considered Christianity worthy of comment, and some agreed with Pliny that the extermination of the new cult was desirable. Celsus, whose work is known only from Origen's reply, the *Contra Celsum*, written some seventy years later, complained that Christianity was incredible and unintelligent. Christians want to:

> convince only the foolish, dishonourable, and stupid, and only slaves, women, and little children. ... Moreover, we see that those who display their secret lore in the market-places and go about begging would never enter a gathering of intelligent men, nor would they dare to reveal their noble beliefs in their presence; but when they see adolescent boys and a crowd of slaves and a company of fools they push themselves in and show off.[6]

This is an unflattering portrait of Christian mission. Celsus wrote in the late second century CE; Galen, in a near-contemporary work, described Christianity and Judaism as schools of philosophy, but considered Christians to be dogmatic and uncritical.[7] Alongside these criticisms there grew a body of Christian literature which both countered pagan arguments and developed a Christian apologetic. To speak of this encounter as between pagan and Christian is rather misleading. There certainly existed both paganism and Christianity, but neither was a monolithic system.

Christianity had not yet developed much of the theology which later characterized it. The great Church councils were still to come. There was Gnostic Christianity, Jewish Christianity, and many differing local varieties.[8] Paganism, too, was a very fluid phenomenon. The difference between Christianity and other religious groups might well be presented more as one of attitude than of belief. O'Donnell and Dodds have noted that Jewish and Christian faith were most obviously contrasted with secular laxity and religious eclecticism.[9]

Christianity (in all but a few Gnostic groups) demanded the convert's entire allegiance. Christians and Jews were committed to their beliefs and worship, and were willing to die for them if necessary. The God of the Bible was the sole Creator and idols, being created, were either useless pieces of wood and metal or the hiding places of evil spirits.

Some scholars have contended that the various religions of antiquity lacked the metaphysical and theological speculation which was fundamental to Christianity. This is not strictly true. Some of the mystery cults were theologically complex, and required special devotion on the part of the adherent. The poet Propertius (c. 50BCE to 2CE) wrote of his mistress Cynthia (in real life the courtesan Hostia) that her devotion to the cult of Isis interfered with his relationship with her. The poem 'The Cult of Isis' says:

> The rites are here again, the lover's blight:
> Ten times has Cynthia worshipped, night by night.
> Down with the cults of sultry Nile, the pest
> That Isis sent to women of the west,
> To part devoted lovers — still the same
> Ill-natured goddess, by whatever name.[10]

Poetry is governed by convention, and it is likely that Propertius is invoking a stock image, when he complains of his mistress neglecting him for her religious devotions. Yet the women of Rome were among the most ardent devotees of the mystery cults, and it is significant that Celsus accuses Christianity of brainwashing women who knew no better. Further evidence of pagan theological complexity and of individual faith and devotion can be found in Apuleius' *The Golden Ass*, which describes the author's state of depression and purposelessness, which is alleviated by initiation into the cult of Isis. Apuleius says that after his initiation: 'I remained for some days longer in the temple, enjoying the ineffable pleasure of contemplating the Goddess' statue, because I was bound to her by a debt of gratitude so large that I could never hope to pay it.'[11]

Christians have spoken similarly of their gratitude to God for the salvation granted them.

The next significant anti-Christian writer, and perhaps the most effective of all, was Porphyry (233–305 CE).[12] He was a learned and intelligent man, born in Tyre, who wrote a biography of the great Neo-Platonic philosopher, Plotinus, and edited Plotinus' *Enneads*. He was acquainted with Origen, and made the Bible central to his criticisms of Christianity. He actually shared many moral and ethical ideas with the Christians, but was offended by their theology. The strength of his criticisms may be inferred from the fact that Eusebius' *Evangelical Preparation* cites Porphyry nearly one hundred times, and Augustine's *Harmony of the Gospels* refers to Porphyry's *Against the Christians* and its arguments about the contradictory nature of the Christian scriptures.

Despite these opponents, Christianity continued to win converts, sometimes in quite spectacular ways. One significant figure here was Gregory Thaumaturgos (the 'Wonder-Worker') who had been converted due to Origen's persuasions. He worked in Cappadocia, and it is said of him that when he died there were only seventeen pagans left in the capital of that province. Latourette says of Gregory's methods:

> To pagan miracles he opposed Christian ones and exposed the fraudulent practices of the priests. He encouraged the Christians to celebrate festivals in honour of the martyrs, substituting these for the feasts of the old gods. By such means the transition from the old to the new was eased and popularised, even though in the process Christianity acquired some of the beliefs and trappings of the cults which it supplanted. Gregory seems frankly to have recognised the fact that for the masses any demand for a complete break with the past would either prevent conversion or could not be realised.[13]

Gregory's methods, and their phenomenal success, are significant because throughout the history of the Christian missions to the pagan Germanic peoples it is precisely these techniques of substitution and cultural transference which were employed.

The conversion of Constantine

At the beginning of the fourth century Christianity was still uncertain of its position, having been persecuted by Diocletian and still being a minority religion in the Empire. In 305, the year of Porphyry's death, Diocletian abdicated, and by 312 Constantine (c. 273–337) was the senior Augustus.[14] The evidence for the life and conversion of Constantine comes from Eusebius of Caesarea and centres on Constantine's victory over Maxentius at the battle of Milvian Bridge in 312. Before this victory Constantine had already shown favour to the Christian community (perhaps because his mother, Helena, was a Christian or because his father, Constantius, pursued a policy of toleration).[15] He had, through the promulgation of the Edict of Milan in 313, granted full toleration to Christians although he clearly was not himself a Christian at that point.[16] Before the battle Constantine allegedly had a vision of the *chi-rho* in the sky, on a banner which bore the legend 'In Hoc Signo Vinces' (by this sign conquer).[17] The suddenness and intensity of the experience (as portrayed in the literature) can be traced to the experience of St Paul on the road to Damascus.[18] As the person in question was a secular and military leader, however, the nature of the experience tended to involve battles and displays of the power of the Christian God over other gods.[19]

The problem with the conversion of Constantine is that he clearly had not become a Christian in the sense that orthodox Christianity required. He had been a worshipper of Sol Invictus, the Unconquered Sun, and it is clear that he effected a fusion of this deity with Jesus Christ and that he continued to associate pagan symbols and connotations with his activities throughout his reign.[20] Although he was not to be baptized until 337, upon his deathbed, by Eusebius of Nicomedia, that his attitude changed after the battle can be seen in the letter he wrote to Anullinus, the proconsul of Africa, in *c.* 312–13.[21] This expresses the opinion that the right treatment of the Christian community is vital for the continued strength of the Empire. He exhorts Anullinus:

> Wherefore we will that, when thou receivest this letter, if aught of those things that belonged to the Catholic Church of the Christians in any city, or even in other places, be now in the possession either of citizens or of any others: these thou shouldest cause to be restored forthwith to these same churches, inasmuch as it has been our determination that those things which these same churches possessed formerly should be restored to them as their right.[22]

Constantine also made clear that he believed that the emperor had a right to decide Church controversies when he summoned the Council of Nicaea in 325, which opened on 20 May. But this is not conclusive evidence of Constantine's personal acceptance of Christianity. The unification of the Empire and the new faith had much to offer, and Constantine's later intervention in the Donatist[23] issue in North Africa was not successful, although he was victorious over the Church in that he asserted, and the Church admitted, his right to influence the direction taken by Church authorities.[24]

Politically, Constantine charted a prudent course with regard to the old and new religions. The Triumphal Arch erected by the Senate in Rome to Constantine depicts the Emperor making offerings to Diana and Sylvanus, among other deities,[25] and the most definite step taken by Constantine to break with the pagan traditions of the Empire, moving the capital from

Rome to Constantinople, is more ambiguous than usually assumed. Alföldi contends that when on 17 May 330CE the Emperor dedicated his new capital, he gave 'his Christian organization of the state a centre free from any touch of paganism'.[26] This certainly offers an interesting perspective on Constantine's intentions, both politically and spiritually. The move to Constantinople also had political significance, however, in that it concentrated power in the Eastern Empire and virtually abandoned the Western Empire to the barbarian invaders. The new city also contained iconography which continued the pagan tradition. The two temples by the Augusteion were dedicated to two goddesses, Tyche and Rhea. The statue of Rhea had been transported from Cyzicus, and Doerries speculates that Constantine interpreted this transition as 'the goddess herself [being] converted',[27] as she clearly had not been identified with Mary or incorporated into Christianity in any other way. The opposite opinion is expressed by Barnes, who believes that Constantine's use of pagan symbols (specifically the sun) 'attests not imperial devotion to a vague solar monotheism; but the dead weight of iconographic tradition'.[28] What is certain is that Constantine did little to persecute or suppress paganism, and died seven years after the dedication of his new capital.

What is significant about Constantine's relationship with Christianity is that it became the pattern for that of later Germanic rulers. The idealized conversion experience story of the victory at Milvian Bridge underlies that of many later rulers, such as Clovis of the Franks. The ambivalent nature of Constantine's acceptance of the new faith also echoes this.

The Germans and the Roman Empire

While Christianity was advancing through the Roman Empire, groups of Germanic, Celtic, and Asiatic peoples were also entering the Empire. Whether this entrance may be termed an invasion or not is questionable; historians currently speak of migrations. Germanic society has been the subject of much research, with scholars seeing very different defining characteristics. In the *Germania* (98CE) Tacitus idealized the Germans, comparing them favourably to the decadent Romans.[29]

Tacitus' broadly anthropological study is, however, an important primary source, written when Germania was a Roman province. It offers valuable material on the function of kingship in Germanic society and the nature of Germanic religion. Although he had not himself visited the province and spoke no Germanic language, his account tallies well with other, later, descriptions of Germanic society. Both Germanic religion and kingship played crucial roles in facilitating the conversion to Christianity of the various German tribes. Tacitus writes in some detail of four deities: Mercury, Hercules, Mars and Nerthus. The first three bear Roman names, and it is reasonable to assume that the Germanic gods behind this classical façade resembled the Roman gods originally bearing those names. Generally Mercury is identified with Woden, Hercules with Thunor, and Mars with Tiw. These identifications are based on resemblances between the Roman and German deities. Mercury is the Roman version of Hermes, the Greek god of those who live by their wits, who assists the dead on their journey to Hades;[30] and Woden/Odin is variously a god of the dead, a sorcerer and a trickster god, and a breaker of oaths who is described as 'foul and untrue'.[31] Tacitus' Mercury and the Scandinavian Odin (the Woden figure) both demand human sacrifices. The presumed identity between Hercules and Thunor/Thor rests on their great physical strength and Mars and Tiw/Tyr are purely war gods. Nerthus, the fourth deity, is an earth mother whose cult survives in the Viking Age in the worship of Njord (which is etymologically the same as 'Nerthus', (although Njord is male) and in the cult of Njord's children Frey and Freya.[32]

Studies in early Indo-European mythology have suggested that Tiw, who appears as a rather faded war god in the Anglo-Saxon and Scandinavian pantheons (as Tyr in the latter) was originally a 'sky-father' deity, and hence the king of the gods. Woden/Odin has the characteristics of a god of the dead and of sorcery, and it has been suggested that this was his original function.[33] It may be that his military function stems from battles being occasions of great slaughter.

In discussing kingship among the Germans of the first century CE, Tacitus distinguished two kinds of leader, saying that the Germans 'choose their kings for their noble birth, their commanders for valour'.[34] The former case has often been taken to mean no more than tracing descent from a god, specifically Woden. This equation of nobility with divine origin is not restricted to the Germans: Celtic sources often feature gods at the top of royal genealogies; Roman emperors traced their descent from classical deities; and it has been argued that the Christian model of kingship resembled the pagan model in that figures such as David were spiritually, if not biologically, sons of God.[35] The Anglo-Saxon kings believed themselves descended from a variety of gods, including Seaxneat and Woden; and the Goths traced their royal line to Gautaz, who is possibly a double of Woden. Moisl observed that: 'belief in descent from a god was an important ideological principle in the ordering of society among the early Germans. It gave ethnic coherence to peoples, and royal authority to the dynasty which ruled them.'[36] Some scholars have claimed that descent from Woden is to be seen as literally biological and that he was a deified mortal, but this seems fairly unlikely.[37]

According to Tacitus, for a man to qualify for kingship he must claim divine lineage. This encourages the view that the king-cult was a major element in Germanic religion. Kings were regarded, if not themselves divine, as channels through which the power of the gods reached the people. The great role played by royalty in the conversion of virtually all the Germanic peoples also lends support to this theory. Tacitus also comments on the existence of an assembly of free men, the fact that chieftains' power is calculated by the strength of their retinues, and the two bonds, that between clan members (the family) and that between men and their lord, which constitute the basis of society. On this last point he observed:

> Furthermore, it is a lifelong infamy and reproach to survive the chief and withdraw from the battle. To defend him, to protect him, even to ascribe to his glory their own exploits, is the essence of sworn allegiance. The chiefs fight for victory, the followers for their chief.[38]

There is corroborating evidence from a variety of sources for this *comitatus* organization of warriors and for the seriousness with which they took their oaths.[39]

The study of sacral kingship, exemplified by Hocart's *Kingship* and Hooke's *Myth, Ritual and Kingship*, was a thriving area of research in the first half of the twentieth century. Most of the material covered was Middle Eastern and related to those cultures which could illuminate the religion of the Old Testament. More recently Indo-European sacral kingship has been examined by scholars such as Dumezil, Gonda, and Lincoln. Indo-European kingship, as evidenced in mythology and in the context of human society, connects the three functions of Dumezil's system; the functions of sovereignty, military prowess and fertility.[40] This makes the king central to the well-being and maintenance of the society: as priest he unites the people with the supernatural realm; as warrior he leads the people to victory and increases his power through appropriating the power of slaughtered enemies; and as guarantor of the fertility of the land he ensures the physical well-being of the whole people.[41] This identification of the king with the well-being of the people is the fundamental factor which informs and illuminates any understanding of the spread of Christianity among the post-Roman Germanic kingdoms.

Of all the Germanic tribes, the Goths made the strongest impression on the Roman world. Prehistorically, the Gothic culture has been identified at two sites, Černjachov, near Kiev in the Ukraine, and Sîntana de Mureş, in central Transylvania.[42] Textual sources for the Goths include Jordanes' *Getica* (which draws on the lost Gothic histories of Ablasius and Cassiodorus and dates from approximately 550), the lost histories of Eunapius and Olympiodorus which were partially preserved by Zosimus, Sozomen and Philostorgios, and the comprehensive works of Ammianus Marcellinus and Procopius. From these sources it is clear that the Goths were a mixed people, with the first instance of a division being observed in 291, between the Tervingi-Vesi and the Greutungi-Ostrogothi.[43] Much of what is known of Gothic society confirms the two-tier theory of leadership described by Tacitus.

Wolfram and Heather concentrate on different aspects of leadership. Wolfram says of the Goths that their kingship carried far greater authority than among other Germanic peoples.[44] Heather, discussing the role of the judge (which corresponds to the Tacitean *dux*), disputes Thompson's contention that the judge among the Tervingi ranked lowly and held power only in times of emergency.[45] He noted that the office of judge descended through a single family, so that in Ariacus (king in 332), his son Aoric, and his grandson Athanaric we have three generations of a ruling family.[46] The role of kings and judges was significant in the later conversion of the Goths to Christianity.

The first indication that the Germanic peoples were on the move was in 166, when there were minor breaks in the frontiers in Venetia and Achaea. The crisis came in the mid-third century when, between 254 and 278, the frontier of northern Germany collapsed and the Germans penetrated Gaul and even Spain. Only Dacia, of all the Roman provinces affected, was actually abandoned to the barbarians.[47]

By the fourth century the Roman Empire, increasingly burdened with the maintenance of enormous frontiers, had been recruiting barbarian soldiers into the army for approximately two hundred years. Many of these men retired with Roman army pensions and a grant of land within the Empire's borders. In addition to this peaceful and piecemeal settlement there were occasional violent attacks and campaigns which sped up the process of barbarian tribes entering the Empire. At the same time Christianity was winning converts and becoming increasingly enmeshed with the Empire. It is as if the German tribes and the Christians were undergoing a parallel process, which resulted in the Romanization of both groups, but also in the Christianization and barbarization of the Empire.

Initially Christianity had little to do with the Germans, for the Western bishops closely associated paganism and barbarism, and efforts were made to convert the barbarians only when their presence threatened ordered civilian life.[48] The Western Empire was in general more vulnerable to the barbarian attacks and the Eastern more secure.

With the marriage of Christianity and the Empire, the perspective on mission to the barbarians changed: it became possible to see the conversion of the barbarian tribes as a valuable opportunity for the Church to increase its ranks. Momigliano analysed the situation as follows:

> The Church managed to have it both ways. ... It succeeded where pagan society had little to offer either way. The educated pagan was by definition

afraid of barbarians. There was no bridge between the aristocratic ideals of a pagan and the primitive violence of a German invader ...

The Christians ... could convert the barbarians and make them members of the Church. They had discovered a bridge between barbarianism and civilization. Alternatively the Church could give its moral support to the struggle against the barbarians: the defence of the Empire could be presented as the defence of the Church.[49]

Christianity and the Goths

The first encounters between Germans and Christians are obscure and undocumented.[50] Bottom-up conversion, with casual contact creating a receptive environment for the spread of Christianity, may have prevailed among those Germans in the Roman army and where Christian traders and hostages lived among the Goths.[51] In 325 Theophilus, bishop of the Goths, attended the Council of Nicaea[52] but nothing further is known of him.

The key figure in the early years of Gothic Christianity is Ulfila (Wulfilas), who was consecrated bishop by Eusebius of Nicomedia in 341 at the Council of Antioch. He was born *c.* 311 in what is now Romania, and died in 383.[53] The complicating factor in the spread of the Gospel to the Goths was the Arian heresy, named after Arius, who taught that the second person of the Trinity (Jesus) was not co-equal with the Father, but was a created being.[54] The Council of Nicaea in 325 was convened to condemn this belief, but it remained popular.[55] Ulfila was an Arian, but this did not affect the legitimacy of his mission, because in the first half of the fourth century 'Arianism ... was orthodoxy at Constantinople, and Athanasius [the champion of orthodoxy] was denounced there as a dangerous heretic'.[56]

The principal source for the mission of Ulfila is Philostorgios, whose work survived only in an *Epitome* compiled by Photius in the ninth century.[57] There is also a letter written by Auxentius of Durosturum, bishop of Milan, a pupil of Ulfila. Both of these sources are pro-Arian and offer an alternative view of fourth-century Christianity, with the Arian missions promoted by Constantius II seen in an heroic light.

Ulfila's parents were a Cappadocian and a Goth; he knew both Latin and Greek, and went to Constantinople while in his twenties as part of a delegation from the Gothic federation to the Emperor.[58] When he was sent as bishop to the Goths it was to the Christians already living in Gothia (the province of Dacia, just outside the boundaries of the Empire). Therefore he was not starting a mission in an area with no Christian presence, but being given pastoral responsibility for Christians (presumably captives and slaves) living among the Goths. These Christians were possibly exerting bottom up influence which made the success of Ulfila's activities more likely. Wolfram argued that the mission of Ulfila was an imperial matter[59] and Heather and Matthews concur, asserting that Ulfila operated with imperial favour, and may have been seen by the Goths as a representative of the Empire.[60]

This is significant when considering the likelihood of the adoption of Christianity by the Goths. It has been demonstrated that Gothic society was closely knit and that leader figures were of considerable significance. Some evidence for Gothic religion has been adduced, suggesting that the kings had a sacral role. The presence of casually transmitted Christianity created a receptive intellectual environment for conversion, and Gothic culture was in a highly unstable condition due to the meeting of its microcosmic, rural and parochial world-view with that of the macrocosmic, international and urban Roman culture.

The roles and interactions of the agents of mission and the secular and religious leaders of the Goths must be considered in Gothic reactions to Christianity. It is known that Christianity was unpopular with the pagan assembly of the people and that converts were ostracized. Evidence for this is found in the *Passion of Saint Saba,* a life of the Visigothic St Saba (Sabas), which tells of how the saint was persecuted by his fellow-villagers, ejected from village society and eventually murdered 'because of his persistent refusal to worship with his fellow villagers'.[61] This incident occurred during the persecution of the Goths of 369–72, and Saba was martyred on 12 April 372.[62]

Ulfila spent seven years ministering to the Goths in Dacia, and then returned to Constantinople although he continued as their bishop for a further thirty-three years, dying in 481. For Auxentius, writing when Arianism was in decline, Ulfila is a heroic figure, described as 'a man of great (spiritual) beauty'.[63] Auxentius says of his missionary methods that 'he never shrank from preaching quite openly'[64] and that his ordination as bishop resulted in 'the salvation of many among the people of the Goths'.[65] Other sources are similarly vague about Ulfila's methods of spreading the Gospel. His greatest achievement, however, was the translation of the Bible (or parts of it)[66] into Gothic. It is assumed that Ulfila translated the Bible into Gothic because he believed that a familiarity with the scriptures in their own tongue would assist the Goths in accepting Christianity.

Philostorgios and Sozomen describe Ulfila's invention of the Gothic alphabet, and his translation of the Bible. Scholars are agreed that what survives shows a careful and literal translation,[67] and Bradley last century commented:

> it was a wonderful piece of work for the age in which it was written. It cannot have been very easy, in the fourth century, for a Goth to acquire such a

thorough knowledge of Greek as to enable him accurately to understand the text of the Scriptures, and to make a faithful translation out of one language into another requires a mind trained in habits of exact thinking. But there are very few passages in which Ulfila appears to have misread the sense of his original.[68]

It is this accuracy and care in the translation which makes Ulfila's Gothic terminology interesting. It may be assumed that while translating two things were uppermost in his mind: how to render the meaning of the Bible accurately without using words which were associated with the old religion; and the knowledge that the predominately illiterate Goths were already in awe of the written word, possibly because of the semi-magical function of runic inscriptions.[69]

The English words 'reading' and 'writing' are both Germanic, and would have had cognates in Gothic. However, Ulfila never used these cognates. It has been suggested that this was because they had religious connotations. 'Write' originally meant to scratch or engrave and 'read' to guess the answer to a riddle. The runic script was generally used only for brief inscriptions and may have been thought to possess magical powers. This would explain Ulfila's avoidance of 'write' (Anglo-Saxon *writan*). The avoidance of the word 'read' (Anglo-Saxon *rædan*) is less easily explained, but might relate to the often bawdy nature of Germanic riddles. *Siggwan*, which Ulfila uses to mean 'read', properly means to 'sing' and it may be that the reading aloud of the scriptures suggested the appropriateness of that verb to him. For 'write' he employs *meljan*, which actually means to paint or to make markings.[70]

Ulfila's terminology also sheds light on how the kings of the Goths were regarded. Normally he uses *weihs* to mean 'holy', but on four occasions he uses *airkns*. This word has been shown to relate to Old Norse *jarteikn* which means of good birth or good origin.[71] *Airkns* also relates to Old English *eorcnanstan* and Old Norse *jarknasteinn*, which mean 'jewel' and preserve the sense of preciousness, while having lost the connection with origins.[72]

The Gothic Bible opens up the question of the transmission of Christianity through missionaries and interpreters, and the ways in which the message changed as it was received. Hard evidence for the actual techniques employed by the missionaries who preached to the Germans is difficult to extract from the sources and it is often necessary to speculate. The increased efficacy of missions conducted in local languages has always been acknowledged,[73] and the close relationship between language and culture has played a part in the flourishing and decline of many religious movements.[74]

Opinion is divided on this issue, but it does appear that linguistic and cultural differences affected the acceptance of Christianity and influenced the political relationships between the Latin-speaking Romans and other ethnic groups. Jones, who attempted to argue that heretical sects were not nationalist movements, failed to note that in Late Antiquity ethnic solidarity was a more appropriate expression of identity than any behaviour which might be recognized as nationalist in the modern sense. Furthermore, his observation that the Arian Vandals and the Berber-speaking Donatists in Africa did not unite to overthrow the Catholic Romans actually supports the contention that language, culture and religious choice are all factors in ethnic self-determination.[75]

There were four major wars between the Visigoths and the Empire during Ulfila's lifetime, and from 367 Valens, Emperor in the East, was reconquering territory in Dacia. This resulted in the intensification of persecution of the Gothic Arian Christians by their pagan fellow-countrymen, who associated the new religion with the Empire which was harrying them. Auxentius reported that Aoric, the father of Athanaric, ordered a persecution in 347/8, which action Heather attributes to the role of the judge in regulating Gothic religious life.[76] Ulfila was in Moesia from around 348, and he eventually petitioned the Emperor Constantius to permit the Visigothic Christians to enter Moesia, which was within the Empire. It is pertinent here to consider the *Passion of Saint Saba* and the persecutions of the Gothic Christians. The first persecution took place in 348 and coincides with Ulfila's departure from Gothia.[77]

The second persecution, for which there is greater evidence, was during the reign of the judge Athanaric. The *Passion* reveals that the Gothic village had its own council, which generally resented interference on the part of the central authorities.[78] There are leaders, including Atharidus, who condemned Saba. This supports the 'casual contacts' model of the spread of Christianity, where the adherents are mostly humble people without influence in the community.[79] The *Passion* also testifies to a variety of Christianities in Gothia, since Saba is a Catholic, not an Arian.[80]

Saba came to the attention of his fellow-villagers not at the time of his conversion, but at a time when the leaders of the Goths were attempting to enforce social conformity, presumably as a prelude to resisting the Empire with force. Pickett's research highlighted the socially cohesive aspects of religion[81] and the mass movement in conversion in particular. Saba, as one of a scattered group of individual converts, was caught when the Gothic leaders devised a test equivalent to Pliny's emperor-worship trial. The *Passion* says:

> when the chief men in Gothia began to be moved against the Christians, compelling them to eat sacrificial meat, it occurred to some of the pagans in the village in which Saba lived to make the Christians who belonged to them eat

publicly before the persecutors meat that had not been sacrificed in place of that which had, hoping thereby to preserve the innocence of their own people and at the same time to deceive the persecutors.[82]

Saba resisted this deception and was expelled from the village for a time. After his return, he interrupted the village authorities swearing to the persecutors that there were no Christians in the village, and was banished again.

The village council attempted to assert the unity of the community, and Saba's aggressive Christianity broke that unity, resulting in his expulsion from it. It is sometimes argued that even to speak in terms of the 'old religion' and the 'new religion' is misleading, and that religious beliefs of all kinds coexisted in a perpetual flux without clear boundaries; but the case of Saba makes clear that the Germanic societies understood the change of loyalties which adherence to Christianity brought. Saba was then apprehended by Atharidus, who repeated the sacrificial meal test, and when the saint resisted had him put to death. The manner of death is interesting:

> Then they took him down to the water, still thanking and glorifying God (until the very end his soul performed worship), threw him in and, pressing a beam against his neck, pushed him to the bottom and held him there.[83]

This method of execution resembles Tacitus' observation in the *Germania* that:

> traitors and deserters are hanged on trees; cowards, shirkers and sodomites are pressed down under a wicker hurdle into the slimy mud of a bog. This distinction in the punishments is based on the idea that offenders against the state should be made a public example of, whereas deeds of shame should be buried out of men's sight.[84]

The parallel is not perfect, as the Goths dragged Saba out of the river and left him unburied, but it is not impossible that they viewed conversion to Christianity as cowardice and shirking of responsibility, a shameful choice which merited death.

The Battle of Adrianople and its consequences for the Goths

More Goths entered the Empire in 376 when their king died. At that time the Goths were broadly divided into two chief parties, one led by Athanaric and the other by Fritigern.[85] Athanaric was anti-Christian and had ordered the persecution of 369, which Heather sees as an attempt to rid the Goths of the religious as well as the political influence of the Empire.[86] Athanaric was judge, rather than *rex*, the heir of a line of judges and a powerful figure who dominated Gothic politics in the 360s and 370s. In 369 he had been forced to conclude a peace with Valens after being sporadically at war for most of the decade.[87] The peace followed a defeat in the area between the Prut and the Dneister,[88] but Valens had to make the treaty as an equal and, due to Athanaric's refusal to conclude it on Roman soil, they met on a ship in the middle of the Danube.[89] This respite allowed the Tervingi to recover, but their later encounters with Rome were complicated by civil strife.

Horton's view of secular and religious leaders as agents of conversion who take an active role in the new world view, having had the greatest stake in the old, is appropriate in the case of the Goths. Valens' reconquest of Dacia, with the Gothic microcosm encountering the Roman macrocosm, and the struggle between the traditionalist Athanaric and the progressive Fritigern also fit Horton's paradigm perfectly.

There is a great deal of confusion in the sources for this period. Socrates Scholasticus and Sozomen wrongly assume that Ulfila was evangelizing during Athanaric's reign, and fail to distinguish between the persecution of 348 and that of 369–72.[90] They accurately describe Fritigern's conversion to Christianity, however, in terms which suggest that he understood the threat to the Goths from the Romans, but was also aware of the power and advantages of Rome and wished to identify with and benefit from that power. Socrates observed that:

> when [Athanaric] had obtained an evident advantage over his rival, Fritigernes had recourse to the Romans, and implored their assistance over his adversary. This being reported to the emperor Valens, he ordered the troops ... to assist those barbarians who had appealed to him ... and ... a complete victory was obtained over Athanaric beyond the Danube .... Because of this, many of the barbarians professed the Christian religion: for Fritigernes, to express his sense of the obligation the emperor had conferred upon him, embraced the religion of his benefactor, and persuaded those who were under his authority to do the same.[91]

Sozomen's account is basically identical,[92] with one interesting variation. He used the conversion of Fritigern as a means of proving that the Arianism of the Goths was entirely due to Valens' influence and that Ulfila was not responsible for the Goths being heretics. This view is endorsed also by the Gothic history of Jordanes.[93]

After concluding the peace with Valens, Athanaric persecuted the Christians in Gothia and hostility increased between him and his enemy Fritigern. By 376 Athanaric had been defeated by the alliance of Fritigern and Valens and a substantial number of Goths had been baptized.[94] The baptism of Fritigern and his followers is the forerunner of many such conversions among the early medieval Germans, where the demonstration of the power of the Christian God is victory in battle and the tribal leader's acceptance of baptism is accompanied by the baptism of his war-band or *comitatus*.

Complicating Fritigern's relationship with Valens were the Huns, who were devastating the Gothic lands. The Goths were incapable of effectively resisting them,[95] and the Gothic Christians argued that flight from the Huns into the Empire offered the only possible deliverance. This resulted in desertion of Athanaric by those who believed that the baptized Fritigern could arrange such a rescue.[96] Valens gave the Tervingi under Fritigern permission to cross the Danube and settle in Thrace. Ammianus Marcellinus presents this as a fatal error,[97] but does not seek to excuse the Romans in the matter.

Valens gave orders that the Goths were to be fed and given lands to occupy, but they were inadequately provided for and were forced to sell their children for food.[98] The Romans had deceived the Gothic leaders at a banquet, and murdered Fritigern's *comitatus*, and only Fritigern's quick wits saved him.[99] The Tervingi, pressed beyond endurance, revolted. They were supported by the Ostrogoths, who had broken the Danube frontier. Disturbed by this news, Valens returned from Antioch and engaged the Goths at Adrianople on 9 August 378, where they were victorious and Valens was killed.

Valens' fellow-Emperor, Gratian, appointed Theodosius as Emperor and placed him in charge of the Gothic campaign. After three years of warfare he succeeded in expelling the Ostrogoths from the Empire (they became subjects of the Huns) and settling the Visigoths in Moesia in return for military service. There was one unusual fact about this settlement: as Jones pointed out, the Goths 'were not *laeti*, subjects of the empire, but *foederati*, a foreign state bound by treaty to Rome.'[100] Therefore, they were able to retain their tribal structure under their own chieftain. This indicates how hard-pressed the Romans were to contain the Goths and how generous they had to be in order to obtain a treaty.

Arianism triumphant

Athanaric died after surrendering to the Emperor in 381. The conservative Goths who had opposed Christianity were now without a leader. Theodosius' treaty was particularly important, because it seems that the major effort made to convert the Visigoths was during the resulting period of stability in Moesia. The Visigoths converted to Arian Christianity, which was beginning to fall into disfavour just as they adopted it. It is known that orthodox Catholic missionaries worked among them,[101] however, so it seems that the choice of Arianism was deliberate. E. A. Thompson argued that Ulfila was unable to convert the majority while in Dacia, because they were outside the Empire and were thus able to maintain religious difference, and that they eventually converted to Arian Christianity as a means of preserving their tribal separateness, as it had been preserved in the treaty with Theodosius.

Relevant to Thompson's first point is Russell's insistence that the conversion of the Germanic peoples was a two-way process in which Christianity became Germanized. Frend had noted that once Germanic tribes came within the boundaries of the Roman Empire 'the real agent of conversion was the social disintegration this vast transfer of life and custom brought about. Religious transformation followed social transformation'.[102] Thompson is certain that the majority of the population only assented to Christianity after their entry into Moesia. The importance of the Gothic Bible is not clear: it may be that it was not widely used (save for reading lessons aloud) because the majority of the population was illiterate. Increased familiarity with Roman culture and the absence of persecution clearly contributed to the conversion.

There are some problems with this perspective. The politically motivated conversion of Fritigern and his followers needs to be analysed further. When Fritigern negotiated with Valens before Adrianople, he sent an Arian priest as his diplomat. Politically motivated conversions are often followed by apostasy in times of trouble,[103] but it appears that the two years of hardship experienced by the Goths[104] after entering the Empire had not caused them to abandon Arian Christianity. Athanaric, who lived to 381, still led and represented traditional Goths, but it was Fritigern the Arian Christian who was in command at Adrianople.[105] The sacral Gothic king, who was the link between his people and the divine, gained prestige through the demonstration of the power of the Christian God in a great military victory. Additional to this evidence is the continued high regard shown to Ulfila. In 376 he led the embassy to Valens to negotiate the entry of the Tervingi into the Empire,[106] and when he died in 383 he was given a splendid funeral[107] despite the Catholicism of the ruling Emperor, Theodosius.

Unfortunately, virtually nothing is known of the mechanism of the conversion in Moesia, the identities of the missionaries who effected it, or the motivation for it. Jordanes identifies ethnic solidarity as the motivation, commenting that:

> Moreover, from the love they [the Visigoths] bore them [other Germans], they preached the Gospel both to the Ostrogoths, and to their kinsmen the Gepidae,

teaching them to reverence this heresy, and they invited all people of their speech everywhere to attach themselves to the sect.[108]

It is reasonable to speculate that moving into a political and cultural entity which had been officially Christian for seventy years (with a two-year apostasy in the reign of Julian) would have exerted considerable pressure to convert on the Visigoths. Thompson, as a Marxist, sees the Visigoths as seduced by the materialist Empire, offering its luxurious and consumer-oriented lifestyle.[109] Whether this is what happened is debatable, but it is noteworthy that only the Rugi, of all the Germanic tribes, converted while outside the borders of the Empire, some time before 482.[110]

Thompson's second claim, that the Visigoths deliberately accepted Arian Christianity to preserve their identity within the Empire, which was becoming increasingly dominated by Roman Christianity, is more difficult to prove. Jordanes' comments suggest that the Goths did seek to spread the Arian faith deliberately among fellow-Germans. Therefore, Arianism may have been identified with being German. Trompf's discussion of how mission-field cultures domesticate or contextualize Christianity and make it their own is relevant here, as is Russell's assertion that Christianity became Germanized. Thompson suggests that the attraction may have been that Arianism was not centrally organized, but was rather a collection of independent Churches, resembling the Visigothic social organization of a loose confederacy of tribes or clans.[111]

Musset suggests that the adoption of Arianism by the Germanic peoples was due to two chance circumstances, the theological persuasion of Ulfila, the first missionary to approach them; and the high prestige of the Goths after their victory at Adrianople. He gives some credence to Thompson's theories by noting that the chief attraction of Arianism was 'the use of the vernacular, which is not in itself an Arian trait but an oriental one shared by all the churches founded by the Byzantine mission'.[112] Musset was wrong, however: these things were not mere accidents. They were inextricably bound up with the retention of ethnic identity: Ulfila evangelized the Goths because he was a Goth; the vernacular gained a hold because of his translation of the Bible and its use by later missionaries; and the Visigoths had prestige and influence after Adrianople because the Germans saw the king as a sacral figure and victory as the gift of the gods.

The Visigoths under Alaric left Constantinople in 395 and cut a swathe across Europe, eventually reaching Rome in 410. In 418 they were settled in the province of Aquitania Secunda and by the end of the century they had expanded their territory to include Spain.[113] This revolt had been occasioned by the death of Theodosius on 17 January 395. Control of the Empire passed to Honorius in the West, assisted by his general Stilicho; and Arcadius in the East, assisted by his general Rufinus.[114] Alaric was a strong leader, a king in every sense,[115] and the Goths followed him successfully across the Empire. When he died in 411 he was, though a Christian, buried as befitted a Gothic monarch. Dawson has observed that: '[German] manners and ideas remained those of a pagan warrior society. The burial of King Alaric in the bed of the River Busento, surrounded with his treasure and his slaughtered slaves, recalls the funeral of Patroclus rather than that of a Christian king.'[116] Claudian portrays Alaric, like Athanaric and Fritigern before him, as dependent on his *comitatus* and threatened with desertion if the men were dissatisfied.[117] Yet Arian Christianity remained the faith of the Visigoths.

Between the conversion of Constantine in 312 and the accession of Justinian in 527 there is no record that the Catholic Church sent missionaries outside the borders of the Empire to convert the barbarians, whether from paganism to Christianity or from Arianism to Catholicism. Therefore two sources, the *Chronicle* of Hydatius, a Gallaecian bishop, written in 468/9, and the *History of the Vandal Persecution*, written by Victor of Vita in 484, are invaluable in providing information about Germanic Christianity in the fifth century. Neither are used by Russell, but both provide evidence which strengthens his Germanization of Christianity thesis. Hydatius lived in an isolated Roman community in southern Galicia, an area being settled by Vandals and Suevi from 411 onwards.[118] As a Catholic bishop he commented extensively on those who departed from orthodoxy in faith, chiefly Arians and Priscillianists. His *Chronicle* testified to enthusiastic Arianism among a number of Germanic groups, chiefly the Vandals:

> In the course of pillaging Sicily Gaiseric undertook a lengthy siege of Panormus and at the instigation of Maximinus, a leader of the Arians in Sicily ... he initiated a persecution of the orthodox in order to force them into the Arian impiety. ... Some succumbed, but a considerable number persevered in the orthodox faith and achieved martyrdom.[119]

Victor of Vita supplemented this picture with details of the Vandal occupation of North Africa under Geiseric (d. 477) and his successor Huneric. Like Hydatius, Victor was a Catholic bishop, but his contact with the occupying Arians was closer than that of his Gallaecian near-contemporary. His *History* presented the Vandals as engaged in a systematic persecution of the Catholics, principally in order to seize the property of the Church. Geiseric is also concerned to aggrandize the Arian Church. 'When the bishop had been driven out, together with the venerable clergy, as we said above, he immediately delivered the church called Restituta, in which the bishops had always had their throne, over to his own religion ...'[120] Victor also noted that individually and collectively

Arians were fervent in their persecution of orthodox Catholics.[121] Geiseric actively promoted the Arian faith, continuing the Germanic king's central role in the conversion and maintenance of the new faith. 'At that time Geiseric, urged on by his bishops, declared that only Arians were to be placed in the various offices within his and his sons' courts.'[122] Geiseric's military successes, and the prosperity of the Vandal kingdom, which even Victor admitted ('the kingdom grew in wealth')[123] must have increased the prestige of the Arian faith.

However, it must be noted that Victor's evidence on this issue of Germanization or indigenization is confusing. It seems that the Arian bishops were concerned for the preservation of their Germanic identity, and were agitated when Catholics wore Vandal dress (the issue of whether these people were ethnically Vandal is not really of significance). Such people were to be refused entry to the Catholic churches by decree of Huneric, as they had evidently confused the social and religious divisions of the rather delicately balanced Vandal state. Failure to do so resulted in persecution and martydom by the Arian authorities.[124] Huneric, too, persecuted the Catholics and aggressively campaigned for the Arian faith. Therefore the question of whether the Germanic conversions were sincere or had any effect on their lifestyle is answered by the references to an enthusiastic Arian Church in Catholic histories[125] and the testimony of Arians such as Auxentius and Philostorgios.

In the West, the Germanic tribes preserved their old traditions and forms of worship much longer, but in the East they followed the Visigothic lead. In the West Odoacer, a Hun, had been proclaimed king by his troops in 476 and while not called Emperor, was virtually in charge of the Western Empire. He was killed in 493 by Theodoric the Ostrogoth, who succeeded him as king of Italy, with a capital at Ravenna. Theodoric did not succeed in gaining recognition from the Emperor either, but he admired Roman society and, although an Arian, maintained friendly relations with the Papacy. Theodoric reigned until 526, and his policy of toleration died with him.

The fifth century was a time of consolidation and growth for the Germanic political units, and there is some evidence for cordial relations between Catholics and Arians during this time. Eugippius' *Life of Saint Severin* tells of a Catholic saint who was acquainted with Queen Giso of the Rugi, a committed, proselytizing Arian. Eugippius wrote between 509 and 511 and his *Life* is centred on Noricum. Severin came to Noricum somewhere between 453 and 468 and struggled against residual paganism and Arianism in his mission.[126] The Arian Rugian royal family depended on Severin for advice[127] and, despite Eugippius' description of Giso as a 'wicked and sinister queen',[128] the saint is not unduly harsh towards her. Thompson comments on Severin's uniqueness, as the 'only cleric of whom we know from the Northern frontier provinces who regularly hobnobbed with the barbarian leaders, advised them, influenced them and occasionally raised opposition to them.'[129] Theodoric's friendly relations with the Papacy have already been mentioned, and he was asked by the Pope on one occasion to resolve a dispute. His court at Ravenna promoted the Arian faith and the beautiful churches of Sant' Apollinare Nuovo and San Vitale and the magnificent *Codex Argenteus*[130] are evidence of the artistic richness of Gothic Arian culture.

Their culture is also attested in law codes issued by the Arian kings of the Visigoths, the Burgundians and the Ostrogoths.[131] The three great codes, the *Lex Romana Visigothorum*, the *Lex Burgundionum*, and the *Edict of Theodoric*, all show the king as central to the nation, both in a military, and in an administrative and judicial sense.[132] Drew also observes the reluctance of the Roman writers to accept that real power now lay with the Germanic kings and that the applicability of Roman law had been severely reduced by their legislative and judicial activities.[133]

Arianism in decline

When Justinian became Emperor in the East in 527 he had many plans. He was concerned to retrieve the Western Empire from the barbarians, and by doing so to eliminate the Arian heresy. Justinian and his wife Theodora both sponsored missions, although they were campaigning for different types of Christianity, Justinian being a Catholic and Theodora a Monophysite. Chesnut observes (in reference to Theodosius):

> The good Christian emperor was expected to attack the pagan cults. This meant closing temples or destroying them or converting them to churches. It also entailed the prohibition of pagan ceremonies. The way in which pagan cult objects were exposed to ridicule or simply put out like museum pieces was recounted with great satisfaction. ... The Christian historian now gloried in the forcible suppression of the worship of the old gods.[134]

Under Justinian, Christian historians gloried in the defeat of Arianism by Catholicism. The *Getica* of Jordanes, and the *History of the Kings of the Goths, Vandals and Suevi* by Isidore of Seville both record with exultation this change of loyalties. Jordanes wrote *c. 551* and his work owes a great deal to a lost Gothic history of Cassiodorus. Isidore of Seville (*c. 560–636*) has as his hero Recared, the Visigothic king of Spain who converted to Catholicism in 587.[135]

Justinian had died in 565, but this conversion was a direct result of his anti-Arian policies. Visigothic Spain was somewhat isolated (for example, the Pope did not hear of Recared's conversion for three years), but it was sufficiently in touch for general trends in the Roman world to be known. By the time of his death, Justinian had reconquered the Western provinces (at great cost to the Empire), and had been equally successful in persecuting both paganism and Arianism (he failed with Monophysitism, as he could not effectively persecute his wife's sect).[136] Spain was disunited and attempts were made to unite it under Arianism: Agila, who was assassinated in 554, was fanatically intolerant of Catholicism, and from 570–580 Leovigild attempted to create a unified Arian kingdom. This was not possible, as the Catholic population had been tolerated earlier in the century by Theudis, who became King in 531 and had married a Catholic and pursued a policy of conciliation with Italy. Eventually Recared:

> then called together a synod of bishops from the various provinces of Spain and Gaul for the condemnation of the Arian heresy; this very religious ruler was present at this assembly and supported its proceedings by his presence and signature; together with all his subjects he renounced the falsehood which the nation of the Goths had up to now learned from the teaching of Arius, and proclaimed the unity of the three persons in God.[137]

Recared had waited for this moment: ten months after his coronation in 586 he had been secretly baptized, possibly as part of the conditions for his marriage to a Catholic Frankish princess. The conversion to Catholicism was supported by the clerics, the aristocracy, and Recared's powerful Frankish in-laws, and there is some evidence that most of sub-Roman Spain had remained Catholic. Schmidt has argued that the Visigoths had never attempted to convert the Roman Spanish to Arianism 'because, if masses of Romans had entered the Arian church, the distinction between Roman and Visigoth would have been blurred in an important respect – and the Visigothic kings of Spain thought it important to keep the distinction sharp and clear-cut'.[138] Again, it seems that the motivating force for this secondary conversion was not only political pressure, but possibly also a popular movement on the part of the Roman population.

In conclusion, the Arian phase of Germanic Christianity was an attempt to find an indigenous faith to replace the traditional religion which had failed to meet the increased demands of the macrocosm that the Germanic tribes had entered. This phase came to an end when the Germans themselves became divided in their Christian allegiance, through the conversion of the Franks to Catholic Christianity and their parallel rise to pre-eminence among the Germanic states.

Notes

1. *The Jerusalem Bible*, ed. Alexander Jones, London, 1968, Matthew 28:18–20, p. 45. The Greek text is in *The Greek New Testament*, ed. Kurt Aland *et al.*, London, 1966, p. 117.
2. H. H. Scullard, *From the Gracchi to Nero*, London, 1959, p. 11.
3. Adolf Harnack, *The Mission and Expansion of Christianity in the First Three Centuries*, London, 1962, pp. 118–19, comments that even images of Jesus which were presented to potential converts, such as that of the Divine Physician, served only to identify him strongly with figures such as Asclepius, who was himself the subject of a fairly fervent cult.
4. Pliny the Younger, *The Letters of the Younger Pliny*, ed. and trans. Betty Radice, Harmondsworth, 1963, letter 96, pp. 294–5. The Latin text is in Elmer Truesdell Merrill (ed.), The Younger Pliny, *Selected Letters*, London, 1903, p. 154.
5. James J. O'Donnell, 'The Demise of Paganism', *Traditio*, XXXV, 1979, says that this means of testing Christians was a stroke of genius because 'Any Christian who complied with the requirement of sacrifice might confidently expect no end of trouble if he attempted then to convince his co-religionists that he was still a loyal Christian at heart', p. 51. E. R. Dodds' *Pagan and Christian in an Age of Anxiety*, Cambridge, 1968, is also interesting in this context, as Dodds demonstrates that attitudes in the two groups to miracles, dreams, supernatural beings and so on were very similar.
6. Origen, *Against Celsus*, III, 49–50, ed. and trans. Henry Chadwick, Cambridge, 1953, p. 162.
7. Robert L. Wilken, *The Christians as the Romans Saw Them*, New Haven, CT, 1984, p. 92. See also R. Walzer, *Galen on Jews and Christians*, Oxford, 1949.
8. The discovery of the Nag Hammadi Codices earlier this century testifies to a lively and varied Christianity in North Africa, and by analogy in other regions of the Empire. This view is supported by the rise of regional heresies such as Montanism.
9. O'Donnell, *op. cit.*, p. 65, and Dodds, *op. cit.*, *passim*. Stewart Perowne, in *Caesars and Saints*, London, 1962, makes much the same point when he comments that 'There is no such thing as 'paganism' as a creed. The word can be used in a negative sense only, to indicate what a [person] did not believe', p. 53.
10. Propertius, *The Poems of Propertius*, ed. and trans. A. E. Watts, Harmondsworth, 1961, p. 116. The Latin text is in Propertius, *The Elegies of Sextus Propertius*, ed. and trans. G. P. Goold, London, 1990, p. 235.
11. Apuleius, *The Golden Ass*, ed. and trans. Robert Graves, Harmondsworth, 1951, p. 287. The Latin text is in Lucius Apuleius, *The Golden Ass*, ed. and trans. W. Adlington, revised S. Gaselee, London, 1965, p. 582. See also Wilken, *op. cit.*, p. 64: 'the idea of "conversion" – that is, a conscious and individual decision to embrace a certain creed or way of life – was wholly foreign to the ancients'.
12. Ferdinand Lot, *The End of the Ancient World and the Beginnings of the Middle Ages*, New York, 1961, p. 153.

13. K. S. Latourette, *A History of the Expansion of Christianity*, vol. 1, London, 1944, p. 90.

14. H. A. Drake, *In Praise of Constantine*, University of California Press, 1976, pp. 17–23.

15. *Ibid.*, p. 17.

16. A. H. M. Jones, *Constantine and the Conversion of Europe*, London, 1965, p. 80, says that 'no ancient author claims that he was during that period a Christian, and the orators who from time to time delivered panegyrics before him had no hesitation in representing the pagan gods as his protectors'. Many scholars have argued that Constantine did not convert to Christianity at all, but merely used the Church for his own ends. Jacob Burckhardt, in *The Age of Constantine the Great*, New York, 1949, says of Eusebius 'In the present instance men find it hard to believe that an important theologian, a scholar weak in criticism, to be sure, but of great industry, a contemporary as close as was Eusebius of Caesarea, should through four books repeat one and the same untruth a hundred times. Men argue from Constantine's zealous Christian edicts, even from an address of the Emperor's "to the assembly of the saints", an expression impossible on the lips of a non-Christian. But this address, it may be remarked in passing, was neither composed by Constantine nor ever delivered; and in writing the edicts, Constantine often gave the priests a free hand. ... It is a melancholy but very understandable fact that none of the ... spokesmen of the Church ... revealed Constantine's true position. ... We can easily imagine the joy of the Christians in finally having obtained a firm guarantee against persecution, but we are not obliged to share that elation after a millennium and a half', pp. 292–3.

17. Accounts from the *Vita Constantini* and the *Historia Ecclesia*, and also Lactantius' *On the Deaths of the Persecutors*, may be found in John W. Eadie (ed.), *The Conversion of Constantine*, Holt, Rinehart and Winston, 1971, pp. 9–14.

18. *Acts of the Apostles*, ch. 9, verses 3–9, *The Jerusalem Bible, op. cit.*, p. 167.

19. Gregory of Tours, *History of the Franks*, ed. and trans. Lewis Thorpe, Harmondsworth, 1974, offers the case of Clovis, who converted somewhere between 496 and 506 after persuasion from his wife and victories in battle.

20. Hermann Doerries, *Constantine the Great*, trans. Roland H. Bainton, New York, 1972, pp. 46–7. This is an apologetic work in which Doerries attempts to rescue Constantine's Christianity from oblivion while having to admit evidence of syncretism. A more intelligent attempt in this direction is Robin Lane Fox's *Pagans and Christians*, Harmondsworth, 1986, in which he makes observations such as 'the interest lies less in the vision's occurrence than in the way in which it was understood: the Christian interpretation was planted in the Emperor's mind, and if Ossius, the Spanish bishop, was already in his company, we must allow for the influence of the man who was to lead so many of the Emperor's subsequent dealings with the Church', p. 617, and 'Constantine first saw a religious sign, and then saw a god who bore it: he responded as pagans so often had, and soon afterwards, he found that this god had a special power. Why should he exclude all other gods?', p. 620.

21. Lactantius also records the text of the Edict of Milan, which extends toleration to Christians and which he refers to as the restoration of the Church: Lactantius, *The Minor Works*, ed. and trans. Sr Mary Francis McDonald, Washington, 1965, pp. 197–9.
22. Eusebius, *The Ecclesiastical History*, ed. H. J. Lawlor, trans. J. E. L. Oulton, vol. II, London, 1938, p. 453. The Greek text is in Eusebius, *op. cit.*, p. 452.
23. Lot, *op. cit.*, p. 211. At the height of Donatist enthusiasm they were alleged to have had three hundred bishops.
24. Jones, 1965, *op. cit.*
25. Doerries, *op. cit.*, pp. 47–9. Doerries acknowledges that it was the Senate, the last bastion of pagan belief, which erected the arch, but suggests that it was unlikely that Constantine disapproved.
26. Andrew Alföldi, *The Conversion of Constantine and Pagan Rome*, Oxford, 1948, p. 110.
27. Doerries, *op. cit.*, p. 73.
28. T. D. Barnes, *Constantine and Eusebius*, Cambridge, MA, 1981, p. 48.
29. Perry Anderson, *Passages from Antiquity to Feudalism*, London, 1974, p. 107, claims that 'A primitive communal mode of production prevailed among them. Private ownership of land was unknown: each year the leading men of a tribe would determine which part of the common soil was to be ploughed and would allocate sections of it to respective clans, who would till and appropriate the fields collectively; the periodic redistribution prevented great disparities of wealth between clans and households, although herds were privately owned and provided the wealth of the leading tribal warriors. There were no peacetime chieftains with authority over a whole people: exceptional military chiefs were elected in time of war. Many of the clans were still matrilineal'. Anderson is a poor scholar, and does not appear to have read many of the primary sources for early Germanic society. This passage is quoted merely as an illustration of his scholarly fantasy.
30. Robert Graves, *The Greek Myths*, vol. 1, Harmondsworth, 1955, pp. 66–7.
31. Hilda Ellis Davidson, *Gods and Myths of Northern Europe*, Harmondsworth, 1964, p. 50; also Snorri Sturluson, *Edda*, ed. and trans. Anthony Faulkes, London, 1987, pp. 26 and 55, where there is reference made to Odin and Loki's oath-relationship and its eventual disintegration. The section on Hermes in Graves emphasizes his untruthfulness, and, by implication, that of Mercury.
32. Ellis Davidson, *op. cit.*, pp. 93–6. Ellis Davidson discusses briefly but thoroughly the similarities between Tacitus' account of the travels of Nerthus through the countryside in a wagon and the account in *Flateyjarbók* of Gunnar Helming, who impersonated the god Frey and went round to villages and homesteads in a cart, accompanied by a priestess. See also Einhard the Frank, *The Life of Charlemagne*, ed. and trans. Lewis Thorpe, London, 1970, p. 29.
33. Hilda Ellis Davidson, *Scandinavian Mythology*, Feltham, 1969, p. 42.
34. Tacitus, *The Agricola and the Germania*, ed. and trans. H. Mattingly, Harmondsworth, 1970, p. 107. The Latin text is in Tacitus, *The Dialogues of*

Publius Cornelius Tacitus, ed. and trans. William Peterson, London, 1932, p. 274.

35. Patrick Wormald, 'Celtic and Anglo-Saxon Kingship: Some Further Thoughts', in Paul E. Szarmach (ed.), *Sources of Anglo-Saxon Culture*, Kalamazoo, 1986, p. 162.

36. Hermann Moisl, 'Anglo-Saxon Royal Genealogies and Germanic Oral Tradition', *JMH*, 7, (3), 1981, p. 217.

37. Kenneth Harrison, 'Woden', in Gerald Bonner (ed.), *Famulus Christi*, London, 1976, p. 351.

38. Tacitus, Mattingly, *op. cit.*, p. 113. The Latin text is in Tacitus, Peterson, *op. cit.*, p. 284. Rosemary Woolf's article, 'The Ideal of Men Dying with their Lord in the *Germania* and in the *Battle of Maldon*', *A-SE*, 5, 1976, addresses the issue of whether dying for a lord had been at one time a social reality which became a literary construct. She points out that Tacitus was comparing the noble German with the decadent Roman, and is therefore a dubious authority.

39. Anglo-Saxon poems such as *The Battle of Maldon* and prose incidents such as 'Cynewulf and Cyneheard' from the *Anglo-Saxon Chronicle* illustrate the same ethic. Woolf argues that what is ultimately important is whether people believed in the ethic, not whether it was customary practice.

40. The ancient Scythian creation myth preserved by Herodotus in *The Histories*, ed. and trans Aubrey de Selincourt, Harmondsworth, 1954, bk 4, sections 5–6, demonstrates this brilliantly with the first king, Kolaxais, receiving three sacred objects: the cup (for sovereignty and priest-kingship, as evidenced by a number of Indo-European ruler-deities such as the Dagda and Sucellos); the sword (for warriors); and the plough for the agriculturists. The myth also contains an example of divining the rightful king, a process common to most Indo-European myth and history.

41. James L. Sauve, 'The Divine Victim: Aspects of Human Sacrifice in Viking Scandinavia and Vedic India', in Jaan Puhvel (ed.), *Myth and Law Among the Indo-Europeans*, Berkeley, CA, 1970, pp. 173–91, *passim*; also J. Gonda, 'The Sacred Character of Ancient Indian Kingship', in *The Sacral Kingship*, VIIIth International Congress for the History of Religions, supplement to *Numen*, Leiden, 1959, pp. 172–80.

42. Peter Heather and John Matthews (eds), *The Goths in the Fourth Century*, Liverpool, 1991, p. 54.

43. Herwig Wolfram, *History of the Goths*, trans. Thomas J. Dunlap, University of California Press, 1988. Wolfram notes that the identification of these groups with 'western' and 'eastern' from Cassiodorus is clearly wrong. The Amali, claiming descent from Ansis and the god Gaut, are Ostrogoths, and the Balthi are Visigoths, as attested by Jordanes. The nomenclature of Tervingi-Vesi and Greutingi-Ostrogothi remained in use until approximately 400.

44. *Ibid.*, p. 41.

45. E. A. Thompson, 'The *Passio S. Sabae* and Early Visigothic Society', *Historia*, IV, 1955, p. 331.

46. Peter Heather, *Goths and Romans 332–489*, Oxford, 1991, p. 99. Athanaric's

status as a judge rather than king is confirmed by Wolfram, who notes that 'the Roman observers described Athanaric more as a spokesman or the executive agent of a number of "Gothic kings", rather than as a royal or princely monarch', Wolfram, *op. cit.*, p. 65.

47. Lucien Musset, *The Germanic Invasions*, trans. Edward and Columba James, London, 1975, p. 11.

48. W. H. C. Frend, 'The Missions of the Early Church 180–700', in W. H. C. Frend, *Religion Popular and Unpopular in the Early Christian Centuries*, London, 1976, p. 14.

49. Arnaldo Momigliano, 'Christianity and the Decline of the Roman Empire', in A. Momigliano (ed.), *The Conflict Between Paganism and Christianity in the Fourth Century*, Oxford, 1963, p. 14. Some of Momigliano's comments are a little extravagant: the 'violence of a German invader' is rather clichéd, and not strictly accurate. See Paulinus of Pella, 'Thanksgiving', in Ausonius, *Works*, ed. and trans. H. G. Evelyn White, vol. 2, London, 1921, pp. 305–51. Paulinus' relationship with the invaders oscillates from requiring their protection to selling them properties: 'Thou didst raise up for me a purchaser among the Goths who desired to acquire the small farm, once wholly mine, and of his own accord sent me a sum, not indeed equitable, yet nevertheless, a godsend, I admit, for me to receive, since thereby I could at once support the tottering remnants of my shattered fortune and escape fresh hurt to my cherished self-respect.', p. 349. The Latin text is on p. 348.

50. L. E. Elliott-Binns, *The Beginnings of Western Christendom*, London, 1948, reviews early evidence of Christianity in Germany as follows: 'The earliest references to Christianity in Germany are naturally vague and general. Tertullian in a highly rhetorical passage can speak of it as having reached even the Germans (*Adv. Jud.* VII); and, a little earlier, Irenaeus is able to refer to the orthodoxy of the faith of the churches in Germany, as though these were well-organised and already of some duration. Origen likewise speaks of Britain and Germany as having had the Gospel preached to them (*On Matt.* 24:9). On the other hand it must be noted that Eusebius omits Germany from his list of provinces (*Vita Const.*, III, 19), as does Athanasius (*Contra Arian.*, I); though the latter makes mention of Britain. Moreover Bede's statement that Severus became Bishop of the Treveri early in the fifth century and preached the Word to the people west of the Rhine (*Hist. Eccles.*, I, xxi) suggests that up to that time Christianity had failed to make any deep impression', p. 190.

51. E. A. Thompson, 'Christianity and the Northern Barbarians', *NMS*, 1, 1957, p. 3.

52. F. F. Bruce, *The Spreading Flame*, The Paternoster Press, 1958, p. 321.

53. E. A. Thompson, *The Visigoths in the Time of Ulfila*, Oxford, 1966, pp. xiii and xxi.

54. Heather and Matthews, *op. cit.*, pp. 136–7.

55. Emperor Constantine himself had been baptized in 337 by the Arian Eusebius of Nicomedia, the same bishop who appointed Ulfila bishop to the Goths.

56. Jordanes, *The Gothic History of Jordanes*, ed. and trans. Charles Christopher Mierow, Cambridge, 1915, pp. 164–5.

57. Philostorgios, *The Ecclesiastical History of Sozomen and the Ecclesiastical History of Philostorgios*, trans. Edward Walford, London, 1855, and Philostorgios, in Heather and Matthews, *op. cit.*, p. 133.

58. Henry Bradley, *The Goths*, London, 1888, p. 57. See also Philostorgios, *op. cit.*, pp. 435–6, 'He [Philostorgios] also says that Urphilas brought over as settlers to the Roman territory a large body of persons who had been driven out of their ancient abodes for the sake of religion. These came from among the Scythians, north of the Ister, and were formerly called Getae, though now they are better known as Goths. And he asserts that this race of men were brought over to the faith of Christ in the following manner ... Scythians ... made an incursion ... [and] took a large quantity of prisoners, among whom were not a few ecclesiastics ... these pious captives ... persuaded them to embrace the Christian religion in the place of heathen superstitions. Of the number of these captives were the ancestors of Urphilas himself. ... This Urphilas, then ... being sent by the then king of the Goths on an embassy ... was ordained bishop of the Christians among the Goths ...'.

59. Wolfram, *op. cit.*, p. 78. He also theorizes about Ulfila's social standing, which is significant for his success as an agent of mission. Thompson, in *The Visigoths in the Time of Ulfila*, had argued for his being of humble origins, but Wolfram suggested that 'he could never have become a member of the Gothic delegation without a certain social standing. ... Ulfilas did not win renown among the Goths and Romans only as a result of his priestly office and how he administered it; rather, he became bishop because he had already possessed some standing. He was, for example, able to rise from lector to bishop without ever having been a deacon or presbyter', pp. 76–7.

60. Heather and Matthews, *op. cit.*, p. 135.

61. Thompson, 1957, *op. cit.*, p 4.

62. Heather and Matthews, *op. cit.*, p. 103.

63. Auxentius, in Heather and Matthews, *op. cit.*, p. 146, although it is important to note that Auxentius was probably making a doctrinal point here, indicating Ulfila's willingness to speak out in defence of his Arian beliefs, rather than of Christianity generally.

64. *Ibid.*, p. 147.

65. *Ibid.*, p. 150. See also p. 151, 'he showed the Christians (among them) to be truly Christians, and he multiplied their numbers'.

66. Thompson, 1966, *op. cit.*, p xxiii.

67. *Ibid.*, p. 155.

68. Bradley, *op. cit.*, p 61.

69. R. V. W. Elliott, *Runes*, Manchester, 1959, p. 11, states that 'all we know is that in some Germanic tribe some man had both the leisure (a factor often forgotten) and the phonetic sense to create the *futhark* from a North Italic model known to him somewhere in the alpine regions in the period *c.* 250 to 150 BC'. Ulfila's development of the Gothic alphabet was probably in order

to avoid using either a script which was associated with the old religion (runic) or one which was associated with the Eastern Roman Empire (the Greek script).

70. Joseph Wright, *Grammar of the Gothic Language*, Oxford, 1954, p. 336 and p. 342.

71. Alan F. Lacy, 'Gothic *weihs*, *airkns* and the Germanic notion of "Holy" ', *JIS*, 7, (3) and (4), 1979, p. 291.

72. *Ibid.*, p. 292.

73. See Chapter 1, section 'Contemporary Christian Approaches to Conversion', especially footnote 32. Also Thompson, 1957, says that 'it has been argued elsewhere that the conversion of the Visigoths must be dated to the period 382–395, when they were settled as Federates in Moesia. Although we know something about certain Catholic missionaries who tried in vain to convert them, there is unfortunately no hint in our sources of the identity of the Arian missionaries who successfully won them over in 382–95; but it is natural to suppose that they were not Romans but Gothic disciples of Ulfila who went among them with the Gothic Bible in their hands', p. 13.

74. See Frend's analysis of the failure of North African Christianity, which centres on the Donatist challenge to Catholic orthodoxy, in 'Religion and Social Change in the Late Roman Empire', in W. H. C. Frend, *Religion Popular and Unpopular in the Early Christian Centuries*, London, 1976, in particular p. 488 where he comments on the cultural and linguistic differences between the nomadic, Proto-Berber-speaking Donatists, and the urban, Latin-speaking Catholics. His analysis has been extended by Peter Brown in two articles, 'Religious Dissent in the Later Roman Empire: The Case of North Africa', *History*, 46, 1961, pp. 83–101, and 'Religious Coercion in the Later Roman Empire: The Case of North Africa', *History*, 48, 1963, pp. 283–305.

75. A. H. M. Jones, 'Were Ancient Heresies National or Social Movements in Disguise?', *JTS*, n.s. X, 1959, p. 283.

76. Heather, *op. cit.*, p. 106. See also Wolfram, *op. cit.*, p. 63.

77. Wolfram, *op. cit.*, p. 79.

78. Heather, *op. cit.*, p. 104.

79. Thompson, 1955, *op. cit.*, pp. 334–5.

80. *Passio*, Heather and Matthews, *op. cit.*, p. 112, 'II.I. Now Saba was orthodox in faith ...'. The Greek text is in Hippolyte Delehaye (ed.), *Passio S. Sabae Gothi*, in *AB*, XXXI, 1912, p. 217.

81. See Chapter 1, section 'Conversion, Christianization and Religious Change'.

82. *Passio*, Heather and Matthews, *op. cit.*, pp. 112–13. The Greek text is in Delehaye, *op. cit.*

83. *Passio*, Heather and Matthews, *op. cit.*, pp. 116–17. The Greek text is in Delehaye, *op. cit.*, p. 221.

84. Tacitus, Mattingly, *op. cit.*, p. 111. The Latin text is in Tacitus, *Germania, Agricola, and First Book of the Annals*, ed. and trans. William Smith, London, 1840, p. 9.

85. Socrates Scholasticus, *The Ecclesiastical History of Socrates*, ed. and trans. unknown, London, 1880, pp. 254–5, states that the Goths 'were divided into

two parties, one of which was led by Fritigernes, the other by Athanaric'. The Greek text is in Socrates Scholasticus, *Ecclesiastical History*, ed. William Bright, Oxford, 1893, pp. 209–10.

86. Heather, *op. cit.*, p. 105.
87. *Ibid.*, p. 106.
88. Wolfram, *op. cit.*, p. 68.
89. Ammianus Marcellinus, *Histories*, ed. and trans. John C. Rolfe, London, 1939, p. 35, writes: 'but since Athanaricus declared that he was bound by an oath accompanied by a fearful imprecation, and thus prevented by his father's orders from ever setting foot on Roman soil, and since he could not be induced to do so, and it was unbecoming and degrading for the emperor to cross to him, it was decided by those of good judgement that ships should be rowed into mid-stream, one carrying the emperor with his guard, the other the Gothic ruler with his men, and that thus a treaty of peace should be struck as agreed'. The Latin text is on p. 34.
90. Heather and Matthews, *op. cit.*, p. 104.
91. Socrates Scholasticus, *op. cit.*, p. 255. The Greek is in Socrates Scholasticus, Bright, *op. cit.*, p. 210.
92. Sozomen, *op. cit.*, p. 305: 'the emperor having commanded the troops in Thrace to assist him, a second battle was fought, and Athanaric and his party were put to flight. In acknowledgement of the timely succour afforded by Valens, and in proof of his fidelity to the Romans, Phritigernes embraced the religion of the emperor, and persuaded the barbarians over whom he ruled to follow his example. It does not, however, appear to me that this is the only reason that can be advanced to account for the Goths having retained, even to this present day, the tenets of Arianism. Ulphilas, their bishop, originally held no opinions at variance with those of the Catholic church ...'. The Greek text is in Sozomen, *Kirchengeschichte*, ed. Joseph Bidez, Berlin, 1960, p. 295.
93. Jordanes, Mierow, *op. cit.*, p. 88: 'Thus the Emperor Valens made the Visigoths Arians rather than Christians'. The Latin text is in Jordanes, *Getica*, in *MGH:AA*, ed. Theodore Mommsen, tom. V, Berlin, 1882, p. 92. See also Theodoret, *History of the Church from AD 322 to AD 427*, ed. and trans. unknown, London, 1864, pp. 197–8, where blame is laid on Valens, Eudoxius, and Urfila (Ulfila).
94. Peter Heather, 'The Crossing of the Danube and the Gothic Conversion', *GRBS*, 27, (3), 1986, pp. 311–12.
95. Wolfram, *op. cit.*, p. 72.
96. Ammianus Marcellinus, *op. cit.*, pp. 399–401, states that the chief motive of the deserters was fear of the Huns, but he is not a Christian, and may have been unaware of possible religious motivations.
97. *Ibid.*, p. 405, 'With such stormy eagerness on the part of insistent men was the ruin of the Roman world brought in. This at any rate is neither obscure nor uncertain, that the ill-omened officials who ferried the barbarian hordes often tried to reckon their number, but gave up their vain attempt.' The Latin text is on p. 404.

98. *Ibid.,* p. 407.
99. *Ibid.,* pp. 411–13 and Jordanes, Mierow, *op. cit.,* pp. 89–90. On the ill-treatment of the Goths by the Romans, see A. H. M. Jones, *The Decline of the Ancient World,* London, 1966, p. 67, 'It was evidently Valens' intention to deal with the Visigoths as Constantine had dealt with the Sarmatians. He enlisted many young Goths under Roman officers in the army of the East and promised deserted lands in Thrace to the remainder. But the situation was mismanaged: the Goths were not promptly dispersed and adequate supplies were not available, while the local *comes* and *dux* exploited the refugees by selling them food at exorbitant prices and buying their children as slaves. Disorders broke out, and in the confusion the Ostrogoths also managed to cross the Danube. The united tribes are said to have numbered 200,000.'
100. Jones, 1966, *op. cit.,* p. 68.
101. Wolfram, *op. cit.,* pp. 78 and 82–3.
102. Frend, *op. cit.,* p. 12.
103. See Chapter 4, section 'The Missionary and the King'.
104. Ammianus Marcellinus, *op. cit.,* pp. 465–7.
105. Heather, 1986, *op. cit.,* p. 312.
106. Heather and Matthews, *op. cit.,* comment that 'Sozomen reports that Ulfila led the embassy to Valens in 376 which negotiated the entry of the Tervingi into the Roman Empire. That there was such an embassy is confirmed by Ammianus (31.4.1), and the relevant chapter of Sozomen seems to consist of genuine information which has been misplaced rather than fabricated material', p. 135.
107. Wolfram, *op. cit.,* p. 74.
108. Jordanes, Mierow, *op. cit.,* p. 88. The Latin text is in Jordanes, *MGH:AA, op. cit.,* p. 92.
109. Thompson, 1966, *op. cit.,* p. 107: 'the conversion took place when the Visigoths were living in close association with the Roman inhabitants of Moesia. Since the optimates were now becoming landowners, their social interests were approximating more and more closely to the interests of the Roman landowners around them. The tribal religion had decayed with the decay of the tribes themselves: and hence, living as they were in a Roman environment, the Visigothic leaders were accepting the outlook of the Roman propertied classes whose social position they hoped to reproduce in their own society ...'.
110. Musset, *op. cit.,* p. 185.
111. Thompson, 1966, *op. cit.,* p. 110.
112. Musset, *op. cit.,* p. 184.
113. E. A. Thompson, *The Goths in Spain,* Oxford, 1969, p. 2.
114. Heather, *op. cit.,* p. 193.
115. Wolfram, *op. cit.,* p. 143 comments: 'scholars who insist that the Tervingian ancestors of the Visigoths did not know the greater kingship and at the same time reject Alaric's election as king are forced to assume that the introduction of the new institution "happened" to Alaric's Goths somewhere

and sometime on the march, because no one doubts any longer that Athaulf, Alaric's brother-in-law and successor, was in fact a king. Such an argument seems illogical in itself, and its justification certainly is.'

116. Christopher Dawson, *The Making of Europe*, New York, 1956, p. 97.

117. Heather, *op. cit.*, pp. 313–14.

118. Hydatius, *The Chronicle of Hydatius and the Consularia Constantinopolitana*, ed. and trans. R. W. Burgess, Oxford, 1993, p. 4.

119. *Ibid.*, p. 95. See also p. 81 for the persecution of the orthodox Bishop John by Eudoxia, the Arian wife of Arcadius; p. 119 for a description of Ajax, 'a Greek apostate and leading Arian' among the Suevi; and *passim* for the activities of Theodoric the Ostrogoth.

120. Victor of Vita, *History of the Vandal Persecution*, ed. and trans. John Moorhead, Liverpool, 1992, p. 8.

121. *Ibid.*, p. 18, 'the Arians learned that our people had opened a church which had been shut at a certain place called Regia, so they could celebrate Easter Day. Straightaway, one of their priests, whose name was Anduit, got together a band of armed men and incited them to attack the throng of the innocent ...'.

122. *Ibid.*, p. 19.

123. *Ibid.*, p. 9.

124. *Ibid.*, p. 27.

125. Theodoret, *op. cit.*, p. 236 discusses John Chrysostom's efforts to convert the Gothic Arians in Scythia to Catholicism. See also Salvian of Marseilles, *De Gubernatione Dei*, translated in Heather and Matthews, *op. cit.*, pp. 166–9, and analysed in Lyn Olson, 'The Conversion of the Visigoths and the Bulgarians Compared', in Olson, *op. cit.*, pp. 22–32. Socrates, *op. cit.*, describes the nocturnal worship of the Arians, pp. 314–15, and Wolfram, *op. cit.*, p. 210, observes that 'on several occasions we read of an Arian court clergy. Of course the exclusively Catholic Roman observers speak disparagingly of them, and it seems that at times even the king did not take them all that seriously. Still, we must believe that these men were capable of assiduous Bible studies and the preservation of Ulfila's heritage through the spoken and written word. We do not know whether Modaharius, who debated with Roman bishops, was part of the court or was even sent to the disputation by Euric. Modaharius' name, however, is in the best Balthic tradition, and so it cannot have been mere coincidence that he spoke up for the *Lex Gothica*, the Arian faith and Law. Toulouse, to be sure, served not only the Suevi but also the Burgundians in matters of the faith.'

126. Eugippius, *The Life of Saint Severin*, ed. and trans. Ludwig Bieler and Ludmilla Krestan, Washington, 1965, p. 29.

127. *Ibid.*, p. 62.

128. *Ibid.*, p. 65.

129. E. A. Thompson, *Romans and Barbarians*, University of Wisconsin Press, 1982, p. 133.

130. Wolfram, *op. cit.*, p. 325.

131. Patrick Wormald, '*Lex Scripta and Verbum Regis*: Legislation and Germanic Kingship, from Euric to Cnut', in Peter Sawyer and Ian Woods (eds), *Early Medieval Kingship*, Leeds, 1977, p. 107.

132. Kathryn Fisher Drew, 'The Barbarian Kings as Lawgivers and Judges', in Robert S. Hoyt (ed.), *Life and Thought in the Early Middle Ages*, Minneapolis, 1967, p. 9.

133. Drew, *op. cit.*

134. Glenn Chesnut, *The First Christian Histories*, Paris, 1977, p. 229.

135. Musset, *op. cit.*, p 43.

136. Monophysitism was an Eastern heresy which held that Jesus had only one nature, and not the two natures (wholly human and wholly divine) that orthodoxy accepts.

137. Isidore of Seville, *History of the Kings of the Goths, Vandals and Suevi*, ed. and trans. Guido Donini and Gordon B. Ford, Leiden, 1966, p. 25. The Latin is in Isidore of Seville, *Historia Gothorum*, in *MGH:AA*, ed. Theodore Mommsen, tom. XI, vol. II, Berlin, 1894, p. 289.

138. E. A. Thompson, 'The Conversion of the Visigoths to Catholicism', *NMS*, 4, 1960, p. 31. It is significant that Thompson cites Schmidt's argument with approval, because it supports his own argument for the Gothic acceptance of Arianism in the first instance.

3 The Franks: Arianism and Catholicism

For a bishop, orthodoxy was the only bridge over which a barbarian could enter civilisation; and in the eyes of John Chrysostom a Goth who was fully identified with the Roman order by pagan standards but who had remained an Arian, might just as well have stayed in his skins, across the Danube (see Theodoret, *Historia Ecclesiastica*, V. 32)

Peter Brown[1]

Change and continuity in Gaul

The process whereby Christianity supplanted other beliefs in Gaul was part of a complex of changes which saw Roman control of the province replaced first by regional 'emperors' and then by the kingdom of the Franks. The Franks were the final inheritors of an area which had been variously controlled by Celtic vigilante bands (the *Bagaudae*), Visigoths, Alans, and other barbarian groups.[2] Gaul had officially received Catholic Christianity along with the rest of the Empire when Constantine promulgated the Edict of Milan in 313, but the migration of Arian Germans brought a divergent version of the faith. The strongest Catholic Christian presences developed around Trier, which was an imperial city and the residence of emperors, and around Tours in the central western region. The presence in Tours was due to the mission of Martin, bishop of Tours from *c.* 371 to 397.[3]

Martin's mission is known from the writings of his friend and hagiographer, Sulpicius Severus, a Gallo-Roman from Aquitaine, who, after a worldly career, retired to the religious life in 395 with Paulinus of Nola and Paulinus' wife, Therasia. This is the kind of second conversion which Stancliffe envisaged when she observed that in the fourth century, conversion generally referred:

not to the widespread adhesion to Christianity at that time, in the sense that people began to fall in with the emperor's religion ... rather, I allude to [conversion] to the ascetic life, opting out of a career and family life in order to devote themselves wholly to the service of Christ.[4]

Sulpicius first met Martin in 393 or 394, three or four years prior to the saint's death, and he published the *Vita Martini* during Martin's lifetime. Martin was one of the first saints to be so regarded because of their life, rather than because of their death by martyrdom. Sulpicius does not give a systematic account of Martin's missionary programme: he concentrates on his powers as an exorcist and healer; his devotion to prayer and asceticism; and his wisdom in preaching to the pagans and heretics.[5] While the veracity of Sulpicius' *Vita* has been questioned,[6] some details have the ring of truth.

Martin not only participated in the conversion of pagans, but was directly involved in the struggle against the Arian Germans; his mentor, Hilary of Poitiers, was the staunchest champion of orthodoxy in Gaul.[7] The methods employed by Martin included the performance of miracles. On one occasion a serf was possessed by a demon:

> Martin, however, protested that he could not go to the unhallowed house of a pagan. For Tetradius at that time was still held fast in the errors of paganism. He therefore promised that, if the demon were expelled from the boy, he would become a Christian. Martin then laid hands on the boy and drove the evil spirit out of him. Tetradius, on seeing this, made a profession of faith in the Lord Jesus ... and was baptized not long afterwards.[8]

Martin also destroyed sacred objects, including temples and sacred trees,[9] and advocated the substitution of Christian rites and feasts for pagan festivals.[10] The case of the sacred tree recalls the Gauls' horror when Julius Caesar commanded the destruction of the sacred groves, indicating, perhaps, that Martin opposed Celtic beliefs as well as the cults of the classical Roman deities.[11] Though Martin's actions were resisted on occasion, his mission conformed to the general pattern throughout the Roman world; preaching and the performance of wonders were followed by the willingness of the people to convert.[12]

The mission of Martin of Tours ensured that the Gallo-Roman population were Christianized and were therefore able to resist, both culturally and religiously, the influx of Franks. For Gregory of Tours, a successor of Martin, the saint functioned on a national and communal level. He stood 'between the helpless and the powerful. ... His immediate goal was to bring about the salvation of the needy, but his ultimate goal was to redeem the oppressors and, thus, society at large.'[13] Similar views are expressed in other Christian writings of late antiquity.[14] The dissemination of Christianity in Gaul was closely linked to the aristocratization of the Gallic Church;[15] the spokesmen for both paganism and Christianity in the fourth century were aristocrats.[16] The distinction between Roman and barbarian hardened into one of language, culture and belief,[17] and the Church identified with the classical past.[18]

The life of Ausonius (*c.* 310–390) illustrates this well; although a Christian, his enthusiasm for the Roman past was boundless and he retained a pride in his family connection with the druids.[19] Gregory of Tours' *Historia Francorum* suggests that some Gallo-Roman senatorial families continued to be ambassadors, diplomats and generals under the Germanic conquerors, with no loss of prestige or status; others were accommodated into the hierarchy of the Church.[20]

Mission in the fifth century

The mid-fifth century was a period of energetic evangelism, in which the Church attempted to conquer and to assimilate the disparate peoples and kingdoms which were emerging from the wreckage of the Roman Empire. Ireland, which had never been part of Rome, was evangelized by Patrick and Palladius in the early fifth century.[21] Patrick is a puzzling figure and the sources for his life have often been interpreted as referring to two or possibly even three different people.[22] Two of his own writings, the *Letter* and the *Declaration*, have been preserved and there is a biography by Muirchu written approximately two hundred years later. It has been claimed that Patrick entered Ireland in 431 or 432 and that Palladius was consecrated bishop of Ireland in 431, which may support the theory that they are one and the same person.[23]

The most tantalizing thing about Patrick and Palladius is that they were bishops, since bishops were generally only sent to existing Christian communities (and in Bede this is definitely the case with Palladius). For a missionary, the situation was much more likely to be like that of Augustine of Canterbury, who was an abbot when sent to the new mission-field of Anglo-Saxon England and was only consecrated bishop after he had baptized ten thousand English and had a flock. It is likely, then, that Christianity first reached Ireland through casual contacts (as in the bottom-up conversion model), but that it had not penetrated greatly, since Patrick's writings indicate that on his arrival the Irish aristocracy were almost entirely pagan.[24] From whence these converts came is not known, and the methods employed by Patrick are similarly shrouded in mystery.[25]

In the fifth century Gaul was overrun by Germanic tribes which eventually divided the province up between themselves, with the Visigoths in the south-west, the Burgundians in the south-east, and the Franks in the north. The Visigoths began to move westwards in 395 under the leadership of Alaric, and eventually came to occupy parts of southern Gaul.[26] They brought their heretical Christianity with them and as a result the Germans in the Western Empire were either pagan or Arian. The lives of Christians such as Sidonius Apollinaris and St Germanus of Auxerre will now be examined to illuminate the transformation of Gallic society in this period.

Germanus was born in the late fourth century and became bishop of Auxerre in approximately 415.[27] He was an aristocrat who had studied law and held a provincial governorship, and his *Vita* was written by Constantius of Lyons around 480, some thirty years after the saint's death in 448. Germanus' aristocratic origins were evident in his confident and outspoken opposition to the heresies of Arianism and Pelagianism and the disruption caused by the settlement of the barbarians. He travelled to Britain to combat Pelagianism, a doctrine which emphasized free will and opposed original sin and predestination, and witnessed one of the early attacks of the Anglo-Saxons on the Romano-British population.[28] Germanus was not a missionary, but he engaged in missionary activity when required. During the Saxon attack, Constantius states that:

> the Saxons and the Picts had joined forces to make war upon the Britons. ... It was the season of Lent and the presence of the bishops made the sacred forty days still more sacred; so much so that the soldiers, who received instruction in daily sermons, flew eagerly to the grace of baptism; indeed, great numbers of this pious army sought the waters of salvation ... and Germanus announced that he would be their general.[29]

Like Martin of Tours, Germanus of Auxerre became the focus of the community in Auxerre; a shrine which he had built in honour of a group of martyrs was rededicated to Germanus himself after his death. The cult of the saints was fast displacing the cults of the regional deities.

Sidonius Apollinaris was born in Lyons in 432. His family was of senatorial rank and he was destined for a great career; in 453 he married Papianilla, the daughter of Eparchius Avitus, who had been praetorian prefect of Gaul. Politics in Gaul at that time was dominated by Flavius Aetius, who was Master of Soldiers for Emperor Valentinian III.[30] Aetius' position was difficult, but he pursued a skilful policy of divide-and-conquer, allying with one barbarian group at a time in order to defeat the other groups. Aetius settled the Visigoths around Toulouse, and Sidonius made diplomatic journeys to that city and became acquainted with the Arian king, Theodoric.[31]

The years 454 and 455 were disastrous: Aetius was murdered at Valentinian III's instigation; Valentinian himself was then murdered; and two barbarian kings, Theodoric the Goth and Geiseric the Vandal were prepared to declare themselves emperor. Independent barbarian groups, taking advantage of the power vacuum renewed their attacks. In Gaul the Saxons, Franks, Burgundians and Gepidae were on the move; in Spain the Suevi sacked Cartagena; the Alamanni crossed the Rhine; and the Goths and the Vandals both conceived of attacking Rome itself.[32]

Sidonius' poetry responds to this chaos with the personification of cities and aspects of civilization and the expression of a profound reverence for Rome and all it stood for.[33] His writings expressed genuine pathos, as he faced the decline of Latin culture throughout Gaul. In a famous letter written around 470 to Arbogast, the Frankish Count of Trier, Sidonius applauded him for preserving what is left of Roman speech and culture in the North.[34] He wrote:

> The Roman speech, if it still exists anywhere, has survived in you, though it has long been wiped out from the Belgian and Rhenic lands: with you and your eloquence surviving, even though Roman law has ceased at our border, the Roman speech does not falter. For this reason, as I reciprocate your greeting, I rejoice greatly that at any rate in your illustrious breast there have remained traces of our vanishing culture. If you extend these by constant reading you will discover for yourself as each day passes that the educated are no less superior to the unlettered than men are to beasts.[35]

Sidonius became bishop of Auvergne, but his life ended with arrest, confiscation of property, exile, and other humiliations after Euric the Visigoth seized Auvergne. He was released in 476, but had to petition Euric for possession of some land bequeathed to him by his mother-in-law, two-thirds of which had been occupied by a Goth. He died sometime between 480 and 490, just as the Franks were gaining power in the north.

The final figure to be discussed before considering the Franks is Caesarius of Arles (470–543), who was a monk of Lérins before becoming bishop of Arles in 503. Since Arles was an important city, he immediately became embroiled in politics. Alaric II, a Visigoth, was effectively king of the region, and for the next forty years Caesarius dealt with rulers of the Visigoths, Burgundians and Franks.[36] He counselled compliance with the civil authorities:

> He always taught, there and everywhere, that men should render to God what are God's and to Caesar what are Caesar's as the Apostle teaches, obey, indeed, kings and powers, when their orders are just, but despise the depravity of King [Alaric's] Arian belief ...[37]

Alaric II was killed in the battle of Vouille against Clovis the Frank in 507, and in 508 Arles was besieged by Franks, Burgundians and Goths. Caesarius' principal missionary concern was the expulsion of syncretistic elements from Christianity. His sermons reveal that his flock mostly followed a Christianity mixed with elements of Greco-Roman, Celtic and Germanic religion.[38] These sermons are evidence for the presence of Christian ideas and practices in the territory the Franks later occupied.[39] Caesarius was also concerned with the making of a Christian people and, though his writings on this theme are not systematic, they foreshadow some of the ideas of Pope Gregory the Great on the creation of a Christian society.[40]

The Franks

Current scholarly opinion is that the Franks, like the Goths, had no real shared ethnic history. 'Goths' means 'the people' and the etymology of 'Franks' has generally been traced to the Germanic *frak* or *frech*, which means 'savage' or 'proud'.[41] The Franks are first mentioned in classical sources in the middle of the third century. The biographer of the Emperor Aurelian observed that: 'Aurelian was tribune of the Sixth Legion (Gallicana) at Mainz when the Franks attempted to overrun the whole of Gaul. He shattered their attack, killing seven hundred of them and selling three hundred prisoners as slaves'.[42] After Aurelian's death the Frankish attacks on Gaul increased. In 358 Ammianus records the Franks as settled in Belgium. At this time a number of Franks were distinguishing themselves in the service of the Empire: Silvanus, who usurped the throne in 355; Bauto who was *de facto* regent to Valentinian II; Richomer, who was military commander in the East from 388 to 393; and Arbogast.[43]

Gregory of Tours' *History of the Franks*, the principal source for this period, was written in the latter half of the sixth century. Gregory was born *c.* 539 to a Gallo-Roman senatorial family with a distinguished tradition of service to the Church and a tendency to be canonized.[44] Gregory's book begins conventionally with the Creation and a brief resume of biblical history. When he reaches more recent events he relies heavily on works such as Orosius' *Historia Adversus Paganum*. Gregory's principal subject is the conversion of the Franks, and his hero and ideal ruler is Clovis, who converted to Catholicism somewhere between 496 and 508.

It is not surprising that Gregory offers little information about the pre-Christian beliefs of the Frankish people, for 'Gregory never had to encounter learned pagans, such as Orosius faced; but paganism he knew well ... and heresy – notably Arianism – was his constant dread'.[45] He does record that the Merovingian dynasty traced its origins to Merovech, who is elsewhere recorded as the son of a sea-monster. It appears that the worship of a war god, which was customary among all the Germanic peoples, was also popular with the Franks. This god was most likely Woden, or a deity resembling Woden.[46]

As with other Germanic societies, kings were vital to the religious life of the Franks, and they played a significant part in their conversion. In discussing the Merovingian kings, Einhard in his *Vita Karoli* comments that 'Whenever [the Merovingian king] needed to travel, he went in a cart which was drawn in country style by yoked oxen, with a cow-herd to drive them'.[47]

This detail, which Einhard supplies to belittle the Merovingian monarchy (in order to excuse the usurpation of the Arnulfing family by whom he was employed), actually recalls the traditional journey of the sacral god-king throughout the villages of his people in a ceremonial cart.

The Frankish kings shared many of the characteristics of the Germanic kings described by Tacitus; the two aspects of leadership, the *dux* and the *rex*, are clearly present. Wallace-Hadrill comments that 'the Tacitean *dux* is not the tap-root but a specialised function of Germanic kingship. Nothing suggests that the *rex* could not be a *dux* or that a *dux* could not acquire the traditional duties of a *rex*. ... *Duces* rise and fall according to need, and so do *reges*'.[48]

Clovis, whom Gregory of Tours likens to Constantine, was a vigorous war-leader and did not desist from military action after his conversion. This suggests the *dux*, but he was also a Merovingian, descended from the half-divine Merovech, and therefore had the noble descent of the *rex*. This lineage recalls the importance of divine descent for Germanic kings.[49] In pagan terms Clovis was a properly constituted king.

The principal archaeological evidence for Clovis' lineage are the grave goods of his father Childeric, whose burial in Tournai was accidentally discovered in 1653. Unfortunately, most of this treasure was stolen from Paris in 1831, but the goods had been drawn and published by Chifflet, so it is possible to speculate about the burial. In addition to jewellery and personal possessions, the burial included a battle-axe, the standard Frankish weapon, and 'his spear and the head of his horse with all its harness, numerous gold buckles, gold mounts from a belt ... a mounted crystal ball. ... No less than three hundred gold cicadas, the symbol of eternal life, their wings inlaid with garnets, were sewn on the king's brocaded cloak.'[50] This burial parallels other royal interments in the Germanic world, such as Sutton Hoo in England and Oseberg in Norway (although Childeric's was not a ship burial). The emphasis on providing the king with all the comforts necessary for the next world reveals the 'this-worldly' and materialistic orientation of Germanic religion already noted by Russell.

Childeric was the first historically attested Frankish leader of any import, although Sidonius Apollinaris referred to a 'Chlodio' or 'Chlodion', who began the Frankish conquests in north-east Gaul in the first half of the fifth century.[51] Childeric had been exiled from his tribal confederation, who had elected Aegidius, a Roman general who had rejected the authority of the Western emperors after 462 and set up an independent kingdom based at Soissons, as their king.[52] It is not clear from Gregory of Tours, but it seems that Childeric returned and challenged Aegidius for control of the Franks, and won a victory at Orléans. This was one in a string of victories which were aimed at the domination of the Gallo-Roman *civitates*.[53] When Childeric died in 481 he was master of half a dozen of these communities, and his son Clovis inherited his territories. Gregory gives Clovis' age at accession as fifteen. Five years into his reign he fought and defeated Syagrius, the son of Aegidius, and had him killed.[54] Gregory styles Syagrius 'King of the Romans', but current scholarship is divided as to his status.[55] Clovis' victory over Syagrius was followed by a campaign against the Thuringians around 491. Clovis' marriage to Chrotechildis, or Clotild, the niece of the Burgundian king Gundobad, also occurred at about this time.

This raises the issue of how Romanized the Franks were? The transition from pre-Christian to Christian in Frankia is complicated by several factors. First, the pre-Christian beliefs were a mixture of Celtic, Germanic and Greco-Roman religious ideas. Second, the process of conversion involved a choice between Arian Christianity and Catholicism. Childeric was dignified by a Roman title and therefore probably ruled with some degree of recognition by Rome.[56] By the time of Clovis' campaigns, however, the area was dotted with barbarian rulers and their federations, with only Theodoric the Ostrogoth in a relationship with the Byzantine emperors in Constantinople.

The conversion of Clovis

Where, when, how, and why Clovis converted to Catholic Christianity are questions which are still hotly debated. There are significant problems with Gregory's account and chronology, and the supporting evidence raises many more questions. Gregory sees Queen Clotild and Clovis' desire for success in war as the key motives for the king's change of faith. Clotild was a devout Catholic Christian from an Arian family, which was unusual for a Germanic princess. The thirteenth-century, and therefore late and unreliable *Les Grandes Chroniques* indicates that Gundobad had killed Clotild's parents, and that she was therefore on bad terms with him, which could explain the religious differences in the family.[57] Gregory's account states that after their first child was born she pressed Clovis to allow her child to be baptized and argued fiercely with him about the power of the old gods. Clovis was not convinced. 'However often the Queen said this, the King came no nearer belief. "All these things have been created and produced at the command of our gods," he would answer. "It is obvious that your God can do nothing, and, what is more, there is no proof that he is a God at all".'[58]

The queen arranged for her son to be baptized, after which he died. This was a powerful sign for Clovis: the power of the old gods seemed stronger than the protection afforded by the new God. The same disagreement occurred when their second son was baptized and became ill; Clovis attributed the illness to the baptism and claimed that had the children been dedicated to his gods they would have come to no harm. Though the second child did not die, more was needed to persuade Clovis.

Gregory's account has its weaknesses. It has been argued that little credit ought to be given to the motivations he supplies, since his kings and queens are primarily literary creations. The factors in the conversion as presented by Gregory, such as a believing wife, victory in battle, and being impressed by miracles, are clichés in conversion literature. Moorhead has suggested these motifs 'were merely things authors thought likely to have been important'.[59] It is true that there is a literary *topos* in which the influence of wives and mothers assists in the spread of Christianity.[60] Gregory also relates that Clotild teased Clovis about his religious beliefs in the words of Virgil, which is possible but feels artificial and 'literary'.[61] (Goffart and Auerbach have pointed out that, however much Gregory protested his rough style and lack of learning, he was a genuine artist, and that his artistry may be recognized in his narration of events.)[62] It cannot be denied, however, that a Christian wife would have been a factor of significance in Clovis' environment, exposing him daily to the beliefs and practices of the new faith. There is also a possibility that Clotild contributed personally to Gregory's *History*. When Clovis died in 511 she retired to Tours, where she died in 548. Gregory was born in 539 and although any personal contact with Clotild must have been slight, his family were of senatorial rank, and would certainly have known her.[63]

According to Gregory, the direct cause for Clovis' conversion was the hostility between the Alamanni and the Franks erupting into war. For Germanic kings success in battle was a sign that the gods' favour was with them. A later source, the anonymous *Liber Historiae Francorum* of 727, follows Gregory closely in its account of Clovis' preparations for the battle. He is said to have vowed that he would be baptized if the victory came to him:

'Jesus Christ,' he said, 'you whom Clotild maintains to be the Son of the living God, you who deign to give help to those in travail and victory to those who trust in you, in faith I beg the glory of your help. If you will give me victory over my enemies, and if I may have evidence of that miraculous power which the people dedicated to your name say that they have experienced, then I will believe in you and I will be baptized in your name. I have called upon my own gods, but, as I see only too clearly, they have no intention of helping me. I therefore cannot believe that they possess any power, for they do not come to the assistance of those who trust in them. I now call upon you. I want to believe in you, but I must first be saved from my enemies.'[64]

Gregory places this battle in 496, but this is problematic, since a letter from Theodoric the Ostrogoth survives referring to the Alamannic campaign of 506 and to Clovis' victory.[65] Were there several campaigns? It seems likely.

At any rate, the date of Clovis' baptism is difficult to establish; dates as disparate as 496 and 508 are possible. Gregory wrote over half a century after the events, at a time when learning had declined greatly, and he had his own reasons for telescoping events to make a better story. Gregory is eager to have Clovis baptized immediately, to the delight of Clotild, and to present his subsequent campaigns against the other Germanic peoples as part of a holy war against Arianism. As Wood has commented, finding a causal link between 'Clovis' Catholicism and his success would have seemed obvious enough to anyone who expected to see divine intervention in human affairs'.[66] Most scholars now suggest that Clovis' baptism did not take place until several years later and that he was therefore rather like Constantine, to whom Gregory ambiguously compares him. Constantine won victory at the battle of Milvian Bridge[67] and adopted Christianity as the imperial religion in 312, but was not baptized until 337 when he was on his deathbed, and Eusebius of Nicomedia, an Arian, administered the rite. Gregory records of Constantine only two facts: that he poisoned his son and murdered his wife.[68] Considering Clovis' conduct towards his relatives at the end of his life, perhaps Gregory intended the comparison ironically.[69]

The extent to which Arianism complicated the conversion of the Franks became apparent with Wood's 1985 article.[70] Gregory presents Clovis as converting from paganism to Catholicism, but Wood used five sets of sources which are much closer to the lifetime of Clovis than Gregory, none of which refer to a conversion experience at the battle of Tolbiac. These sources are: the *Vita Genovefae*, an early sixth century life of St Geneviève of Paris; the three letters of Bishop Remigius of Rheims; the three works of Bishop Avitus of Vienne, including a letter to Clovis; six letters of Theodoric the Ostrogoth; and Clovis' letter to the bishops of Aquitaine.[71] Remigius of Rheims wrote to Clovis on his accession in terms which suggests that the young king was not a Christian,[72] supporting Gregory's account. The later letter of Avitus of Vienne, congratulating Clovis upon his baptism, is the best contemporary evidence available. Avitus' other writings, a lost homily *De conversione Lenteildis Chlodovaei sororis* ('The Conversion of Lenteildis Sister of Clovis') and a letter to the Pope announcing the conversion of an unidentified king, are also important.[73]

Avitus' letter to Clovis places his baptism in a Byzantine imperial context, from which Wood deduced that it occurs after 500, when Gundobad had become a tributary of the Franks and the Byzantine Emperor Anastasius was moving against the Arian Theodoric the Ostrogoth.[74] Wood also suggested that the second letter was more logically associated with Clovis than the Burgundian Sigismund to whom it is traditionally believed to refer.[75] Avitus preached the homily at the Catholic baptism of Clovis' sister Lenteildis (Lantechild), who had apparently received Arian baptism before converting to Catholicism. From these sources, Wood marshals evidence to suggest that Clovis had been an Arian Christian before his baptism as a Catholic.

How reasonable is this hypothesis? James conceded the possibility, but Barlow shrewdly argued that if Clovis had converted from Arianism the bishops of Frankia would have used him as an *exemplum* in their campaign against Arianism, which was not the case.[76] Daly, in a revisionist article, wishes to dismiss the traditional picture of Clovis as a barbarian warrior converted to Catholicism. He portrays Clovis as thoroughly Romanized and intimately acquainted with Christianity. His evidence for this includes Childeric's acquaintance with St Geneviève, the Arian Christianity of at least two of Clovis' sisters (Audofled, who was married to Theodoric, and the aforementioned Lenteildis), and the dedication to virginity of his other sister Albofled. This would be an example of incidental contacts with Christianity preparing the way for the conversion of kings. With regard to the *Vita Genovefae*, however, the evidence is not quite so clear. Frye notes that in this text 'Childeric appears not as a friend, ally or peaceful administrator, but as conqueror of the Gallo-Roman Parisii'.[77] Daly also seems not to distinguish between Catholic Christianity and Arian Christianity particularly, the sense that two of Clovis' sisters started out as Arians, and only the third, Albofled, chose Catholicism, and we do not know the dates of the baptisms of these princesses. What is established beyond doubt is that Clovis could not have been entirely ignorant of Christianity.

The details in Gregory's description of Clovis' baptism are interesting, since they show the dependence of the Germanic king on his *comitatus*. The bishop-saint, Remigius of Rheims, visited Clovis at the invitation of Clotild and preached to him. Clovis responded: 'I have listened to you willingly, holy father. There remains one obstacle. The people under my command will not agree to forsake their gods. I will go and put to them what you have just put to me'.[78] Conveniently, the people decide to worship the God of the saint; three thousand of Clovis' army are baptized along with the king and his two sisters, Albofled and Lenteildis. This conforms to the classic model of the sacral king, imbued with power and religious significance, but still dependent on the oaths of his supporters, who elect to change beliefs with him. Gregory presents Clovis as the first Frankish Christian, though assuredly he was not, as his Arian sister demonstrates. It is not even certain that he was the first Catholic king of the Franks;[79] Barlow argues that Childeric's Frankish followers had abandoned him for Aegidius, who was a Catholic, and that Aegidius was therefore the first Catholic king of the Franks, despite not being ethnically Frankish.[80]

After his victory against the Alamanni, Clovis spent a number of years subduing other Germanic tribes, including the Burgundians and the Goths.

Gregory presents Clovis as saying: 'I find it hard to go on seeing these Arians occupy a part of Gaul. ... With God's help let us invade them. When we have beaten them, we will take over their territory.'[81] To modern eyes this may appear to be a cynical exercise on Clovis' part to expand his territory and add to his power, and it calls to mind Wallace-Hadrill's comments about the Germanic 'desire for booty' and 'ancient quarrels'.[82] The result resembled a primitive form of the later medieval institution of vassalage, in which the power of a ruler was assessed by the number of minor rulers who were oath-bound to him. The Anglo-Saxon *bretwalda* or over-king is another example of this type of arrangement.[83] For Clovis, however, making war was a contest of power between different deities and an essential part of his role as king.

The reaction to Clovis' conversion (meaning either his identification with Christianity or his baptism, whenever that took place) from the clergy of Western Europe was positive. Bishop Avitus of Vienne, a notable opponent of heresies (chiefly those of Sabellius and Eutyches), wrote to Clovis comparing him to the Eastern Emperor in Constantinople and reassuring him of the noble stature of Christian monarchs. This letter has been referred to above. It is a fascinating document, raising questions about the nature of Germanic sacral kingship. Avitus advised Clovis:

> Many others, in this matter, when their bishops or friends exhort them to adhere to the True Faith, are accustomed to oppose the traditions of their race and respect for their ancestral cult. ... Of all your ancient genealogy you have chosen to keep only your own nobility, and you have willed that your race shall derive from you all the glories which adorn high birth. ... You follow your ancestors in reigning in this world; you have opened the way to your descendants to a heavenly reign.[84]

Avitus described a phenomenon which will appear in subsequent Germanic conversions, the reluctance of the people to abandon their ancestral ways. He also is concerned to transfer the Germanic concept of the king as peculiarly connected with the gods into a Christian context, where there were many precedents (such as the close relationship of David and Solomon with Yahweh in the *Old Testament*, and Jesus' sonship in the *New Testament*). He encouraged Clovis to retain his regard for his ancestors, but not to worship them or view them as in any way divine.

On the basis of this, Moisl contended that the pagan Germanic kings had a special sacral role which they feared would be lost with conversion. He argued that Avitus was concerned to:

> reassure Clovis about the effects of Christian conversion on his *nobilitas*. Some aspect of it was lost: Clovis is now 'satisfied with a *nobilitas* drawn solely from a

lineage of ancient origin'. In other words, his pre-conversion *nobilitas* had consisted of something more than the antiquity of his line. What aspect of it had been lost? ... According to a contemporary witness, therefore, the pagan Merovingian king Clovis had claimed a *nobilitas* based only partly on antiquity of descent, and had had a *reverentia* for his ancestors which involved religious ritual. This cultic *reverentia* presupposes a mythology of native origin; as we have seen, Gregory of Tours associates long-established cult practices with the name of Merovech.[85]

This lends support to the contention of this book that the king is a figure of religious significance for the Late Antique and Early Medieval Germans.

The interactions of the Franks with the Gallo-Roman clergy and administration, with the Byzantine emperors and, to a lesser extent, with the quasi-imperial court of Theodoric in Ravenna, fit Horton's 'microcosm encountering macrocosm' paradigm. Theodoric, as a powerful German ruler and Clovis' brother-in-law, may have functioned as an over-king for Clovis, making his adoption of Catholicism more likely later in his career when Theodoric's power was waning. Avitus' letter to Clovis supports this contention somewhat, encouraging Clovis to extend his Catholic overlordship over other Germanic peoples, specifically mentioning those 'still living in natural ignorance, [who] have not been corrupted by the seeds of perverse doctrines'.[86]

However, the relationship between Clovis and the Byzantine court is worthy of particular attention. Gregory describes Clovis' visit to Tours in 508:

> Letters reached Clovis from the Emperor Anastasius to confer the consulate on him. In Saint Martin's church he stood clad in a purple tunic and the military mantle, and he crowned himself with a diadem. He then rode out on his horse and with his own hand showered gold and silver coins among the people present all the way from the doorway of Saint Martin's church to Tours cathedral. From that day on he was called Consul or Augustus. He left Tours and travelled to Paris, where he established the seat of his government.[87]

The general outline is clear. Clovis had defeated the Visigothic kingdom of Toulouse, a victory which was also in the interests of the Byzantine Empire, and received a title from the Emperor in recognition of this service. The precise nature of the honour has been debated at length,[88] but Clovis is here clearly a Catholic ruler, which accords with Wood's analysis of the chronology of his reign. Gregory's account indicates imperial approval of Clovis but also makes clear his independence from Constantinople.[89] McCormick believes that the Merovingian rulers, like many others, appropriated the ceremonial of the Empire.[90] This included ceremonial appropriate to Byzantine generals as well as to the Emperor himself; it is quite understandable that the aspects of imperial life which had the greatest appeal to the Franks were military.

The agents of conversion in the case of the Franks differ from those in the general Germanic conversion paradigm. The Goths (in the late Roman period) and the Anglo-Saxons were outside the Empire, in the barbarian hinterland. The Franks were within the citadel and therefore encountered established non-missionary Gallo-Roman clergy and Christians from all levels of society. Many took Christian wives, and Christianity expanded the role of royal women; they became involved in the foundation of monasteries and convents and often remained faithful in times of apostasy, being outside male networks of allegiance.[91]

At this point it is necessary to deal with the relationship between conversion and the acceptance of baptism. James commented that a late date for Clovis' baptism does not imply a late date for his *conversion*, as the latter is often difficult to identify.[92] For example, Constantine, to whom Gregory compares Clovis at the moment of his baptism,[93] was baptized twenty-five years after his acceptance (in some sense) of Christianity. Relevant here is Wallace-Hadrill's observation that Clovis probably believed in the Christian God as 'the giver of victory (most precious of gifts) and as a better god than any his fathers had known, under whose providence and with whose priests it was proper to fight on'.[94]

For the argument of this book it matters little whether Clovis flirted with Arianism before baptism in the Catholic Church, or exactly when his baptism took place. The Christian context of Clovis' reign and personal life is clear, as are the conceptual structures which facilitated the transition to the new religion. For Clovis the need for powerful protection in battle, the efficacy of rituals such as baptism, and the possibility of political alliances were paramount motivations. For the agents of conversion it was more significant to ensure the support of the monarch than his baptism; mere acceptance of a rite implied no policy change towards the new faith. Ideally, baptism and the change of policy would go together, but in cases such as Clovis' and Constantine's, the Church was satisfied with the imperial support provided.

Possibly because most of the continental Germans were already Arian Christians, in the Frankish case there was no parallel to the continual uncertainty about the relative power of the rival gods which plagued the Anglo-Saxons after their conversion. While pre-Christian practices persisted, the Franks were surrounded by Christianity, and gradually became permeated by it. The Franks were a minority ruling a Gallo-Roman population which was already substantially Christianized and which identified Christianity with *Romanitas*.[95]

The most striking thing about Gregory's Clovis is that though he accepted baptism, he was still a barbarian chieftain in essence, as were his successors. Tales were told of his ruthless extermination of his rivals, many of whom were his relatives, and his skilful absorption of their wealth and retinues. His lawcode, the *Pactus Legis Salicae* (Lex Salica), shows little (if any) Christian influence, and Wallace-Hadrill observed that it continued to protect the sacrificial pigs of pagan subjects, that pre-Christian practices such as name-giving on the tenth day are ratified, and that heavy fines are imposed 'on plunderers of corpses, burned or not; and [it] makes a special case of the plundering of a body in a *tumba*, or the destruction of a *tumba*'.[96] '*Tumba*' here means a tumulus, and Wallace-Hadrill sensibly assumed that Clovis' law was intended to protect those buried as pagans (which may explain how the grave of his father Childeric survived). In addition to the evidence of lawcodes, Gregory's writings tell of the continuing practice of polygyny and other pre-Christian customs within the family unit. As with many Germanic peoples, the Church tried hard to regulate Merovingian family life.[97]

Archaeology offers supporting evidence for the continuation of pagan customs. Cemeteries up to the eighth century contain a majority of graves with goods, which are generally considered a sign of paganism. (Although it has been pointed out that Christian clergy were never averse to being buried fully clothed and with the symbols of their office.)[98] As evidence for polygyny, Lavoye burial 319, excavated early this century, contains three women and one man in a central tomb with Christian artefacts.[99]

These practices illustrate the continuities involved in the conversion of the Franks. As with Rædwald of East Anglia, whom Bede records as having erected an altar to Christ in his pagan temple, the Franks appear to have been respectful to all gods, or at least aware that others were. Gregory of Tours had no time for pagans or heretics, but he had acquaintances, such as his Spanish visitor Agilan, the envoy of the Arian king Leuvigild, who reported a proverb that 'no harm is done when a man whose affairs take him past the altars of the Gentiles and the Church of God pays respect to both'.[100] Gregory is highly critical of this attitude, but he nonetheless reports it as current, and the remainder of the conversation shows Agilan to be an educated and articulate man, well able to argue his case. This is interesting in the context of Gregory's hostility to Arian Christianity and the Germanic peoples who adhered to it.[101]

While Clovis accepted Christianity, this acceptance could not blot out the victories of the past, won under the aegis of the old gods. Wallace-Hadrill has argued that by the time of the reign of Clovis' son Childebert I the royal attitude to Christianity had changed: that Childebert accepted Christ as a complete substitute for the pagan gods and that Christian ritual had been fully integrated into the calendar of seasonal festivals, obliterating or at least obscuring other associations.[102] This is, however, virtually impossible to prove, although his point that the transition from paganism to Christianity was not one which involved a spiritual revolution is important, encouraging as it does the view that such practical substitutions took place and were acceptable over time.[103]

Gregory of Tours presented a lurid vision of Frankish society, where adultery, murder, and other violences were daily occurrences. He sees God as watching the activities of the Merovingians constantly, with the intention of ultimately punishing them for their appalling crimes. The private lives of the Merovingians are interesting because by the time of Gregory, Christianity is firmly established as a national faith. The Frankish aristocracy was a Germanic warrior aristocracy which had converted to Christianity, but had not changed its mode of living at all. Inevitably the new faith was concentrated in the cities and where the clergy were; in most missions of this period little or no effort was made to convert the country people, and the conversion of the lower classes was effected due to their ties of loyalty to the aristocracy.[104]

The indigenization of Catholicism

The final stage to be recognized in the model of conversion used in this book is that of indigenization, where Christianity becomes an integral part of the ethnic or national culture. James has noted that there were few clergy with Frankish names recorded in the first century of Catholicism.[105] The growth of monasticism, with attendant schools and native pupils and novices, played a crucial role in the dissemination of Christianity, and its integration into Frankish society. This is precisely the pattern of events suggested by J. W. Pickett's research into Christian conversion in India.

The Christianization of Frankia was furthered by the activities of St Columbanus, an Irish monk born in 540 whose twin passions were evangelism and monasticism. Although he had no official mission to the Frankish Church, his arrival at the end of the sixth century was opportune, since the Merovingian Church was in a disorderly state. Columbanus is known to us through a hagiography written by Jonas of Bobbio in the mid-seventh century. He established himself in Gaul, disregarded the Gallic bishops, and appealed to the Pope to support his activities when the local clergy complained. He was not afraid to criticize the monarchies, being accustomed to the Irish situation, where Celtic monks, 'like Old Testament prophets . . . condemned sinners and pronounced terrible maledictions upon them'.[106] As mentioned earlier, he incurred the wrath of Theudoric of Burgundy and Brunhild by refusing to bless the children of a royal concubine. They attempted to exile him, but he sought refuge with Chlotar II of Neustria, then with Theudebert of Austrasia, and finally settled in Italy at the court of the Lombard king, Agilulf. Columbanus used this base in Lombardy to effect a revival in Frankish monasticism. One by one the monasteries began to adopt insular customs and to become more disciplined and productive. The bishops continued to be hostile, however, and the Columbanan reforms did not affect the secular clergy at all.

The Frankish kings had never attempted to convert neighbouring Germanic peoples to Christianity. After his baptism Clovis received Avitus of Vienne's letter of congratulation, which contained advice that he should evangelize others,[107] but Clovis ignored this advice, and his conquests of Arian peoples were based firmly on territorial imperatives. One reason for this reluctance may be that the old Roman concept of the barbarian hinterland was still operational and that the Christian Germanic kingdoms were happy that their borders dissolved into a different culture.

Columbanus and his disciples evangelized enthusiastically: Gall among the Alamans; Eustasius among the Varasci; and Amand among the Basques, Slavs and the Flemish.[108] Columbanus himself worked among the Suevi, and Jonas' *Life* gives some idea of his missionary methods:

> at length they arrived at the place designated, which did not wholly please Columban; but he decided to remain, in order to spread the faith among the people, who were Swabians. Once, as he was going through this country, he discovered that the natives were going to make a heathen offering. They had a large cask that they called a *cupa*, and that held about twenty-six measures, filled with beer and set in their midst. On Columban's asking what they intended to do with it, they answered that they were making an offering to their God Wodan (whom others call Mercury). When he heard of this abomination, he breathed on the cask, and lo! it broke with a crash and fell in pieces so that all the beer ran out. Then it was clear that the devil had been concealed in the cask, and that through the earthly drink he had purposed to ensnare the souls of the participants. As the heathens saw that, they were amazed and said Columban had a strong breath, to split a well-bound cask in that manner. But he reproved them in the words of the Gospel, and commanded them to cease from such offerings and to go home. Many were converted then, by the preaching of the holy man, and turning to the learning and faith of Christ, were baptized by him. Others, who were already baptized but still lived in the heathenish unbelief, like a good shepherd, he again led by his words to the faith and unto the bosom of the church.[109]

Saints' lives are highly stylized works and notoriously unreliable as historical sources. Jonas' *Life* follows the standard heroic model. In the above extract it does not seem likely that the Swabians would have realized that the devil was in the cask (indeed, their comment about Columbanus' breath would indicate that their chief concern was their lost beer), but, since heathens should be impressed and receive spiritual revelations when a sign is performed in their presence, Jonas provides an appropriate response from them.

The great influence of Columbanus fits in well with the Frankish understanding of the role of the saint. Gregory of Tours recorded and commented on the stories of a multitude of saints. Martin of Tours, his favourite saint, is praiseworthy because he was a godly bishop, was involved in the establishment of monasteries, and contributed to 'establishing and maintaining ... an orderly, law-abiding, just, and merciful society'.[110] The miracle stories of the saints also had a function: the letter of Nicetius of Trier, writing in the 560s to Clovis' granddaughter Clotsinda, mentions the detail that Clovis was greatly impressed by the miracles attributed to St Martin of Tours.[111] The saints, alive and dead, were the guardians of Christian society. Medieval society has been described as a pyramid in which the dead and living mingled, with God at the top. In this pyramid 'in the popular view, the saints performed a function akin to that of the Gods in Homer: alive, active, intensely interested in mortal affairs, each enjoying his or her own local cult centres and intervening for the protection of their subjects – a kind of superior aristocracy'.[112]

It is this *de facto* aristocratic status which allowed Columbanus to rebuke the Frankish monarchs without fear and Gregory of Tours to attack the reputations of kings and queens with such relish. There is a sense, however, in which the veneration of saints replaced polytheism in the religious life of the people; this confusion between the old and the new faiths was exacerbated by the missionaries' habit of reconsecrating pagan sites for Christian worship in their pursuit of continuity.[113]

Sources for the seventh century are sparser and in general less reliable than those for the sixth. Jonas' *Vita Columbani* and the *Chronicle* of Fredegar are of greatest interest. Fredegar offers the information that Clovis' baptism took place at Rheims, which is not intrinsically unlikely.[114] The *Chronicle* covers the missionary activity of Columbanus favourably and dwells on incidents such as the baptism of Recared, king of Visigothic Spain, which caused his nation to adopt Catholicism.[115] The *Vita Amandi*, written shortly after the death of St Amand, one of Columbanus' followers, details his struggle with King Dagobert, who tried to limit Amand's missionary work to areas where it served Frankish interests.[116]

The conversion of the Franks was not a national conversion because the area they occupied was divided into a number of small kingdoms and, while these peoples acknowledged their relationship with each other, there was no Frankish nation as such. It was also an atypical Germanic conversion because of the presence of Arian Christianity. Nevertheless, many of the factors encountered in other Germanic conversions were present. Clovis accepted the new faith in a military context, with the Christian God demonstrating his power over the Germanic gods by his gift of victory in battle. After his baptism there is evidence that he continued to support and even favour pagan customs and rituals, which would have rendered the transitional period easier to accept for not only Clovis, but also his people. Even later, when Christianity was firmly established as the religion of the Franks, pagan culture lived on in the habits and lifestyle of the Frankish monarchy and aristocracy. Like Olaf Tryggvason, who began as a viking for Odin and became a viking for Christ, the Frankish people maintained their Germanic warrior lifestyle. This points to an acceptance of the this-worldly orientation of Frankish religion by Christianity, as Russell suggests.

The conversion of the Franks was also complicated by the presence of Gallo-Roman Christianity with its established clergy. As a result they did not have to establish fresh Church structures and an energetic native clergy took much longer to emerge, with the chief ecclesiastical figures being either Gallo-Roman, like Gregory of Tours, Remigius of Rheims and Avitus of Vienne, or foreign, like Columbanus. The Church in Frankia established itself independently of the monarchy, and consequently enjoyed an independence entirely lacking in Anglo-Saxon England, for example. This made the Church powerful, for, as le Bras has commented:

> the sociology of Heaven has a direct bearing on the sociology of the church and of the profane world. The saints are agents of local, regional and universal integration. They protect the city and the nation and watch over the bands of pilgrims that they attract. Through one of the saints, the Apostle Peter, the Pope is enabled to be present in many different places at the same time; this serves the cause of unity.[117]

In Frankia it was sometimes necessary to call on the saints, and even the Pope, in struggles against the Frankish monarchs, whereas in England the monarchs more frequently volunteered to consult the Pope and to accept his arbitration. This is possibly because the conversion of the Franks was sabotaged from within, as it were, by the non-Christian groups living around them. Because there was no attempt to convert these peoples, a sense of an entirely Christian world was difficult to maintain. Charlemagne's conversion of the surrounding populations in the late eighth and early ninth centuries was therefore of vital importance: he was building an empire, to be sure, but it was to be a Christian empire, and he would be Holy Roman Emperor, ruling with the consent and support of the Pope, Christ's vicar on earth.

Notes

1. Peter Brown, 'The Religious Crisis of the Third Century AD', in Peter Brown (ed.), *Religion and Society in the Age of Saint Augustine*, Harper and Row, 1972, pp. 74–93.

2. Raymond van Dam, *Leadership and Community in Late Antique Gaul*, University of California Press, 1985, pp. 25–44.
3. A. H. M. Jones, *The Decline of the Ancient World*, London, 1966, p. 268, notes that the election of Martin, a former Roman soldier, was supported by the people but opposed by the bishops, who declared that he was 'a contemptible person, unworthy of the episcopate, a man of despicable appearance, with dirty clothes and unbrushed hair'. Martin founded the first monastery in Gaul at Tours, but monasticism did not take off quickly, no doubt partly due to the political turmoil of the next century.
4. Clare Stancliffe, *St Martin and his Hagiographer*, Oxford, 1983, p. 27.
5. *Ibid*, pp. 154–5.
6. G. K. van Ardel, *The Christian Concept of History in the Chronicle of Sulpicius Severus*, Amsterdam, 1976, discusses Sulpicius' classical education, and his casting of contemporary affairs in classical moulds (for example, his treatment of the Priscillianist affair as a contemporary Catiline Conspiracy).
7. van Dam, *op. cit.*, p. 67, mentions Martin being driven from several towns by hostile Arians before being appointed bishop of Tours, and van Ardel, *op. cit.*, notes Sulpicius Severus' hatred of both heresy and the persecution of it, due to accusations of Priscillianism having been brought against Martin and his associates, p. 3 and p. 107. See also Daniel H. Williams, 'The Anti-Arian Campaigns of Hilary of Poitiers and the *Liber Contra Auxentium*', *CH*, 61, (1), 1992, pp. 7–22, which discusses Hilary's struggles with Auxentius, Arian bishop of Milan, whose apologetic writings concerning Ulfila were discussed in Chapter 2. The interesting point is that Hilary failed to oust Auxentius, indicating that the push for doctrinal orthodoxy was limited to Frankish Gaul and that Arianism was the norm in Northern Italy and probably in a majority of Frankish Gaul's neighbouring states.
8. Sulpicius Severus, *The Life of Saint Martin*, in F. H. Hoare (ed. and trans.), *The Western Fathers*, London, 1954, p. 31.
9. *Ibid.*, pp. 26–7.
10. Raymond Chevallier, 'Des Dieux Gaulois et Gallo-Romains aux Saints du Christianisme. Recherches sur la Christianisation des Cultes de la Gaule', in *La Patrie Gauloise d'Agrippa au VIeme Siècle*, Lyon, 1983, pp. 283–326, and also K. S. Latourette, *A History of the Expansion of Christianity*, London, 1944, vol. 1, p. 201: 'at the time of his accession to the see, Christianity appears to have been restricted chiefly to the city of Tours, then probably a place of only a very few inhabitants. The surrounding countryside seems to have been pagan. Martin led his monks in preaching, in destroying temples and in baptizing. As a rule he built on a site of non-Christian fame a Christian church or monastery'.
11. Lucan, *Pharsalia*, ed. and trans. J. D. Duff, London, 1969, bk III, ll. 399–453, pp. 142–7.
12. Stancliffe, *op. cit.*, pp. 328–9.
13. Kathleen Mitchell, 'Saints and Public Christianity in the *Historiae* of Gregory of Tours', in Thomas F. X. Noble and John J. Contreni (eds), *Religion, Culture and Society in the Early Middle Ages*, Kalamazoo, 1987, p. 80.

14. Erich Auerbach, *Literary Language and its Public in Late Latin Antiquity and in the Middle Ages*, trans. Ralph Manheim, London, 1965, p. 85.

15. van Dam, *op. cit.*, pp. 122–3.

16. It is significant that Martin, who was not aristocratic, left no writings of his own, but was immortalized by Sulpicius Severus.

17. J. M. Wallace-Hadrill, *The Barbarian West 400–1000*, London, 1985, p. 23.

18. Pierre Riche, *Education and Culture in the Barbarian West*, trans. John J. Contreni, Columbia, SC, 1976, p. 11.

19. W. H. C. Frend, 'Romano-British Christianity and the West: Comparison and Contrast', in Susan M. Pearce (ed.), *The Early Church in Western Britain and Ireland*, BAR, British Series 102, 1982, p. 9. See also Nora K. Chadwick, *Poetry and Letters in Early Christian Gaul*, London, 1955, pp. 31–5.

20. van Dam, *op. cit.*, p. 153.

21. Ludwig Bieler, 'The Mission of Palladius: A Comparative Study of Sources', *Traditio*, 6, 1948, pp. 1–32, refers to O'Rahilly's belief that Patrick and Palladius (who was surnamed Patricius) are identical.

22. Josiah Cox Russell, 'The Problem of Saint Patrick the Missionary', *Traditio*, 12, 1956, pp. 393–8.

23. A. B. E. Hood (ed. and trans.), *St. Patrick*, Phillimore, 1978, says in his introduction, 'Patrick was the effective founder of the Christian Church in Ireland. He was consecrated bishop and came to Ireland in 432. He stayed in Ireland until his death, about 30 years later, and was the first Christian to make any substantial number of converts, and to leave behind him a lasting organised church', p. 1. Bede, in his *A History of the English Church and People*, ed. and trans. Leo Sherley-Price, Harmondsworth, 1975, states that 'In the eighth year of his reign the Roman Pontiff Celestine sent Palladius to the Scots who believed in Christ to be their first bishop', p. 53. The Latin text is in Bede, *The Ecclesiastical History of the English People*, ed. and trans. Bertram Colgrave and R. A. B. Mynors, Oxford, 1969, p. 46.

24. Ludwig Bieler, 'The Christianization of the Insular Celts During the Sub-Roman Period and its Repercussions on the Continent', *Celtica*, 8, 1968, p. 114.

25. E. A. Thompson, *Who Was Saint Patrick?*, The Boydell Press, 1985. Thompson says at the beginning of the chapter entitled 'The Mission to the Irish' that 'Nothing could give more pleasure to the student of St Patrick than a description of what happened when he entered for the first time a pagan, or almost wholly pagan, Irish village. What sort of person did he first seek out? What kind of thing did he say to them? How did he set about expounding the new religion and undermining their faith in the gods which had satisfied them and their ancestors hitherto? The answers to these and countless similar questions are utterly beyond us. We cannot ever hope to find them', p. 79.

26. See Chapter 2, section 'Arianism Triumphant'.

27. van Dam, *op. cit.*, p. 142.

28. Constantius of Lyons, *Life of Saint Germanus*, in F. H. Hoare, *The Western Fathers*, London, 1954, pp. 296–302.

29. *Ibid.*, p. 301. The Latin is in Constantius, *Vita Germani Episcopi*, in *MGH:SRM*, ed. B. Krusch and W. Levison, tom. VII, par. I, Hannover, 1919, pp. 263–4.
30. C. E. Stevens, *Sidonius Apollinaris and His Age*, Oxford, 1933, p. 20.
31. Chadwick, *op. cit.*, p. 307.
32. Stevens, *op. cit.*, p. 25.
33. *Ibid.*, p. 34.
34. *Ibid.*, p. 81.
35. Sidonius Apollinaris, *Poems and Letters*, ed. and trans. W. B. Anderson, London, 1965, vol. II, IV 17, pp. 127–9. The Latin text is *ibid.*, pp. 126–8.
36. William M. Daly, 'Caesarius of Arles, a Precursor of Medieval Christendom', *Traditio*, XXVI, 1970, p. 9.
37. *Vita Caesarii*, in J. N. Hillgarth, *The Conversion of Western Europe 350–750*, Englewood Cliffs, NJ, 1968, section 23, p. 36. The Latin is in *Vita Caesarii*, in *MGH:SRM*, ed. Bruno Krusch, tom. III, Hannover, 1896, p. 465.
38. Pierre Audin, 'Césaire d'Arles et le Maintien de Pratiques Païennes Dans la Provence du VIe Siècle', in *La Patrie Gauloise d'Agrippa au VIème siècle*, Lyon, 1983, *passim*.
39. Caesarius of Arles, *Sermons*, vol. 1, ed. and trans. Sr Mary Magdaleine Muller, New York, 1956, sermon 53, 'An Admonition to Destroy the Shrines of Idols' and sermon 54, 'An Admonition to Those Who Not Only Pay Attention to Omens, but, What Is Worse, Consult Seers, Soothsayers, and Fortune Tellers in the Manner of Pagans', pp. 263–70.
40. Daly, *op. cit.*, p. 28.
41. Wallace-Hadrill, 1985, *op. cit.*, p. 65.
42. Robert Latouche, *Caesar to Charlemagne*, trans. Jennifer Nicholson, London, 1968, p. 78, quoting *Historia Augusta*, 31: vol. ii, p. 141.
43. Edward James, *The Franks*, Oxford, 1988, pp. 42–3.
44. Gregory of Tours, *The History of the Franks*, ed. and trans. Lewis Thorpe, Harmondsworth, 1974, p. 8.
45. J. M. Wallace-Hadrill, *The Long-Haired Kings*, London, 1962, p. 57.
46. J. M. Wallace-Hadrill, *The Frankish Church*, Oxford, 1983, p. 22.
47. Einhard the Frank, *The Life of Charlemagne*, ed. and trans. Lewis Thorpe, London, 1970, p. 29. The Latin text is in the *Vita Karoli Magni*, *MGH:SRG*, ed. G. H. Pertz and G. Waitz, Hannover, 1911, p. 3.
48. J. M. Wallace-Hadrill, *Early Germanic Kingship*, Oxford, 1971, p. 15.
49. See Chapter 2, section 'The Germans in the Roman Empire'.
50. Peter Lasko, *The Kingdom of the Franks*, London, 1971, pp. 25–6.
51. Latouche, *op. cit.*, pp. 211–20.
52. David Frye, 'Aegidius, Childeric, Odovacer and Paul', *Nottingham Medieval Studies*, XXXVI, 1992, p. 4.
53. David Frye, 'Transformation and Tradition in the Merovingian Civitas', *Nottingham Medieval Studies*, XXXIX, 1995, pp. 1–2.
54. Gregory of Tours, Thorpe, *op. cit.*, II. 27, p. 139.
55. Gregory of Tours, Thorpe, *op. cit.*; James, 1988, *op. cit.*, pp. 72–3, considers Syagrius' 'kingdom' to be an 'historical myth'.

56. James, 1988, *op. cit.*, p. 75.
57. Robert Levine (trans.), *France before Charlemagne: A Translation from the Grandes Chroniques*, Studies in French Civilization, vol. 3, Lampeter, 1990, p. 38.
58. Gregory of Tours, Thorpe, *op. cit.*, p. 142. The Latin text is in Gregory of Tours, *Libri Historiarum*, in *MGH:SRM*, ed. Bruno Krusch, tom. I, par. I, fasc. I, Hannover, 1937, p. 74.
59. John Moorhead, 'Clovis' Motives for Becoming a Catholic Christian', *JRH*, 1985, p. 335.
60. Kate Cooper, 'Insinuations of Womanly Influence: An Aspect of the Christianization of the Roman Aristocracy', *JRS*, LXXXII, 1992, pp. 150–64.
61. Gregory of Tours, Thorpe, *op. cit.*, II. 29, p. 141, 'Jovisque et soror et coniunx', *Aeneid*, I, 46–7.
62. Walter Goffart, *The Narrators of Barbarian History*, Princeton, NJ, 1988, and Auerbach, 1965, *op. cit.*, *passim*. Also Chapter 4, 'Sicharius and Chramnesindus', in Erich Auerbach, *Mimesis*, trans. Willard R. Trask, Princeton, NJ, 1953, pp. 77–95.
63. Latouche, *op. cit.*, p. 223.
64. Gregory of Tours, Thorpe, *op. cit.*, p. 143. The Latin text is in Gregory of Tours, *MGH:SRM*, *op. cit.*, p. 75. See also Bernard S. Bachrach (ed. and trans.), *Liber Historiae Francorum*, Coronado Press, 1973, p. 45.
65. James, 1988, *op. cit.*, pp. 84–5.
66. Ian Wood, 'Gregory of Tours and Clovis', *RBPH*, LXIII, (2), p. 258.
67. See Chapter 2, section 'The Conversion of Constantine'.
68. Gregory of Tours, *Lives of the Fathers*, ed. and trans. Edward James, Liverpool, 1985, p. 13.
69. Goffart, *op. cit.*, pp. 218–19.
70. Wood, *op. cit.*, pp. 249–72.
71. William M. Daly, 'Clovis: How Barbaric, How Pagan?', *Speculum*, 69, (3), 1994, pp. 619–64, considers all these sources and provides a convenient summary of them.
72. Wood, *op. cit.*, p. 264.
73. Avitus of Vienne, *Epistolae*, *MGH:AA*, ed. Rudolfus Peiper, tom. VI, Berlin, 1883, pp. 1–157.
74. Wood, *op. cit.*, pp. 268–70.
75. *Ibid.*, p. 266.
76. Jonathan Barlow, *The Success of the Franks: Regional Continuity in Northern Gaul in Late Antiquity*, unpublished doctoral thesis, awarded 1994 University of Sydney, Chapter 8, 'Catholicism and the Legitimisation of North-East Gaul', p. 21. The Gallic bishops were concerned to prevent the spread of Arianism and convened councils (for example, Arles in 353, Béziers in 356 and Paris in 360–1), see Ralph W. Mathisen, *Ecclesiastical Factionalism and Religious Controversy in Fifth Century Gaul*, Washington, 1989, pp. 10–12. They would certainly have drawn attention to the fact if Clovis had been a convert from Arianism to Catholicism. I take this to confirm, indirectly, Barlow's argument.

77. Frye, *op. cit.*, 1992, p. 9.
78. Gregory of Tours, Thorpe, *op. cit.*, II. 31, pp. 143–4. The Latin text is in Gregory of Tours, *MGH:SRM*, *op. cit.*, p. 76.
79. James, 1988, *op. cit.*, p. 124.
80. Barlow, *op. cit.*, ch. 8, p. 17.
81. Gregory of Tours, Thorpe, *op. cit.*, p. 151. The Latin text is in Gregory of Tours, *MGH:SRM*, *op. cit.*, p. 85.
82. Wallace-Hadrill, 1985, *op. cit.*, p. 70.
83. See Chapter 4, section 'The Anglo-Saxons'.
84. Avitus of Vienne, in Hillgarth, *op. cit.*, 1968, pp. 75–6. The Latin text is in Avitus of Vienne, *MGH:AA*, *op. cit.*, p. 75.
85. Hermann Moisl, 'Anglo-Saxon Royal Genealogies and Germanic Oral Tradition', *JMH*, 7, (3), 1981, p. 225.
86. Hillgarth, *op. cit.*
87. Gregory of Tours, Thorpe, *op. cit.*, p. 154. The Latin text is in Gregory of Tours, *MGH:SRM*, *op. cit.*, pp. 88–9.
88. Michael McCormick, *Eternal Victory*, Cambridge, 1986, and most recently 'Clovis at Tours: Byzantine Public Ritual and the Origins of Medieval Ruler Symbolism', unpublished typescript.
89. McCormick, 'Clovis', *op. cit.*, p. 7.
90. *Ibid.*, p. 16.
91. Pauline Stafford, *Queens, Concubines and Dowagers*, London, 1983, p. 123 and p. 143.
92. James, 1988, *op. cit.*, p. 123.
93. Gregory of Tours, Thorpe, *op. cit.*, p. 144, II. 31, says: 'Like some new Constantine he stepped forward to the baptismal pool ...'. The Latin text is in Gregory of Tours, *MGH:SRM*, *op. cit.*, p. 77.
94. Wallace-Hadrill, 1967, *op. cit.*, p. 70.
95. Barlow, *op. cit.*, chapter 8, p. 23; also Arnaldo Momigliano, cited in Chapter 2, section 'The Germans and the Roman Empire'.
96. Wallace-Hadrill, 1983, *op. cit.*, p. 27.
97. Edward James, *The Origins of France*, London, 1982, comments: 'we can obviously know very little about family life from our sources – most of which, indeed, were written by celibates', p. 73, and 'there was also the question of concubinage and the legitimacy of children. It has sometimes been said that the Merovingian kings were polygamous: Chlothar I did have seven known wives (two of whom were sisters), Charibert I four and others three. But it is quite probable that death or divorce separated those marriages. ... Merovingian kings did however have concubines on occasion, and not surprisingly the Church was worried about the legitimacy of the children of such liaisons. The quarrel between the Irish monk Columbanus and King Theuderic and his grandmother Brunhild which led to the monk's exile from Gaul began by a refusal to bless the king's two sons born to a concubine, born in adultery as Columbanus put it', p. 79.
98. *Ibid.*, p. 97.
99. P. J. Geary, *Before France and Germany*, Oxford, 1988, p. 104, states that

the site contains 362 tombs, 192 from the late fifth and early sixth centuries.

100. Gregory, Thorpe, *op. cit.*, p. 310. This is discussed in Wallace-Hadrill, 1962, *op. cit.*, p. 172.

101. John Moorhead, 'Gregory of Tours on the Arian Kingdoms', *Studi Medievali*, serie terza, anno XXXVI, fasc. II, 1995, pp. 903–15.

102. Wallace-Hadrill, 1983, *op. cit.*, p 33.

103. *Ibid.*, p. 35.

104. *Ibid.*, p. 32.

105. James, 1988, *op. cit.*, p. 128.

106. Pierre Riché, 'Columbanus, His Followers, and the Merovingian Church', in H. B. Clarke and Mary Brennan (eds), *Columbanus and Merovingian Monasticism*, BAR, International Series 113, 1981, p. 63.

107. Avitus wrote: 'do not fear to send them envoys and to plead with them the cause of God, who has done so much for your cause. So that the other pagan peoples, at first being subject to your empire for the sake of religion, while they still seem to have another ruler, may be distinguished rather by their race than by their prince ...', Avitus, *Letters*, in Hillgarth, 1968, *op. cit.*, pp. 76–7. The Latin text is in Avitus, *MGH:AA, op. cit.*, p. 76.

108. Russell, *op. cit.*, pp. 154–66.

109. Jonas, *Life of Saint Columban*, ed. and trans. Dana Carleton Munro, Philadelphia, 1895, pp. 31–2. The Latin text is in Jonas, *Vita Columbani*, in *MGH:SRM*, ed. Bruno Krusch, tom. IV, Hannover, 1902, pp. 102–3.

110. Mitchell, *op. cit.*, p. 78.

111. Nicetius writes: 'do these things happen in Arian churches? They do not. ... But no demon is permitted to rove where the Saints dwell. ... You have heard how your grandmother, Lady Clotilde of good memory, came into France, how she led the Lord Clovis to the Catholic Law, and how, since he was a most astute man, he was unwilling to agree to it until he knew it was true. When he saw that the things I have spoken of were proved he humbly prostrated himself at the threshold of the Lord Martin [at Tours] and promised to be baptized without delay ...', Nicetius, in Hillgarth, 1968, *op. cit.*, p. 79. The Latin text is in Nicetius of Trier, *Epistolae Duae*, in J.-P. Migne (ed.), *PL*, tom. 68, Turnholt, n.d., pp. 378.

112. Christopher Brooke, 'The Cathedral in Medieval Society', in Wim Swaan, *The Gothic Cathedral*, Paul Elek, 1969, p. 13.

113. Lawrence Walter Montford, *Civilization in Seventh Century Gaul as reflected in Saints' Vitae composed in the Period*, Ann Arbor, MI, 1974, p. 367.

114. Fredegar, *The Fourth Book of the Chronicle of Fredegar with its continuations*, ed. and trans. J. M. Wallace-Hadrill, London, 1960, p. xii.

115. *Ibid.*, p. 7.

116. James, 1988, *op. cit.*, pp. 136–7.

117. Gabriel le Bras, 'The Sociology of the Church in the Early Middle Ages', in Sylvia Thrupp (ed.), *Early Medieval Society*, New York, 1967, p. 51.

4   The Anglo-Saxons: reclaiming the lost province

Looking at them with interest, [Gregory] enquired from what country and what part of the world they came. 'They come from the island of Britain,' he was told, 'where all the people have this appearance.' He then asked whether the islanders were Christians ... 'They are pagans,' he was informed ... 'What is the name of this race?' 'They are called Angles,' he was told. 'That is appropriate,' he said, 'for they have angelic faces, and it is right that they should become joint-heirs with the angels in heaven.'

Bede[1]

The Anglo-Saxons

Roman interest in Britain began with Julius Caesar's raid in 55BCE and continued with the invasion of the Emperor Claudius in 43CE, which resulted in the establishment of permanent garrisons and the eventual absorption of Britain into the Roman Empire. The first writings which mention Christianity in Britain are by Tertullian and Origen and date from c. 200 and 240 respectively.[2] Tertullian claimed that Christianity had spread to 'parts of Britain inaccessible to the Romans' which may refer to the highlands of Scotland.[3] This has been the focus of much debate, because it is contemporary evidence for the extent of Christianity in Britain, but the degree of Christian penetration claimed seems rather too extensive given the archaeological record: very few early Romano-British churches have been identified and a comparably small number of distinctly Christian objects have been found. The Water Newton hoard, found in 1975, is a collection of Christian plate which contains pieces for which a third century date could be argued.[4] It consists of nine vessels and eighteen votive plaques, and is the earliest Christian plate within the Empire. The size of the hoard indicates that it was probably located at a shrine, rather than the equipment of a travelling priest.[5]

Whatever its early vicissitudes, Christianity flourished in Roman and post-Roman Britain, producing one prominent martyr's cult, that of St Alban,[6] and one prominent heretic, Pelagius (though he was probably from

Ireland). Both Augustine of Hippo and Jerome mention Pelagius, and oppose his teaching that if the human will is not free, then people are puppets without responsibility.[7]

The Roman administrative withdrawal from Britain in the early fifth century did not result in the cessation of Roman habits and customs. The economic and social life of Britain appears to have remained stable for some years, becoming unsettled only around 430. Evidence for this comes from the *Life of Saint Germanus of Auxerre*,[8] which was written shortly after the saint's death, probably between 472 and 491, by Constantius, a Merovingian cleric. The account of St Germanus' visit in 429 offers a picture of conditions in Britain after the Roman withdrawal; the impression is of a generally peaceful and stable society, save for one incident, an attack by Saxons and Picts. Where this raid took place is not told: all that is related is that the British were unprepared to meet the enemy and that the saint assisted in organizing their successful resistance. Thus it is clear that the Saxons had commenced raiding the coasts of southern Britain by 429.

The Venerable Bede provides the traditional account of the invasion of Britain by the Angles, Saxons and Jutes in the *Historia Ecclesiastica*. He relies on *De excidio et conquestu Brittaniae*, a work by the sixth century British monk Gildas, as his principal source. This text is frustrating to work with and extremely difficult to interpret. It is a key source for the history of sub-Roman Britain, and yet can scarcely be called history. As the title suggests, the work deals with the 'ruin and conquest of Britain' by the Germanic invaders, but it provides few precise names or dates and consists largely of biblical quotations and moralizations on the sins of the British leaders. The following passage, on the arrival of the Saxons, illustrates this:

> 'The stubborn servant', says Solomon, 'is not corrected with words'. The fool is flogged, but feels nothing. For a deadly plague swooped brutally on the stupid people, and in a short period laid low so many people, with no sword, that the living could not bury all the dead. But not even this taught them their lesson, so that the word of the prophet Isaiah was fulfilled here also: 'And God has called to wailing and baldness and girding with sackcloth: look at the killing of calves and the slaughter of rams, the eating and drinking, and people saying: Let us eat and drink, for tomorrow we must die'. The time was indeed drawing near when their wickedness, like that of the Amorites of old, would be complete. And they convened a council to decide the best and soundest way to counter the brutal and repeated invasions and plunderings by the peoples I have mentioned.[9]

There is dispute over Gildas' accuracy. Morris has argued that one hundred years is a reasonable estimate for reliable transmission of historical material. Therefore Gildas, writing about 540, could be relied upon for information about events a century earlier.[10] Collective memory can be tenacious under the right conditions, while being unreliable on points of detail. The real significance of Gildas' work, however, is that it demonstrates Bede's concern for sources and his desire that his history be accurate: Gildas' was the nearest to an eyewitness account available.

The Angles, Saxons and Jutes arrived in Britain in the middle of the fifth century, raiding the coastal areas at first, but later settling. The conquest had several phases, with battles being fought and a British resistance holding the invaders at bay until approximately 500. The traditional account, of which Bede's version is the most polished[11] is also found in the *Anglo-Saxon Chronicle*. This, in all its variant forms, was a product of the reign of King Alfred the Great of Wessex, who ruled from 871 to 900. It is a vernacular source, but of dubious reliability because it was compiled late from earlier sources. Where the *Chronicle* can be compared to its sources, however, it appears to be reliable. The account is as follows:

443

In this year the Britons sent oversea to Rome and asked them for troops against the Picts, but they had none there because they were at war with Attila, king of the Huns; and then they sent to the Angles and made the same request to the princes of the Angles. ...

449

... Vortigern invited the Angles hither, and then they came hither to Britain in three ships at a place *Heopwinesfleot* [Ebbsfleet, Kent]. King Vortigern gave them land to the south-east of this land on condition that they fought against the Picts. They then fought against the Picts and had victory wherever they came. Then they sent to Angel; ordered [them] to send more aid and to be told of the worthlessness of the Britons and of the excellence of the land. They then at once sent hither a larger force to help the others. These men came from three nations of Germany: from the Old Saxons, from the Angles, from the Jutes. ... Their leaders were two brothers, Hengest and Horsa; they were the sons of Wihtgils. Wihtgils was the son of Witta, the son of Wecta, the son of Woden; from this Woden sprang all our royal family and that of the peoples dwelling south of the Humber.[12]

The Anglo-Saxons upon arrival in Britain were apparently entirely unacquainted with Christianity, but this state of affairs is likely to have been short-lived. The usual bottom-up spread of Christianity probably commenced immediately, despite language difficulties and the likely low status of the conquered British Christians.

There is an acute scarcity of reliable textual evidence for Anglo-Saxon religion. Tacitus locates the focus of Germanic religion within the sacred groves which were the gods' sanctuaries. The chief concerns of Germanic religion in the first century CE were warfare and agriculture, concerns which remained constant beyond the 'doom' of the old gods, when Iceland converted in 1000. The *Poetic Edda*, from thirteenth century Iceland, provides the only detailed written source of Germanic mythology. This collection of poems is from the Christian era and very late, so there is disagreement among scholars as to its accuracy. From Anglo-Saxon England itself the only text which provides detail about pre-Christian beliefs and practices is Bede's *De Temporum Ratione* (On the Reckoning of Time), which is hardly encyclopaedic. Most of Bede's references to the former faith of his country concern the names for the months and the dates of the various festivals. He states, for example, that the old heathen year commenced on the twenty-fifth of December and that the night of the following day was called the 'mothers' night', and that the fourth month of the year was named for the goddess Eostre.[13]

The traditions concerning Anglo-Saxon religion preserved by Bede are supplemented by evidence from a variety of sources, including archaeology and royal genealogies and regnal lists. The latter shed light on the religious role of the Anglo-Saxon kings, which was to be decisive in the conversion of the English. It was common practice among the Germanic peoples to trace royal family trees back to a deity, most frequently Woden/Odin.[14] The Frankish royal family, the Merovingians, claimed as their eponymous ancestor Merovech, who was the son of a sea-monster, perhaps a serpent/ dragon such as Grendel, the foe of Beowulf.[15] Jordanes speaks of a similar belief in divine ancestry among the royal families of the Goths. The East Saxon kings claimed descent from Seaxneat, and the Kentish kings from Woden. The *Anglo-Saxon Chronicle* ties all Anglo-Saxon royal lines to the god Woden. As Moisl has noted, even the most cursory study of these genealogies raises several questions.

Was the keeping of extensive genealogical records an authentic pre-Christian Germanic custom, or were the genealogies constructed as a result of the encounter with Christianity? Although the Germanic peoples possessed a script — the Runic *futhark* — from approximately the first century BCE, it was only used for brief inscriptions[16] and the regular keeping of written records was only introduced with conversion to Christianity. Works such as Snorri Sturluson's *Prose Edda* make it clear that European learning came to the Germanic peoples along with the new faith. Snorri traces the origins of the Scandinavian gods back to the Trojan War, linking them in with the main tradition of European history.[17] The royal genealogies with divine roots present in the writings of almost every Germanic society are not unquestionably native.

What role did these genealogies play in Germanic society? Kingship in Germanic society involved both secular and religious powers and responsibilities.[18] To become king a man could either be elected or belong to the ruling dynasty. The sacral nature of kingship is best illustrated by the view of the king as the 'luck of the people', through whose success or failure the favour or displeasure of the gods was visible to the people. That kings had great personal power which was believed to continue after death is supported by the existence of burial mounds which were places of great power.[19]

The tracing of ancestry back to a divine origin served ideological purposes,[20] some simple (merely emphasizing the right of the particular dynasty to rule), and some complex (playing a part in the ordering of society). Whether the information was transmitted orally or in written form made no difference to its function. The learned classes, pagan and Christian priests, poets and scholars, were patronized, protected and paid by the kings and therefore preserved versions of history which were consistent with existing realities. As Dumville observed:

> it is now common ground for social anthropologists that pre-literate peoples only preserve versions of their history which explain current social groupings and institutions, and that these versions may bear little relation to an historical sequence of events. In other words, their oral tradition constitutes both a validation of existing social relationships and a mnemonic device for their transmission and explanation. This applies with particular force to genealogies.[21]

Stressing the pragmatic role of the genealogies, Dumville is positive that, for the Venerable Bede, Woden's presence in the Kentish royal line only made it suitably royal: Woden was a convention and nothing more, having lost all his attributes as a pagan deity.[22] This may be so, but a willingness to reduce everything to simple ideology may inhibit profitable lines of enquiry.[23]

The gods chiefly associated with Anglo-Saxon royal genealogies were Woden and Seaxneat. Very little is known about Seaxneat, a tribal god of the Saxons. Woden is a far more frustrating deity: there is much more evidence regarding his nature and attributes, but this evidence is fragmentary and allusive. In order to fill out the picture, scholars have often been tempted to use the greater detail which is available concerning Odin, the Scandinavian cognate of Woden. This has confused the issue in two ways. Firstly, Anglo-Saxon religion and Scandinavian religion, while undeniably related, are by no means the same thing. Secondly, there is a distinction between Woden and Odin.[24]

Nevertheless, comparative information about Odin, along with information about Tacitus' Mercury, is useful. In each case, the Mercury/ Woden/Odin figure was king of the Germanic pantheon, at least as far back as there is written evidence, and seems to have achieved this position by a tortuous route, having originally been a god of death.[25] This early identification of Odin with death belies his complexity in later sources: in the *Poetic Edda* he has become a super-shaman, simultaneously on both sides of death. Haugen suggested that 'Odin, more than any other god in Germanic myth, embodies this questioning, ambiguous aspect of divinity. He is the union in his own person of the sullied and the sacred.'[26]

Anglo-Saxon kings needed a divine lineage and were, if not divine themselves, channels through which the power of the gods reached the people. The decisive role played by royalty in the conversion of the Anglo-Saxons becomes immediately comprehensible in the light of this fact.

The prelude to the conversion

When Augustine arrived at Thanet in 597, approximately one hundred and fifty years after the arrival of the Anglo-Saxons, Britain had become England (from 'Angleland'), with established kingdoms and royal houses which had emerged over the previous century and a half. Scholars are hampered in speculation about this period of Anglo-Saxon occupation because of the paucity of source material.

The genealogies of the Anglo-Saxon kingdoms help in piecing together the time-scale of development, but they tell us nothing about the establishment of political entities or the survival of Christianity.[27] Although time must have brought familiarity between the Anglo-Saxons and the British, there is little evidence that the Anglo-Saxons knew much about Christianity at the time of Augustine's arrival. It has been argued that Christianity had been wiped out among the British in areas settled by the Anglo-Saxons, and that it survived only in remote regions untouched by the conquerors, principally Wales.[28] This view is at one end of a continuum of opinion: at the other some scholars argue for the extensive survival of Christianity among the conquered British (although it lacked influence, being perceived by the Anglo-Saxons as the religion of the conquered class).[29]

Augustine's mission to England was sent by Pope Gregory the Great and the motivations behind it were complex. The quotation prefacing this chapter charmingly suggests that Pope Gregory had the highest possible reasons for desiring the conversion of the Anglo-Saxons. It is unwise to accept such an anecdote at face value, however. Gregory's own spiritual vision sought the creation of a Christian society and he placed great value on individual souls: 'not only is man a noble creation, but in Christ, God has even favored human weakness above the angels'.[30] There were significant political advantages for the Papacy to be gained from a mission to Britain. In the late sixth century the Papacy was still relatively lacking in international influence and was seeking opportunities to extend its sway over the Christian population of Europe. The breach between the British and Roman Churches caused by Pelagianism had not yet healed, and

Gregory the Great 'could not have been indifferent to the political advantages that would follow from the reunion of a lost province of the empire to the church of its capital'.[31]

The status of the Papacy when Gregory occupied that office was ill-defined. Justinian, who had ruled the Eastern Empire from 527 to 565, treated the popes ruthlessly, managing to depose Silverius (536–37); imprison Vigilius (537–55) and appoint an inappropriate candidate, Pelagius I (556–61).[32] Gregory the Great became Pope in 590, when the spectre of this imperial maltreatment persisted. The most powerful kingdom in the West, that of the Franks, was Catholic but was generally unwilling to recognize the spiritual suzerainty of the Vatican.[33] As a result, missionary activity was inextricably bound up with Rome, which desired political relationships with the newly-converted peoples. Peoples such as the Anglo-Saxons lived on the fringe of European life, due to geographical isolation, paganism, and their own seeming indifference to the wider political scene.

Mission was also becoming more sophisticated in the sixth century. One of the most important accounts of how to convert a rural audience, Martin of Braga's sermon titled 'On the Castigation of Rustics' was written *c.* 574 CE, and contains much valuable information. Martin was concerned to instil into his converts basic Christian precepts and behaviour: 'Prepare your way by good works. Often visit the church or the shrines of the saints to pray to God. Do not despise the Lord's Day. ... Do no servile work on the Lord's Day. ...'[34] But in addition to this simple advice, Martin (who is writing a model sermon which he intends for use by many other clergy) provides quite detailed arguments to refute the ways that the adherents of the 'old religion' might view the world. He explains the pagan gods as devils, fallen angels in the Christian scheme, and emphasizes the reward that the new faith brings after death to people who have toiled all their lives. This more sophisticated persuasion in missionary activity is evident in the mission to the Anglo-Saxons.

Bede provides the fullest account of the mission, and a number of supplementary sources support parts of his story. Bede was born around 672 and, according to the autobiography appended to the *Historia Ecclesiastica*, entered the monastery of Wearmouth at seven and lived within the confines of the double monastery of Wearmouth-Jarrow until his death in 735. He has been called the most learned man of his age,[35] and his works include the *Historia Ecclesiastica*, *De Temporum Ratione*, *De Arte Metrica*, and a number of saints' lives. Bede's writings are characteristic of his time: his history is that of the inevitable and triumphant progress of Christianity over paganism and contains much that is miraculous and unverifiable. Bede had access to a formidable array of source materials, however, and he is careful to cite the origins of the information he is preserving. Bede's learning and scholarly attitude are indubitable,[36] but his information is not exhaustive. Recent research and the discovery of other traditions for the conversion of the Anglo-Saxons in the Welsh sources[37] have demonstrated that Bede was often reticent and restricted the information he provided. (It is understandable that topics such as the old religion, which remained powerful in Bede's lifetime, should have been sensitive.)[38] The dedication to King Ceolwulf in the *Historia* shows this:

> should history tell of good men and their good estate, the thoughtful listener is spurred on to imitate the good; should it record the evil ends of wicked men, no less effectually the devout and earnest listener or reader is kindled to eschew what is harmful and perverse, and himself with greater care pursue those things which he has learned to be good and pleasing in the sight of God.[39]

In the areas where Bede is reticent, evidence from place-name studies, archaeology, and other texts is sometimes of assistance. The missionary selected by Gregory to evangelize the English was Augustine, an Italian monk. He and his companions did not relish their task. Bede reports that:

> In obedience to the Pope's commands, they undertook this task and had already gone a little way on their journey when they were paralysed with terror. They began to contemplate returning home rather than going to a barbarous, fierce, and unbelieving nation whose language they did not even understand.[40]

Several factors may have contributed to the mission's terror at the prospect of Britain. Procopius' *Gothic War* speaks of an island called Brittia (which he distinguished from Britain but which clearly resembles it)[41] which is the home of the souls of the dead.[42] He is openly sceptical of this tradition, but includes it as it is widely held.[43] Augustine and his companions could well have been aware of this alarming information concerning their destination, since Procopius' *Discourses about the Wars* was published in 552. Their distress at their inability to speak the Anglo-Saxon language was understandable.[44]

Gregory's reply was understanding but firm: he insisted that the mission continue and that the group be not swayed from their purpose, and advised them to think of the heavenly reward which would be theirs. This advice might seem lofty and impractical, but Gregory shrewdly reassured them by promoting Augustine from prior to abbot. The Pope's letters demonstrate that he had been considering a mission to England for some time and that his plans were intimately connected with his policy towards the Frankish Church.[45] Many Frankish bishops were asked to support the mission and responded warmly.[46] While in Frankia the missionary party acquired Frankish interpreters to overcome their language problem. It is not clear whether Frankish could be understood by Anglo-Saxons, or whether the interpreters were Franks who were also able to speak Old English.[47]

Augustine's mission arrived at Thanet, an island off the coast of Kent, early in 597. They were not the first mission to Britain since the late Roman period: the entry for 565 in the *Anglo-Saxon Chronicle* states that:

> in this year Æthelberht succeeded to the kingdom of Kent and ruled fifty-three years. In his days Gregory sent baptism to us, and the priest Columba came to the Picts and converted them to the faith of Christ – they are inhabitants along the northern mountains – and their king gave him the island which is called Iona. ... There that Columba built a monastery ... his heirs still have that holy place. The South Picts had been baptized much earlier: bishop Ninian, who had been educated in Rome, preached baptism to them. His church and collegiate minster is at Whithorn, consecrated in the name of Saint Martin.[48]

Columba of Iona is an historically attested figure but there is some doubt about Ninian.[49] The dedication of Ninian's church to St Martin of Tours is suggestive because of Martin's profound influence on missionary methods.[50] The recent excavations at Whithorn in Wigtownshire in south-west Scotland have unearthed significant remains from the sixth and seventh centuries,[51] which confirm the historicity of Ninian's church and the identity of Whithorn as Bede's 'Candida Casa'.[52]

It seems likely that the Gregorian mission went first to Kent because the Kentish king, Æthelberht, had contacts with Frankia through his marriage to the Frankish princess Bertha and hence was already aware of both the wider European political scene and of Christianity. The date of Æthelberht's marriage and the chronology of his reign are uncertain.[53] Bertha married him before he became king, and a condition of the marriage was that she should have the freedom to practise her religion unhindered. She was accompanied by her chaplain, Liudhard,[54] and there is some evidence for Bishop Liudhard's influence in Kent.[55] The extent to which Æthelberht was influenced by the Christianity of his wife or her chaplain is hotly debated; the circumstances of the first meeting between Æthelberht and Augustine suggest that Æthelberht knew next to nothing about Christianity. It has been noted that 'Frankish princesses were not always distinguished for their piety',[56] and a date around 560 for Bertha's marriage to Æthelberht would suggest that she had had little success in persuading her husband to accept Christianity (although it says nothing about the frequency or ingenuity of her efforts to do so). However, Wood's article, using Gregory of Tours' *Historia* as evidence, argues forcefully that Æthelberht's reign should be dated from around 589, telescoping events dramatically.[57] Wood sees the Merovingian Church and monarchy as intimately involved with the mission.[58] This goes far beyond Wallace-Hadrill's suggestion that Bertha's marriage to Æthelberht may have involved some political dependence of the Kentish kingdom on Frankia.[59]

There was much in Anglo-Saxon, and more precisely Kentish, culture which constituted a receptive environment for Christianity. Æthelberht's Christian wife and her chaplain must have had an effect merely by their presence, both as representatives of the new faith and as emissaries of the broader world. Pragmatically, Augustine's approach to Æthelberht made sound sense; before a mission could commence, the permission of the secular authorities had to be obtained (a pattern which continues to this day).[60] As discussed, the king had sacral as well as secular status and the society was bound to him by oaths of allegiance like those among the Goths and Franks.

Augustine sent greetings to Æthelberht and eventually a meeting between the King and the missionaries was arranged. Æthelberht 'took care that they should not meet in any building, for he held the traditional superstition that, if they practised any magic art, they might deceive him and get the better of him as soon as he entered.'[61]

Despite this early wariness on Æthelberht's part, his relations with the missionaries were cordial and he treated them with every courtesy. Bede records his response to Augustine's initial address:

> The words and promises you bring are fair enough, but because they are new to us and doubtful, I cannot consent to accept them and forsake those beliefs which I and the whole English race have held so long. But as you have come on a long pilgrimage and are anxious, I perceive, to share with us things which you believe to be true and good, we do not wish to do you harm; on the contrary, we will receive you hospitably and provide what is necessary for your support; nor do we forbid you to win all you can to your faith and religion by your teaching.[62]

Here Æthelberht is demonstrating the hospitality that Michael Richter has drawn attention to, and is therefore functioning as an agent of conversion.[63] Augustine had prepared well for the encounter: Bede records it as an impressive spectacle, with the missionaries singing a hymn and carrying a cross and a likeness of Christ.[64] As a result of their fair reception, the mission found itself housed in Canterbury, the capital of Kent, and provided with a Romano-British church dedicated to St Martin for their use. (This was the same church which had been used by Bishop Liudhard and Bertha, which may indicate that Liudhard had died.)

The missionary and the king

Augustine and his companions set about the business of converting the Anglo-Saxons to Christianity. Their position was slightly different to that of the missions discussed in previous chapters. The Franks were surrounded by Christianity and its attendant culture, the established Gallo-Roman Church and secular bureaucracy.

The Goths, outside the Roman Empire as they were, were perhaps closer to the Anglo-Saxon case, but Christianity had increased greatly in power and organization by the late sixth century. It is important to keep in mind that there was no full-scale encounter between two monolithic systems, Christianity and paganism, and it is unhelpful to regard the two religious allegiances as coherent enough to permit such an encounter.[65]

Little is known of the actual methods which Augustine employed in converting the Anglo-Saxons, except that his behaviour and that of his companions was admired and won them converts who were inspired by their holiness.[66] Augustine's party reached Britain early in 597 and Pope Gregory wrote to Bishop Eulogius of Alexandria: 'Moreover, at the solemnity of the Lord's Nativity which occurred in this first indiction, more than ten thousand Angli are reported to have been baptized by the same our brother and fellow-bishop.'[67]

Even allowing for some exaggeration, ten thousand converts in ten months, given Augustine's linguistic difficulties and his failure to join forces with the British Christians of Wales, demands an explanation. Although scholars are still unable to agree on a date for the baptism of Æthelberht (the suggested dates range from 597 to 601),[68] the most likely explanation of the mass baptism is that Æthelberht was baptized at this time and that the ten thousand accepted baptism because of their ties of loyalty to him. As the date of Æthelberht's baptism is still disputed, the argument for an early date, very probably Christmas 597, is concluded by the dismissal of the discredited theory that a letter of Gregory's to Bertha indicates that Æthelberht was still not a Christian in 601.[69] In the letter Gregory is severe with Bertha, but it is clear that she is being criticized for the slowness of her husband's conversion, and not because he is still unconverted.[70] The companion letter to Æthelberht compares him to Constantine (as Bertha has been compared to Helena), and exhorts Æthelberht:

> And now let your Majesty hasten to instil the knowledge of the one God, Father, Son, and Holy Spirit, into the kings and nations subject to you, that you may surpass the ancient kings of your race in praise and merit, and since you have caused others among your subjects to be cleansed from their sins, so you yourself may become less anxious about your own sins before the dread judgement of Almighty God.[71]

It is unlikely that the Pope would have written such a letter to a king who was still a pagan.

The ties of loyalty between Germanic kings and their followers, which

Whitelock has termed 'the bonds of society', were fundamental. For Anglo-Saxon England, the later story of Cynewulf and Cyneheard, preserved in the *Anglo-Saxon Chronicle*, offers evidence that the ideal of dying for and with one's lord was a custom both venerated and practised. Cynewulf, king of Wessex, was treacherously killed by Cyneheard while visiting a mistress. Of the retainers who accompanied him to this tryst only one survived to carry the news of his murder to his other retainers. These men then rode to the scene of the crime, and when Cyneheard attempted to make terms with them, they told him 'that no kinsman was dearer to them than their lord, and they never would follow his slayer. ... And they went on fighting around the gates until they forced their way in and slew the prince and the men who were with him ...'[72] These bonds operated at all levels of society: the nobility were oath-bound to the king; the nobles had retainers; and the yeomanry and slaves were bound to the lords on whose land they lived and worked. The practical consequence of this tightly-woven social organization for the success of missionary work was that 'the conversion of the *folc* stemmed from the conversion of the king to the more powerful deity, since it was the king's relationship to the gods which "saved" his people as much as did the gods themselves'.[73] If the conversion of the king could be secured, then that of his nobility and their retainers was virtually assured.

Augustine's attempts to establish a relationship with the remnant of the Romano-British Church were abortive. Reasons for this can be conceptualized in terms of the insider and outsider roles considered in Chapter 1. Pope Gregory had given Augustine authority over the British Church in Wales and the flourishing Irish Church which had its headquarters at Iona (Hii), an island monastery off the west coast of Scotland. Augustine had two meetings with the British bishops, but on neither occasion was he successful in persuading them to accept his, and Rome's, authority. Augustine's position among the British clergy can be seen as that of an insider: they were all Christians, all communicated in the ecclesiastical *lingua franca*, Latin; and all might be assumed to have the evangelization of the Anglo-Saxons as a fairly high priority. The British almost certainly saw him as an outsider. Bede described their meeting as follows:

> Augustine ... summoned the bishops and teachers of the neighbouring British kingdoms to a conference at a place which is still called in English ... Augustine's Oak. ... He proceeded to urge them with brotherly admonitions, that they should preserve catholic peace with him and undertake the joint labour of evangelizing the heathen for the Lord's sake ... then the Britons confessed that ... they could not disown their former customs without the consent ... of their own people. They therefore asked that a conference should be held for a second time and that more should attend. When this had been

decided on ... they went first to a certain holy and prudent man who lived as a hermit among them to consult him as to whether they ought to forsake their own traditions at the bidding of Augustine. He answered, 'If he is a man of God, follow him' ... they said, 'But how can we know even this?' He said, 'Contrive that he and his followers arrive first ... if he rises on your approach, you will know that he is a servant of Christ'.... They did as he had said. Now it happened that Augustine remained seated while they were coming in; and when they saw this, they forthwith became enraged ... saying between themselves that if he was even unwilling to rise at their approach now, he would despise them much more if they were to begin to give way to him.[74]

This was the end of the negotiations between the Roman and British churches.

That such a small misunderstanding could be the cause of a decisive breakdown in communications indicates the precarious state of relations between the two parties, both committed to Christianity but uncertain of their status. Even Stenton, who doubted Bede's anecdote, postulated a 'cultural' reason for the failure to communicate: the conservative and ascetic Welsh church, he claimed, would have had nothing in common with the learned and relaxed Italian monastic tradition.[75] However, the anecdote sounds authentic, especially since it is told against Augustine. This is an example of the difficulties in communication discussed in Chapter 1.

Augustine, working with a group which was apparently culturally similar, easily offended the expectations of the British clergy. It hardly seems likely that, while working among the Anglo-Saxons, a group whose culture he did not understand, he could have won ten thousand converts in the space of ten months (especially as his preaching must have been conducted through the Frankish interpreters) without the acceptance of baptism by the king.

Augustine's relationship with Æthelberht would also have been constrained by potentially negative outsider roles. Augustine had been sent by the Pope, from mainland Europe, a political entity on whose fringes England lay. He therefore had an emissary role, bringing information from powers which were hostile to the paganism and isolationism of the English. He had travelled through Frankia, where Bertha's family were powerful, and might therefore be perceived by Æthelberht as a 'policeman', checking on both the physical and spiritual welfare of his wife. An alternative to this negative perception of the mission is Wood's bold suggestion that the Angles actually petitioned the Pope for a mission.[76] Wood notes the anomaly of Bede's suggestion that the Angles only show interest in Christianity when it is forced upon them by an outside agency, given that ample evidence exists to suggest interest in Christianity on the inside.[77] This recalls Fritigern's request for missionaries, motivated by a realization of the might of Rome and an understanding of how becoming Christian might enable him to more effectively resist, and perhaps ultimately defeat, his rival Athanaric.[78]

Another point to stress is that, in view of Anglo-Saxon social organization, the ten thousand baptized would not have been capable of turning to the new God as individuals. That kind of individuality, where a person could make decisions and perceive them as affecting only themselves, was quite alien to the early medieval mind. The notion of society was pre-eminent: it has been argued that the concerns of primal religions and societies (loosely defined as pre-literate societies) are essentially communal. Trompf wrote of the characteristics of 'fundamental' religion that:

> The hopes of abundance, fertility and health, in fact, are both integral to the wish for individual and group vitality. For, the few pacifistic-looking exceptions aside, a hallmark of the fundamental is warriorhood, or (more inclusively) prowess.[79]

This fits the Anglo-Saxon case exceptionally well. As further evidence that the conversions which took place in Anglo-Saxon England were not individual decisions, it appears that even kings did not change their religious allegiance without consultation. This is seen most clearly in the case of Edwin of Northumbria, which will be considered in the next section.

Bonds of loyalty also applied to the kings. England in the sixth century was not one but seven kingdoms: Kent, Wessex, Sussex, Essex, Mercia, East Anglia and Northumbria. The seven kings swore fealty to an over-king, the *bretwalda*.[80] The line of descent of the *bretwaldas* throughout the conversion period (approximately eighty years) was linked to the vicissitudes of Christianity. Æthelberht was the over-king at the time of his conversion, and his power resulted in the baptism of other monarchs (for example, Saberht of Essex). Æthelberht's enthusiasm for the culture brought by the monks is further evidenced by that fact that he promulgated a written legal code.[81] This phenomenon was also observed with the Burgundians and the Franks. The connection with religion is evidenced by Wormald's comment that 'the Anglo-Saxons soon learned to use documents as proof, but their charters continue to *look* like objects of reverence rather than record'.[82]

When Æthelberht died in 616 his kingdom, Kent, abandoned Christianity because his son, Eadbald, was not a Christian. This makes it very clear that the acceptance of Christianity was dependent on ties of loyalty to the monarch; Christianity could be jettisoned when a new king required oaths of loyalty and served the old gods. The *bretwalda* who filled the power vacuum was Rædwald of East Anglia, whose dealings with the new religion are fascinating. Persuaded to accept baptism by his lord

Æthelberht, he returned to East Anglia to negotiate with his wife and *witan*.
His unnamed wife justified Pope Gregory's belief in the power of spouses
as religious persuaders.[83] According to Bede:

> his wife and certain perverse advisers persuaded him to apostatize from the true
> faith. So his last state was worse than the first: for, like the ancient Samaritans,
> he tried to serve both Christ and the ancient gods, and he had in the same
> shrine an altar for the holy Sacrifice of Christ side by side with a small altar on
> which victims were offered to devils.[84]

It is clear that Rædwald saw the powers of another god as important:
perhaps the new religion could be added to the old? It is also clear that he
had originally accepted baptism due to his obligations to the *bretwalda*, and
when that mantle devolved upon himself, he gave up any pretence of
supporting Christianity where it conflicted with the old religion. This
solution was naturally unacceptable to the Christian historians who
chronicled this period, but it demonstrates that the Christianity accepted by
the Anglo-Saxons was syncretistic, involving elements of the old pagan
religion. Rædwald's solution is regarded more sympathetically by scholars,
who can recognize the inherent pragmatism: 'Redwald ... was clearly
unwilling to offend the God ... by rejecting him altogether. To him it
seemed at least feasible to maintain friendly relations with more than one
god.'[85] Sharpe argued that the Germanic peoples were accustomed to
having more than one god in a temple or sanctuary and that among the
vikings there were those who added the White Christ to the deities they
already worshipped, revering whichever god was appropriate to their
situation.[86]

A 'personal' conversion?

The next significant conversion was that of Edwin of Northumbria by
Paulinus, a member of Augustine's party who was sent as chaplain to the
Northumbrian court when Edwin married Æthelburh, the Christian
daughter of Æthelberht. Paulinus was a bishop, consecrated in 625. He
was a vigorous missionary, but initially had little success in converting the
Northumbrians. 'But although he toiled hard and long in preaching the
word, yet as the apostle says, "The god of this world blinded the minds of
them that believed not, lest the light of the glorious gospel of Christ should
shine unto them." '[87] So Paulinus concentrated his efforts on persuading
King Edwin. What followed was the closest thing to an individual
conversion in the modern sense in all the material covered so far. Paulinus
utilized every opportunity to convince the king, from the successful
avoidance of assassination to the queen's safely giving birth to her first

child.[88] Edwin frequently committed himself to conversion if a certain event came to pass, and just as frequently delayed accepting baptism until some further sign.

Paulinus finally precipitated a decision from Edwin by placing his right hand on the king's head, recalling the action of a stranger who had offered Edwin solace when he was a friendless exile some years earlier. This was a sign which could not be ignored.[89] He summoned the pagan high priest Coifi and his *witan*, the council of advisers which supported his kingship. There was no contest as such (as there was, for example, between Elijah and the prophets of Baal in I Kings 18, verses 17-40), and Paulinus did not perform a miracle, as happens elsewhere in Bede. Instead there was a lengthy discussion, and Coifi spoke on the relative merits of the old and the new gods:

> Notice carefully, King, this doctrine which is now being expounded to us. I frankly admit that, for my part, I have found that the religion which we have hitherto held has no virtue or profit in it. None of your followers has devoted himself more earnestly than I have to the worship of our gods, but nevertheless there are many who receive greater benefits and greater honour from you than I do and are more successful in all their undertakings. If the gods had any power they would have helped me more readily, seeing that I have always served them with greater zeal. So it follows that if, on examination, these new doctrines which have now been explained to us are found to be better and more effectual, let us accept them at once without any delay.[90]

He offered to be the first to profane the altars and temples of the old religion to signify the acceptance of the new; this involved his breaking the taboos on riding a stallion and bearing arms. This is a textbook illustration of Horton's contention that it is those who have most at stake in the old religion who become the leaders in adopting the new faith. Here the king and the high priest combine to precipitate the change of religious allegiance. The result of Coifi's actions and the decision of the *witan* was that 'King Edwin, with all the nobles of his race and a vast number of the common people, received the faith and regeneration by holy baptism in the eleventh year of his reign, that is in the year of our Lord 627'.[91]

The decision of Edwin and the assembly to convert was probably motivated by similar considerations to those that had swayed Æthelberht. Significantly, the *bretwalda*ship of Rædwald of East Anglia had ended, and his son Eorpwald ruled East Anglia. Edwin was well placed to become *bretwalda* himself and could therefore afford to take the lead in religious matters. The new God had ambassadors (for example, Paulinus) with powerful employers, and the king had married a Christian and would have been aware of the importance of pleasing her relatives. Northumbria also needed to keep on peaceful terms with both Kent and Essex, which were firmly Christian.

The motive of greater prosperity and benefits for the people, achieved through the establishment of a relationship with the new God through the king, was also a strong one. Coifi's reasoning was that the Christian God seemed likely to provide greater material and spiritual rewards, so he was the more powerful and should be worshipped. Bede approved of Coifi's argument, referring to his 'wise words', and recorded the arguments of other nobles, including the oft-quoted 'anonymous *thegn*' who compared human life to a sparrow flitting through the king's guest hall, briefly in the warmth and comfort, but returning to the cold and storm from whence it flew.[92] Eschatology, therefore, was clearly an important issue in the conversion process. Christianity spoke with power and authority on the matter of life after death.

Bede says of Edwin:

> But first he made it his business, as opportunity occurred, to learn the faith
> systematically from the venerable Bishop Paulinus, and then to consult with the
> counsellors whom he himself being a man of great natural sagacity would often
> sit alone for long periods in silence, but in his innermost thoughts he was
> deliberating with himself as to what he ought to do and which religion he
> should adhere to.[93]

This indicates a great deal of individual thought and consideration on Edwin's part. However, he must have been aware that any decision he made would be a decision for the Northumbrian people and not simply for himself. The responsibility of kingship was to ensure the spiritual and physical welfare of the people by having a good relationship with the supernatural powers. Therefore, the king's conversion meant the conversion of the kingdom. Any failure of the new god meant the possible removal of the king and reversion to the old gods. What is important is the connection between the king and the religion of the people. 'Thus, while the tribal culture was still strong enough after the conversion to bring royal apostasy, both the old and the new religions related the fate of the kingdom to the cult of the king'.[94] Edwin's recognition of the tribal nature of Northumbrian society is clearly indicated by the meetings he convened with his *witan*.

One of the most interesting elements of the conversion of the Northumbrians was the crucial role of the pagan high priest, Coifi, and of the Christian womenfolk of the royal household. Coifi is evidence for Horton's contention that it is those who are most intimately involved with the old religion who will take the lead with the new. Unfortunately, nothing is known of the career of Coifi after his dramatic change of allegiance. Meaney wondered whether Coifi was rewarded for his dramatic role in the conversion, or whether Edwin 'discard[ed] him once he played his vital part?'[95] The role of the Christian royal women and children is less dramatic, but equally significant. Æthelburh brought Christianity to the Northumbrian court, and with it political ties to the Christian court of her brother Eadbald. Her daughter Eanfled was the first Northumbrian baptized, and the child's trouble-free birth was used by Paulinus to demonstrate the power of the Christian God's protection.

Nora Chadwick has examined other sources associated with the conversion of Edwin. She refers to a very late *Life of Saint Oswald*, written in 1165, which records traditions about Edwin's years of exile in Wales. This Welsh tradition suggests that Edwin was baptized during his exile by Rhun, son of Urien, at the court of Gwynedd.[96] She admits that this tradition may be a late invention, possibly coloured by the conflict between the Roman and Celtic Churches. Hunter Blair has argued that the ready abandonment of their religion by the Northumbrians indicates that the old religion was much weaker in the north, and that there were many Celtic Christians who became part of Paulinus' flock.[97] This is possible: indeed it is probable that there were many underground Christians scattered throughout the Anglo-Saxon kingdoms, especially among the slaves. None of these hypotheses significantly alters the argument of this chapter, however, as the initial stimulus for an official conversion (whether Welsh or Anglo-Saxon) still comes from the royal family.

Christianity advances

The subsequent history of Christianity in the Anglo-Saxon kingdoms further illustrates the points made in the analysis of the conversions of Æthelberht and Edwin. Progress was not always smooth, however. Mayr-Harting has observed of the conversion period in England that the missionaries were able, the political reasons for conversion were compelling, and yet nearly a century passed with just the conversion of the kings and the aristocracy being achieved, and in every case with apostasy and reconversion indicating the strength of the old religion.[98] These relapses illustrate the dependence of Christianity on the personal support of kings. When the heirs of Christian monarchs were not themselves Christian, the changeover of government also involved a change of faith; oaths had to be sworn to the new kings and, as they served the old gods, the new god had to be renounced.

Essex was converted when its king, Saberht, was baptized due to the preaching of Mellitus. Here again there were political motives for the acceptance of the new religion. Saberht was the nephew of Æthelberht of Kent and Mellitus was a companion of Augustine's who had been consecrated bishop by Augustine in 604, doubtless with Æthelberht's approval of the proposed mission to Essex. After the death of Saberht of Essex, his pagan sons demanded the communion wafer from Mellitus and, when he refused them, they drove him from their kingdom.[99] This incident clearly indicates that many unbelievers understood Christianity only in terms of outward physical manifestations and believed that there was some power or nourishment to be gained from taking communion. This fits in with the great importance the old religion attached to symbols of power and acts of magic.[100] The incident also recalls Æthelberht's fear of the 'magic' of Augustine and his companions, and another incident in Bede's *Historia* where Æthelfrid of Northumbria defeated the British in a battle near Chester. Three hundred monks of Bangor had come to the battle to pray for the success of the British. As soon as Æthelfrid became aware of their role, he had them slaughtered.[101]

Although it is impossible to know how soon after Saberht's death Mellitus' eviction happened, the story suggests that some people remained Christian. But Essex was not effectively re-converted until the mission of Cedd, who was sent to the court of King Sigbert (distinct from King Sigbert of East Anglia) in 653. Sigbert was murdered by two of his relatives shortly after his conversion, which may be evidence for the persistence of the old religion: perhaps his acceptance of Christianity rendered him unacceptable to the powerful nobles in his kingdom.

Kent had a brief lapse into paganism when Æthelberht's son Eadbald ascended the throne. Eadbald's loyalty to the old religion is not explained in the sources: both Bede and the *Anglo-Saxon Chronicle* stress the fact that he married his stepmother as evidence of Eadbald's ungodliness.[102] The apostasy was shortlived: after an initial shock at being driven from their mission field and a despairing flight to the continent, the missionaries returned to England to pursue their mission. Kent was quickly salvaged when Eadbald became a Christian under the influence of Justus in 616.

The conversion of Northumbria by Paulinus, in 627, has been described in the last section. Lindsey, a satellite kingdom of Northumbria, also converted. Both kingdoms were rocked by apostasy following the death of Edwin in a battle against Penda, the pagan king of Mercia. Edwin's death resulted in an interregnum of approximately one year in Northumbria, and the kingdom broke into its traditional two regions: Deira (which was ruled by the Christian Osric, cousin of Edwin) and Bernicia (which was ruled by Eanfrid, the son of Æthelfrid, a former king of Northumbria). Bernicia apostasized and both Osric and Eanfrid were killed in battle against Cadwalla, a British prince. The ruler who eventually emerged in Northumbria was Oswald, a Christian who had been in exile and had received baptism through the preaching of the Irish monks of Iona.

So Northumbria returned to the Christian fold, but to a different type of

Christianity. The Irish Church was not in communion with the Roman Church, with disagreement on two main points: the reckoning of the date of Easter and the type of tonsure worn by the monks. Oswald sent to Iona for a bishop and was sent Aidan, a man with methods very different to the Roman missionaries. The Irish clergy placed great emphasis on the establishment of monastic communities and on general education. Oswald gave Aidan the island of Lindisfarne for a monastic site, and a distinctively Celtic Christianity, characterized by a love of learning and by personal austerity, developed. Aidan's spiritual excellence was recognized despite his repudiation of the dignities befitting a bishop. Stenton says of him that 'He was intimate with Northumbrian kings and nobles, and honoured by churchmen in the south, but his achievement was due to the popular veneration in which he was held'.[103]

While Northumbria was apostate, East Anglia was being evangelized. Bede states that East Anglia was officially converted in 627 when Rædwald died and his son Eorpwald (a much less powerful person – Rædwald had been *bretwalda* of England, but upon his death that honour passed to the Christian Edwin of Northumbria) was baptized under the aegis of Edwin. This is another case where a political motive, that of pleasing the over-king, is foremost in the conversion to Christianity.[104] Eorpwald's conversion in 627 was soon followed by his death at the hands of a pagan called Ricbert. Three years of apostasy on the part of East Anglia ensued, before Eorpwald's brother Sigbert took over and ruled stably as a Christian, assisted in the task of converting the province by Archbishop Felix, a Burgundian clergyman whom he had met while in exile.[105] Felix intelligently set about ensuring that no further apostasy would occur by founding a school to spread knowledge of Christian doctrine.[106]

Mercia remained pagan until the death of Penda. Penda serves an important role in Bede's *Historia*, that of the noble pagan. He indicated his willingness for the missionaries to preach in Mercia, merely adding that if any converts proved false to any tenet of their new faith, he will punish them severely. Naturally, the missionaries did not win many converts because the king himself was uninterested in conversion and his retainers could not be persuaded to prove faithless to him.[107] Individual conversion was discouraged by the king's declared intention to ensure all Christians rigorously observed the new faith. Christianity only made real progress in Mercia in the mid 650s, when Peada, son of Penda, wished to marry Alchfled, daughter of Oswy of Northumbria, whom Bede names as the seventh *bretwalda* of England.[108] Oswy made Peada's acceptance of baptism a condition of the marriage, and he was baptized by Finan and brought four priests, Cedd, Adda, Betti and Diuma, back to Mercia with him. Mercia, ruled in sequence by the sons of Penda, Peada and Wulfhere, was one of the few kingdoms which never apostasized.

The king of Wessex, Cynegils, had been baptized by Birinus in 635, with Oswald of Northumbria standing as sponsor. Bede knew little Wessex history and all that is known of Birinus is that he was probably Germanic, but that he came to England 'on the advice of Pope Honorius I, and the Church he founded was presumably organized on an Italian model'.[109] In a now familiar pattern, apostasy followed the death of Cynegils. His successor Cenwalh was baptized due to the persuasions of Anna, king of the East Angles, with whom he sojourned as an exile from 545 to 548. Such a delay in the conversion of the heir suggests that Birinus did not have a great deal of success in his initial mission. After Cenwalh returned to Wessex, however, the kingdom was firmly Christian, with no further record of apostasy.

The final kingdom to convert was Sussex in 681. This was preceded by the Synod of Whitby, which in 664 established the supremacy of Roman Christianity in England. Sussex converted due to the evangelism of Wilfrid of Hexham, an exile from Northumbria. King Æthelwahl had been baptized under the influence of King Wulfhere of Mercia, and Wilfrid baptized the nobility as a result of the king's decision. Wilfrid's mission differed from others, in that he also made genuine efforts to reach the ordinary people. He was assisted in this by a drought which had troubled the kingdom and produced famine for three years, and which broke on the day he baptized the *thegns*. Wilfrid also taught fishing techniques to the hungry people and they were willing to listen to his preaching, because they believed that they owed him their lives. The Isle of Wight received the new faith in 686, as the result of their conquest by the West Saxons. Again Wilfrid was the missionary. This conversion ensured the future political overlordship of Wessex over Wight.[110]

The indigenization of Christianity

Chaney's study, *The Cult of Kingship in Anglo-Saxon England*, explores kingship in England in both pre-Christian and Christian contexts. He argued that the sacral role of the king in Germanic religion facilitated, rather than hampered, acceptance of Christianity, because the role could so easily be translated from one context to another. Christianity could stress the *rex pacificus* and invoke the pagan association of peace and plenty with a king on good terms with the gods. Christian kings who died at the hands of pagans were often venerated as saints and hagiographers recorded miraculous occurrences at their tombs. These miracles were a translation of the *mana* of the king, which formerly remained after death at his grave mound. Grave mounds were particularly holy in pre-Christian Anglo-Saxon religion and it has been argued that:

People who buried their kinsmen in the ground with his possessions about him evidently believed or hoped that those possessions would be used in some life like their own by the dead man in the form in which they knew him. Those who cremated the dead and burned his possessions with him evidently believed that the fire worked some metamorphosis; the spirit of the dead one (and his possessions) was apotheosized to some other plane by the act of cremating.[111]

Objections can be raised to the above reasoning: it may be that inhumation and cremation were quite free of these speculations about the afterlife, reflecting only family or local tradition with regard to the disposal of the dead.[112]

However, the treatment of the burial places of the Christian dead seems to bear out some of the speculations concerning the pre-Christian attitudes to the dead. Oswald of Northumbria is a good example of this: he evangelized enthusiastically with Aidan, even interpreting for him, since Aidan spoke no Old English when he arrived in Northumbria, only Irish.[113] Oswald died in battle against Penda of Mercia in 642 after a nine-year reign. Bede assures us that his grave was a miraculous site:

> Indeed in that place where he was slain by the heathen fighting for his fatherland, sick men and beasts are healed to this day. It has happened that people have often taken soil from the place where his body fell to the ground, have put it in water, and by its use have brought great relief to their sick. ... Many miracles are related which took place either at that site or through the soil taken from it.[114]

These martyred and miracle-working kings were the Christian answer to several problems raised by the passing of the old religion. The death of a king at the hands of heathen enemies did not necessarily mean the disfavour of the Christian God, or imply his weakness and the strength of the pagan gods. Martyrdom, with its noble status in Christian thought, nullified the purely physical victories that pagan armies achieved. It was not difficult to make the Anglo-Saxons understand the concept of martyrdom, because they were accustomed to a king-cult in which the sacrifice of the king for the common good was at least a familiar idea. Chaney's enthusiasm for king-sacrifice is more muted than that of Margaret Murray, but he believes that it was a traditional concept and may actually have occurred, albeit infrequently. He is interested in Murray's observation that ten out of the twelve kings whose names began with the prefix 'Os' (which she identifies with the first syllable of *Aesir*, probably spuriously) died violent deaths. Chaney suggests that 'sainthood bestowed upon kings who die violent deaths may well be regarded as a Christian substitute for the ritual king-slaying of paganism'.[115] Functionally, Christianity was replacing the old religion perfectly adequately.

Pope Gregory had written to Mellitus in 601 suggesting that Anglo-Saxon temples and holy days should be converted to Christian ones to facilitate the process of conversion.[116] The result of this policy was a tendency to build churches near sacred springs and a link between the rite of baptism and pre-Christian ceremonies. Morris commented that:

> the water which forms part of Christian initiation embodies a bundle of ideas; a cleansing in *fons vitae*; the crossing of a boundary; an exchange of one life and family for another; and an image of death and rebirth. These concepts came to be reflected in the architectural, locational and symbolic contexts of baptism. Thus, in a medieval parish church the baptismal ceremony began *ad valves ecclesiae*. Churches were sometimes positioned close to springs and water courses, or even superimposed upon them.[117]

The indigenization of Christianity in Anglo-Saxon society can also be seen from the rapid growth of monasteries.[118] These were often founded by monarchs and attracted novices through networks of patronage which worked much as pre-Christian ties of loyalty had.[119] These monasteries were the source of the Anglo-Saxon literature which has survived to this day. This literature is very powerful evidence for the emergence of an indigenized form of Christianity in Anglo-Saxon England. The most famous of these literary products, *Beowulf*, has been analysed both as a remembrance of the Germanic pagan past and as a Christianized work. What can be determined from *Beowulf* is the kind of stories the Anglo-Saxons enjoyed; stories about fellow-aristocrats, which also preserved their heritage from the Continent.[120] *Beowulf* tells of a Danish king, Hrothgar, whose court (the great hall, Heorot) is menaced by a monster, Grendel. The hero, Beowulf, a Geat (Swede), delivers Hrothgar's hall from Grendel and his mother, reigns long and well, and eventually perishes in battle with a dragon. The action of *Beowulf* never touches England, but appears to preserve a memory of the Scandinavian origins of the Germanic peoples.

The status of *Beowulf* in Christian England raises many questions. Alcuin of York wrote in approximately 797CE, 'Let the word of God be read at the priestly repast. There should the reader be heard, not the harpist (*citharistam*); the sermons of the Fathers, not the songs of pagans (*carmina gentilium*). What has Ingeld to do with Christ? The House is narrow, it cannot hold both.'[121] From this it has been assumed that Alcuin disapproved of tales and poems which recalled the pagan past of the Anglo-Saxons, and believed that they should be replaced with appropriate Christian literature. However, he is writing for a clerical audience, and it therefore does not seem unlikely that the Anglo-Saxon aristocracy enjoyed *Beowulf* and tales like it. Robert Hanning, commenting on the poem, says that although intellectually the gap between the

Christian present and the pagan past is absolute, there are as many continuities as discontinuities.[122]

The critical debate over *Beowulf* is possible because of the ambiguous nature of the poem itself. *Beowulf* can be interpreted as the classic Germanic hero; a courageous lone warrior who achieves heroic status and then dies in combat. But *Beowulf's* role as a slayer of giants and monsters has caused him to be viewed as an agent of God, or even a Christ-figure. This is partly because the giants and monsters are referred to as the offspring of Cain on two occasions, which seems to place them firmly in a Christian or biblical context. Tolkien and Horowitz both see the themes of the poem as linked to the tales of biblical heroes, seeing a particular parallel with David.[123] In addition, God is continually invoked throughout the poem, and there are Christian concepts such as heaven, hell and judgement which are referred to and understood by the characters in the drama. However, the layers of meaning are ambiguous, as *feond* still means 'enemy' (as well as 'fiend'), and *helle* means both 'hell' and 'sky'.

Ultimately, whether *Beowulf* is a pagan or a Christian poem is irrelevant. What it demonstrates is that pagan and Christian concepts and values were entwined by the Anglo-Saxon clergy in their preservation of the pre-Christian culture of the English, and that there was an audience for this type of literature. In *Beowulf* a traditional tale has been partly Christianized; in poems like *Christ* and *Christ and Satan* Christian material has been partly paganized. This literature lends powerful support to the arguments of Trompf and Russell that the indigenous, microcosmic culture, may come to dominate the international, macrocosmic culture.

Notes

1. Bede, *A History of the English Church and People*, ed. and trans. Leo Sherley-Price, Harmondsworth, 1975, pp. 99–100. The Latin text is in Bede, *The Ecclesiastical History of the English People*, ed. and trans. Bertram Colgrave and R. A. B. Mynors, Oxford, 1969, pp. 132–4.
2. W. H. C. Frend, 'The Christianization of Roman Britain', in M. W. Barley and R. P. C. Hanson (eds), *Christianity in Britain 300–700*, Leicester, 1968, p. 37.
3. Ralph Whitlock, *The Warrior Kings of Saxon England*, Bath, 1977, p. 20. The Latin text is in Tertullian, *Adversus Judaeos* 7 (AD 209), in A. W. Haddan and W. Stubbs (eds), *Councils and Ecclesiastical Documents relating to Britain and Ireland*, vol. 1, Oxford, 1869, p. 1.
4. Peter Salway, *The Oxford Illustrated History of Roman Britain*, Oxford, 1993, pp. 514–15.
5. Salway, *op. cit.*
6. Bede, Colgrave and Mynors, *op. cit.*, pp. 28–35.
7. G. F. Browne, *The Church in These Islands Before Augustine*, London, 1899,

p. 80. See also W. H. C. Frend, *Saints and Sinners in the Early Church*, London, 1985, pp. 123–39 for a good summary of the Pelagian controversy.

8. See Chapter 3, section 'Change and Continuity in Gaul' and also Leslie Alcock, *Arthur's Britain*, Harmondsworth, 1971, pp. 100–3.

9. Gildas, *The Ruin of Britain and Other Works*, ed. and trans. Michael Winterbottom, Phillimore, 1978, pp. 25–6. The Latin text is on pp. 96–7.

10. John Morris, 'The Literary Evidence', in Barley and Hanson, *op. cit.*, p. 63.

11. Bede, Sherley-Price, *op. cit.*, pp. 55–8. Another source which provides essentially the same account is Nennius, *British History and the Welsh Annals*, ed. and trans. John Morris, Phillimore, 1980, pp. 12–15. The Latin text is on pp. 54–6.

12. G. N. Garmonsway (ed. and trans.), *The Anglo-Saxon Chronicle*, London, 1972, The Laud Chronicle, p. 13. The Anglo-Saxon is in C. Plummer and J. Earle (eds), *Two of the Saxon Chronicles Parallel*, Oxford, 1972, The Laud MS, p. 13.

13. Brian Branston, *The Lost Gods of England*, London, 1957, p. 51. It has been noted that in the case of the days of the week (Tuesday = Tiw's Day, Wednesday = Woden's Day, Thursday = Thunor's Day, and Friday = Frigg's Day) it is a mistake to assume that a genuine pre-Christian survival has been preserved, as 'this association of heathen Saxon deities with the days of the week is nothing more than a consequence of a wholly artificial correlation of the four concerned with the four Roman deities from whom the corresponding days in the Roman week were called, namely Mars, Mercury, Jupiter and Venus', Peter Hunter Blair, *An Introduction to Anglo-Saxon England*, Cambridge, 1970, p. 123. What is being questioned here is not the similarity between the Germanic and Roman deities which was established in the discussion of Tacitus in Chapter 2; it is the authenticity of a tradition which involves the substitution of Germanic gods for Roman gods in an already-established classical framework.

14. See Chapter 3, section 'The Franks'.

15. Hermann Moisl, 'Anglo-Saxon Royal Genealogies and Germanic Oral Tradition', *JMH*, 7, (3), September 1981, p. 225.

16. See Chapter 2, note 69.

17. Snorri Sturluson, *Edda*, ed. and trans. Anthony Faulkes, London, 1987, pp. 64–5.

18. William A. Chaney, *The Cult of Kingship in Anglo-Saxon England*, Manchester, 1970, p. 11.

19. *Ibid.*, p. 105.

20. David N. Dumville, 'Kingship, Genealogies and Regnal Lists', in P. H. Sawyer and I. N. Wood (eds), *Early Medieval Kingship*, Leeds, 1977, p. 74.

21. *Ibid.*, p. 85.

22. *Ibid.*, pp. 78–9.

23. Patrick Wormald, 'Celtic and Anglo-Saxon Kingship: Some Further Thoughts', in Paul E. Szarmach (ed.), *Sources of Anglo-Saxon Culture*, Kalamazoo, 1986, p. 152.

24. Audrey Meaney wrote of Woden and Odin: 'The first was brought to

England by the Angles, Saxons and Jutes in the fifth century AD, and was defeated, along with his co-deities Thunor, Tiw, and Frig, by Christ between 597 and about 700. [Odin] was imported by the vikings from the middle of the tenth century onwards, but was always on the retreat. It is doubtful if his worship could ever have gained a real foothold in England, with the possible exception of Northumbria, and little can have been heard of him after the conversion of Cnut in the eleventh century', in 'Woden in England: A Reconsideration of the Evidence', *Folklore*, 77, 1966, p. 105.

25. Einar Haugen, 'The *Edda* as Ritual: Odin and his Masks', in Robert Glendinning and Haraldur Bessason, *Edda*, University of Manitoba Press, 1983, p. 8.

26. *Ibid.*

27. Margaret Gallyon, *The Early Church in Wessex and Mercia*, Lavenham, 1980, makes use of such materials in researching the origins of the two kingdoms.

28. Peter Hunter Blair, *The World of Bede*, London, 1970, p. 42.

29. James Campbell, 'The First Century of Christianity in England', in *Essays in Anglo-Saxon History*, London, 1986, pp. 49–68, mentions Wilhelm Levison's acceptance of Bede's assertion that at St Albans the cult of St Alban continued unbroken from Roman times.

30. Carole Straw, *Gregory the Great*, Berkeley, CA, 1988, p. 46.

31. Frank Merry Stenton, *Anglo-Saxon England*, Oxford, 1971, p. 104.

32. Geoffrey Barraclough, *The Medieval Papacy*, London, 1968, p. 22.

33. *Ibid.*, p. 50.

34. Martin of Braga, 'On the Castigation of Rustics', in J. N. Hillgarth (ed.), *Christianity and Paganism 350–750*, University of Pennsylvania Press, 1986, p. 63.

35. Charles W. Jones, 'Bede as Early Medieval Historian', *M&H*, 4, 1946, p. 26.

36. Campbell, 'Bede I' and 'Bede II', in Campbell, *op. cit.*, pp. 1–28 and 29–48.

37. Nora K. Chadwick, 'The Conversion of Northumbria: A Comparison of Sources', in N. K. Chadwick (ed.), *Celt and Saxon*, Cambridge, 1964, p. 147. Chadwick discussed Welsh sources for the conversion of Edwin of Northumbria which contradict Bede's version, among them Nennius. She does not accuse Bede of knowingly suppressing this evidence, merely observing that 'Bede's informants told him the story which he has told us. It may not be the whole story, but it is the story cultivated in the eastern and most completely Anglicized and articulate part of the country', p. 166.

38. Rosalind Hill, 'Bede and the Boors', in Gerald Bonner (ed.), *Famulus Christi*, London, 1976, comments that Theodore of Tarsus, who became archbishop of Britain in 664, in his *Penitential*: 'makes it clear that the house where a person had died was widely believed to be under some sort of taboo until grain had been burned "for the health of the living and the dead". Binding spells seem to have been commonly employed: Æthelfrid thought that the monks of Chester were trying to bind the strength of his army by their incantations (which was probably true)', p. 98.

39. Bede, Colgrave and Mynors, *op. cit.*, p. 3. The Latin is on p. 2.

40. *Ibid.*, p. 69. The Latin text is on p. 68.

41. E. A. Thompson, 'Procopius on Brittia and Britannia', *Classical Quarterly*, n.s., XXX, 1980, pp. 498–507, argues that 'Brittia' is Britain and 'Britannia' is Brittany in Procopius' geography.

42. Procopius, *History of the Wars*, ed. and trans. H. B. Dewing, V, London, 1928. *Gothic War* bk 8, ch. xx, says of Brittia, 'They say, then, that the souls of men who die are always conveyed to this place', p. 267. The Greek text is on p. 266.

43. *Op. cit.*, 'Since I have reached this point in the history, it is necessary for me to record a story which bears a very close resemblance to mythology, a story which did not indeed seem to me at all trustworthy, although it was constantly being published by countless persons'. The Greek text is also *op. cit.*

44. See Chapter 1, section 'Contemporary Christian Approaches to Conversion'.

45. Ian Wood, 'The Mission of Augustine of Canterbury to the English', *Speculum*, 69, (1), 1994, *passim*.

46. *Ibid.*, p. 5.

47. Campbell, 1986, *op. cit.*, p. 54.

48. Garmonsway, *op. cit.*, The Laud Chronicle, p. 19. The Anglo-Saxon is in Plummer and Earle, *op. cit.*, The Laud MS, p. 19.

49. A. C. Thomas, 'The Evidence from North Britain', in Barley and Hanson (eds), *op. cit.*, *passim*.

50. Frend, 1968, *op. cit.*, p. 43.

51. P. Hill, *Whithorn II*, Whithorn Trust, 1988.

52. Candida Casa (*hwitærn* in Anglo-Saxon) is mentioned by Bede as the site of Ninian's church. The name is generally taken to mean 'shining house'. See further discussion in A. C. Thomas, *Christianity in Roman Britain to 500 AD*, London, 1981 and A. A. M. Duncan, 'Bede, Iona and the Picts', in J. M. Wallace-Hadrill and R. H. C. Davis (eds), *The Writing of History in the Middle Ages*, Oxford, 1981, pp. 1–42.

53. Wood, *op. cit.*, pp. 10–11, argues that Æthelberht becomes king after 589, which makes more sense for the chronology of the conversion than the traditional date of 561 given by Bede.

54. A. J. Mason, *The Mission of Saint Augustine to England*, Cambridge, 1897, dates the marriage *c.* 560.

55. Margaret Deanesly, 'Canterbury and Paris in the Reign of Æthelberht', *History*, n.s. XXVI, 1941–2, pp. 97–104, comments on Liudhard's minting 'of coins on the Frankish model', p. 97.

56. D. P. Kirby, *The Making of Early England*, London, 1967, p. 41.

57. Wood, *op. cit.*, p. 11.

58. *Ibid.*, p. 9.

59. J. M. Wallace-Hadrill, *Early Germanic Kingship*, Oxford, 1971, p. 97.

60. Stephen Neill, *A History of Christian Missions*, Harmondsworth, 1964, *passim*.

61. Bede, Colgrave and Mynors, *op. cit.*, p. 75. The Latin is on p. 74.

62. *Ibid.*

63. Michael Richter, 'Practical Aspects of the Conversion of the Anglo-Saxons', in Próinséas Ní Chatháin and M. Richter (eds), *Irland und die Christenheit*, Stuttgart, 1987, p. 354.

64. Bede, Sherley-Price, *op. cit.*, p. 76. Wood, *op. cit.*, has cast doubt on Bede's account of this scene, noting that the Rogation hymn the missionaries allegedly sang was unlikely to have been known to them, p. 3. However, it is probable that Bede is accurate in indicating that the missionaries made an impression by the use of spectacle, which may well have been alive in memory and tradition in his lifetime.

65. E. J. Sharpe, 'Salvation, Germanic and Christian', in E. J. Sharpe and J. R. Hinnells (eds), *Man and His Salvation*, Manchester, 1973, p. 246.

66. Bede, Sherley-Price, *op. cit.*, p. 70.

67. Gregory the Great, *The Book of Pastoral Rule and Selected Epistles*, trans. Rev. James Barmby, *NP-NF*, XII, Grand Rapids, 1979, p. 240. The Latin text is in Gregory the Great, *Opera Omnia*, in J.-P. Migne (ed.), *PL*, tom. LXXVII, Paris, 1896, pp. 931–2.

68. R. A. Markus, 'The Chronology of the Gregorian Mission to England: Bede's Narrative and Gregory's Correspondence', *Journal of Ecclesiastical History*, XIV, 1963, p. 16. This article basically reviews the chronological arguments of Dom Suso Brechter and the opposition to them from Margaret Deanesly and Père Grosjean.

69. *Ibid.*, pp. 16–30 discusses the theories of Dom Suso Brechter, who asserts as indicated above.

70. Gregory the Great, *Selected Epistles*, trans. Rev. James Barmby, *NP-NF*, XIII, Grand Rapids, 1979, bk XI, ep. XXIX, pp. 56–7.

71. Bede, Colgrave and Mynors, *op. cit.*, p. 113. The Latin text is on p. 112.

72. Garmonsway, *op. cit.*, The Parker Chronicle, p. 48. The Anglo-Saxon text is in Plummer and Earle, *op. cit.*, The Parker MS, p. 48. Rosemary Woolf, in 'The Ideal of Men Dying with their Lord in the *Germania* and in *The Battle of Maldon*', *A-SE*, 5, 1976, pp. 63–81, discusses this incident also, and compares it to the retainers dying with Byrhtnoth in *The Battle of Maldon*, observing: 'But the point at which political and heroic motives mingle is crucial to the patterning of the story. For what the members of Cynewulf's bodyguard courageously reject is not a strategic withdrawal from the fight coupled with the hope of fighting another day (as, by implication, is the case in *Maldon*) but an agreement to serve as king the man who has just killed their lord', pp. 70–1. However, she allows that the Cynewulf and Cyneheard instance does indicate that the practice of dying with one's lord was recognized and did occur in Anglo-Saxon England, indicating the strength of the 'bonds of society'.

73. William A. Chaney, 'Paganism to Christianity in Anglo-Saxon England', in S.L. Thrupp (ed.), *Early Medieval Society*, New York, 1967, p. 74.

74. Bede, Colgrave and Mynors, *op. cit.*, pp. 135–7. The Latin is on pp. 138–40.

75. Stenton, 1971, *op. cit.*, p. 110. However, my colleague Tony Swain has commented that the reasons for being accepted as insider or outsider often have nothing to do with the message that the alien brings. An example from his fieldwork was that of the case of a missionary working in an Australian Aboriginal group whose message was largely ignored, but who was an insider because he had a truck.

76. Wood, *ibid.*, pp. 9–11.
77. Gregory the Great, *The Book of Pastoral Rule and Selected Epistles*, *op. cit.*, bk VI, ep. LVIII, 'To Theodoric and Theodebert', p. 205. It should be noted that Gregory says the Angles are desirous of being converted, but he cites no evidence in support.
78. See Chapter 2, section 'Christianity and the Goths'.
79. Garry W. Trompf, 'Salvation and Primal Religion', *Prudentia*, supp. no., 1988, p. 209.
80. Patrick Wormald, 'Celtic and Anglo-Saxon Kingship: Some Further Thoughts', in Paul E. Szarmach (ed.), *Sources of Anglo-Saxon Culture*, Kalamazoo, 1986, pp. 151–84, *passim*, and Henry Mayr-Harting, *The Coming of Christianity to Anglo-Saxon England*, London, 1972, *passim*.
81. Clare E. Stancliffe, 'Kings and Conversions: Some Comparisons between the Roman Mission to England and Patrick's to Ireland', *Frühmittelalterliche Studien*, 14, 1980, p. 62.
82. Patrick Wormald, 'Bede and the Conversion of England: The Charter Evidence', *Jarrow Lecture*, 1984, p. 13.
83. Wood, *op. cit.*, p. 6.
84. Bede, Sherley-Price, *op. cit.*, p. 133. The Latin text is in Bede, Colgrave and Mynors, *op. cit.*, p. 190.
85. Eric J. Sharpe, *Seasons of Light and Darkness*, unpublished typescript, p. 78.
86. Sharpe, 1973, *op. cit.*, p. 257.
87. Bede, Colgrave and Mynors, *op. cit.*, p. 165. The Latin text is on p. 164.
88. I am grateful to Sheleyah Niven, my student in 1993 and 1994, for her shrewd comments on the role of infant females (and males) as actors in the drama of conversion.
89. Stenton, 1971, *op. cit.*, p. 114.
90. Bede, Colgrave and Mynors, *op. cit.*, p. 183. The Latin text is on p. 182.
91. *Ibid.*, p. 187. The Latin text is on p. 186.
92. The discovery of the Anglo-Saxon palace at Yeavering, the royal seat of Northumbria, and its great hall, has lent credence to the thegn's speech, showing a building with doors at either end. Yeavering also contains a building which is possibly a temple converted into a church, and a timber grandstand focused on a platform, presumably a place of assembly, which may have been the site of Paulinus' preaching. See Brian Hope-Taylor, *Yeavering: Anglo-British Centre of Early Northumbria*, Department of the Environment Archaeological Reports no. 7, London, 1977.
93. Bede, Colgrave and Mynors, *op. cit.*, p. 167. The Latin text is on p. 166.
94. Chaney, 1967, *op. cit.*, p. 75.
95. A. L. Meaney, 'Bede and Anglo-Saxon Paganism', *Parergon*, n.s., 3, 1985, p. 21.
96. Chadwick, *op. cit.*, p. 155. She comments that both the *Annales Cambriae* and Nennius' *Historia Brittonum* record the same tradition, Nennius saying 'And Edwin in the following Easter received baptism, and 12000 persons were baptised with him. If anyone should wish to know who baptised them, Rum map Urbgen baptised them and for forty days ceased not to baptise', p. 156.

The 'Urien' or 'Urbgen' is generally taken to be the king of Rheged, a kingdom probably centred on Carlisle.

97. Hunter Blair, *An Introduction to Anglo-Saxon England, op. cit.*, p. 119.
98. Mayr-Harting, *op. cit.*, p. 29.
99. Bede, Sherley-Price, *op. cit.*, pp. 112–13
100. E. J. Sharpe, in conversation, holds the view that Christianity functions in exactly the same way. It has a lofty doctrinal superstructure, but at ground level also attaches great importance to physical manifestations, symbols of power, and acts of magic.
101. Bede, Sherley-Price, *op. cit.*, p. 103. Of this passage A. L. Meaney, 1985, *op. cit.*, comments, 'Considering the dangerous powers ascribed to this high priest [Coifi] (whose enemies would no doubt usually believe in his powers and who would therefore be far less resistant to his magic than Wilfrid's party), it is not surprising that King Æthelfrith, at the Battle of Chester, took the first opportunity of killing the monks of Bangor, when he was told that they were present for the purpose of praying for the opposing side. ... The South Saxon priest, then, would seem to have been very similar to those whom Tacitus describes in the *Germania*, who took the *effigies et signa*, "images and symbols", from the sacred groves and carried them into battle', p. 19.
102. Garmonsway, *op. cit.*, p. 23.
103. Stenton, 1971, *op. cit.*, p. 119.
104. Frank Merry Stenton, 'Lindsey and Its Kings', in Doris M. Stenton (ed.), *Preparatory to Anglo-Saxon England*, Oxford, 1970, observes that 'There can be no doubt that the attitude of each local king determined the date at which Christianity reached his people. But except for brief intervals, England south of the Humber formed a primitive kind of confederacy under a common overlord, and too little attention has been given to the influence of this overlordship on the progress of the conversion. This influence might well be adverse; the stagnation of the Kentish mission in the later years of Archbishop Laurentius is due in part to the dubious attitude of Rædwald, the new overlord of the southern English. But the relationship between lord and man required that an under-king should visit his overlord's court, and the visits of under-kings to overlords like Edwin and Oswald must have carried some elementary knowledge of the new religion into regions which no missionary had yet explored', p. 127.
105. Bede, Sherley-Price, *op. cit.*, pp. 130–1.
106. Stenton, 1971, *op. cit.*, pp. 116–17.
107. Bede, Sherley-Price, *op. cit.*, pp. 177–8.
108. *Ibid.*, pp. 107–8, states that the sequence was Ælle of Sussex, Cælin of Wessex, Æthelberht of Kent, Rædwald of East Anglia, Edwin of Northumbria, Oswald of Northumbria, and Oswy of Northumbria. It is interesting to see that since the arrival of the missionaries in 597 four out of the five *bretwaldas* were Christian and influenced the conversion of the Anglo-Saxons. The absence of Penda of Mercia is also significant, as he killed in battle Edwin and Oswald, as well as Sigbert of East Anglia, and was evidently never a loyal vassal of any of these over-kings.

109. Stenton, 1971, *op. cit.*, p. 117.
110. Campbell, *op. cit.*, p. 77.
111. Gale R. Owen, *Rites and Religions of the Anglo-Saxons*, London, 1981, p. 79.
112. Hilda Ellis Davidson has expressed this view to me in a letter.
113. Hunter Blair, *The World of Bede, op. cit.*, comments that 'It was one thing for Aidan to move from one island site at Iona to another at Lindisfarne where he had the help of an English king who had already been baptised and could speak Irish well enough to act as Aidan's interpreter. It was another thing for Augustine to journey a thousand miles from Rome with no more than a Frankish queen to help him at the end of his journey in a deeply pagan land. Yet comparing the two missions, if comparison is valid where the evidence is so slight, particularly from Canterbury, we are struck at once by the importance which the Irish attached to the teaching of both children and older people. The Irish may have lacked the skill, and probably the desire, to create an organised church such as Gregory had wanted to see, but until Theodore reached Canterbury in 669, we can find little trace among the Roman missionaries of that zeal for scholarship and teaching which was so characteristic of the Irish monks', pp. 104–5. An examination of the differences between the Irish and Roman missionaries in methods and in their attitude to education was made as early as 1928, in an article by P. F. Jones entitled 'The Gregorian Mission and English Education', *Speculum*, III, (3), 1928, pp. 335–48.
114. Bede, Colgrave and Mynors, *op. cit.*, p. 243. The Latin text is on p. 242.
115. Chaney, 1970, *op. cit.*, p. 76.
116. Bede, Sherley-Price, *op. cit.*, pp. 91–2. An extract from the letter is in Chapter 8.
117. Richard Morris, 'Baptismal Places: 600–800', in Ian Wood and Niels Lund (eds), *Peoples and Places in Northern Europe 500–1600*, Woodbridge, 1991, p. 18.
118. Eric John, 'The Social and Political Problems of the Early English Church', in Joan Thirsk (ed.), *Land, Church and People*, Reading, 1970, p. 58.
119. Patrick Wormald, 'Bede, *Beowulf* and the Conversion of the Anglo-Saxon Aristocracy', in R. T. Farrell (ed.), *Bede and Anglo-Saxon England*, BAR 46, 1978, p. 53.
120. John McGalliard, 'Beowulf and Bede', in Robert S. Hoyt (ed.), *Life and Thought in the Early Middle Ages*, University of Minnesota Press, 1967, p. 102. McGalliard commented: 'If, as Alcuin insisted, Ingeld has nothing to do with Christ, he has a great deal to do with the poetry of Northern Europe. ... Evidently people like these stories of their Continental past. Otherwise they would not have been handed down.'
121. Alcuin, *Epistolae*, ed. E. Dummler, *MGH*, Ep. Sel. Karolini Aevi, p. 183, quoted in Wormald, 1978, *op. cit.*, p. 43.
122. Robert W. Hanning, '*Beowulf* as Heroic History', *M&H*, n.s. 5, 1974, pp. 77–102.
123. Sylvia Huntley Horowitz, 'Beowulf, Samson, David and Christ', *Studies in Medieval Culture*, XII, 1978, p. 20.

5 Anglo-Saxon missions to the continent

Egbert, the man of the Lord, saw that he was not permitted to go and preach to the nations himself, but was retained to be of some other use to the holy Church, as he had been forewarned by a prophecy ... yet ... [he] still attempted to send holy and industrious men to the task of preaching the Word.

Bede[1]

Wilfrid of Hexham

The conversion of the Anglo-Saxons was to have important consequences for the spread of Christianity in Northern Europe. Anglo-Saxon missionaries took the initiative in converting their continental German brethren in the seventh and eighth centuries.

The first of these missions was a brief interlude in the career of Wilfrid of Hexham, the controversial archbishop of York. Eddi's *Life*, written in approximately 720, agrees with Bede in portraying Wilfrid as shrewd and resourceful, a substantial landowner as well as a missionary, and well aware of the necessity of cultivating advantageous friendships and investments, due to the risky and costly nature of missionary activity.[2] His lifestyle attracted criticism and his relationships with the Anglo-Saxon royal families were fraught with difficulties.[3] Mayr-Harting has suggested that Wilfrid was part of a monastic missionary movement which had at its centre a Northumbrian nobleman called Egbert. Egbert was a *peregrinus*, who lived as an exile in Ireland and confined his own missionary activities to converting the Celtic Church to observation of the Roman Easter. Wilfrid, also Northumbrian but slightly younger than Egbert, had been Rome's champion at the Synod of Whitby, and Egbert's best-known protégé, Willibrord, had been a pupil of Wilfrid's at Ripon.[4] Wilfrid was approximately two years younger than Cuthbert, abbot of Lindisfarne, and he began his education at that monastery, where he must have met Aidan, the bishop instrumental in the conversion of Northumbria.[5]

An energetic traveller, Wilfrid had been in Gaul in the 650s, when Amand and Eligius were evangelizing. (Amand, bishop of Maastricht, had a see at Antwerp and a diocese extending to Frisia, and Eligius, bishop of

Tournai, worked in Flanders.)[6] Before being exiled to Sussex from 680 to 685/6 (where he was successful in converting the South Saxons) Wilfrid spent a brief period evangelizing among the Frisians. In 678 he was *en route* to Rome to appeal to the Pope, having been driven from his see by Ecgfrith of Northumbria. Eddi gives a detailed account of this appeal, and may have accompanied Wilfrid on one of his journeys to Rome. Bede disagrees with Eddi on a number of points, but both record that Wilfrid visited Frisia during his journey and engaged in mission.[7] Eddi states that Wilfrid was welcomed by King Aldgisl of the Frisians and 'that year he baptised all but a few of the chiefs and many thousands of the common people',[8] which would fit the familiar pattern. Whatever the case, Wilfrid was unable to follow up his success, and there was little enduring conversion.[9]

In the wake of Wilfrid's pioneering efforts among the continental Germans, Anglo-Saxon connections with the continent strengthened. Other clergy were eager to evangelize in Frisia and Saxony and many realized their ambition. Early efforts were made by Wihtberht, whose failure may have been due to the power vacuum created by the assassination of Dagobert II. The next major figure was Willibrord, whose success was linked to the consolidation of political power by Pepin II.[10]

Willibrord

Evidence for Willibrord's life is slender. His own correspondence has been lost, and his *Vita*, written by Alcuin of York some fifty years after his death, is primarily a collection of miracle stories. Willibrord went to the continent in 690 when he was thirty-two, after twelve years of study in Ireland, where he had come under the influence of Egbert. In Frisia, Willibrord received the support and protection of Pepin II, the Austrasian Frankish king who sought to conquer the Frisians but had so far been resisted by Radbod, the Frisian king. Willibrord also sought the approval of Pope Sergius I, who consecrated him archbishop in 695, giving him the name Clement; his see was at Utrecht and his flock the Frisians.[11] Willibrord's mission 'succeeded whenever the Frankish supremacy gave him protection'.[12] The cultural factors within Frisian society which favoured the new faith were not strong, and the political pressure which Pepin II exerted was not sufficient to force conversion except as a result of direct conquest.

Alcuin recorded few details about Willibrord's missionary techniques, but it appears that he was a formidable traveller, visiting towns, villages and outlying homesteads. Alcuin stated that: 'as the number of the faithful increased day by day and a considerable multitude of believers came to the knowledge of God's Word, many began in their zeal for the faith to make over to the man of God their hereditary properties. These he accepted.[13] This demonstrates the need for missions to be financed and also offers an indication of how the converts perceived the missionary. Bede's contribution to knowledge of Willibrord's methods is limited to noting that Willibrord intended to destroy idols and found churches, and therefore sought a supply of relics of the saints to place in the churches.[14] This ties in closely with the transfer of loyalties from people with power in the old world-view to those with power in the new.[15] Missionaries are frequently depicted in hagiographies performing significant acts which demonstrate their power and greatly impress their audience.

The Germans were accustomed to people with supernatural powers and sacred status, since their primary political and religious institution was the sacral king. The German converts were willing to transfer their reverence for the sacral king to others.

Dawson observed that:

> in this twilight world it was inevitable that the Christian ascetic and saint should acquire some of the features of the pagan shaman and demi-god: that his prestige should depend upon his power as a wonder-worker and that men should seek his decision in the same way as they had formerly resorted to the shrine of a pagan oracle.[16]

Despite Dawson's old-fashioned image of early medieval Europe as a dimly-lit and declining society, the point is valid.

Willibrord's most incendiary act was when he took shelter on an island off the German coast, where the Frisian population worshipped a god called Fosite. Their cattle and spring were sacred to the god.

Alcuin reported that:

> [Willibrord] set little store by the superstitious sacredness ascribed to the spot, or by the savage cruelty of the king, who was accustomed to condemn violators of the sacred objects to the most cruel death. Willibrord baptized three persons in the fountain in the name of the Blessed Trinity and gave orders that some of the cattle should be slaughtered as food for his company.[17]

Radbod decreed that lots be cast among the monks to determine if they would die for their sacrilege. For three days they cast lots three times daily and all escaped, until the last casting, when the lot fell on one of the monks. Radbod deemed, however, that atonement had been made, and they were allowed to leave unharmed.[18] Significantly, the three whom Willibrord baptized were probably ransomed boys from Denmark, not native inhabitants of Heligoland. Although Radbod was sufficiently impressed by Willibrord's courage to release him, he did not accept baptism and the mission's gains were few. On another occasion, Willibrord was not so fortunate; he was injured after overturning an idol on the island of Walcheren.[19]

Radbod's hostility to Christianity was a persistent problem for Willibrord's mission. This hostility was partly a response to Pepin II's imperialist designs on Frisia. It was also a response to Radbod's perception of Christianity as a divisive element in Germanic society. This attitude has permeated Germanic encounters with Christianity since Atharidus condemned St Saba to death in 372. Radbod's political discontent led him to revolt in 714, the year of Pepin of Heristal's death. It is probable that Radbod's rebellion took advantage of the Frankish power vacuum. Earlier, Wulframn, bishop of Sens, had visited Frisia briefly and nearly persuaded Radbod to accept baptism. The *Life of St Wulframn* states that:

> Prince Rathbodus made a prayer and, when he was wet to receive baptism, inquired of the holy bishop Vulframnus, binding him with oaths in the name of the Lord, where the greater number of kings, princes or nobles of Frisian nation, whether in this manifestly heavenly place, which, if he believed and was baptised, he was promised he was going to see, or in that, which was spoken of, nether hell. Then the blessed Vulframnus said: 'Make no mistake renowned prince, the number of your chosen with God is determined. For it is certain that your predecessors, princes of the Frisian nation who died without the sacrament of baptism, received the sentence of damnation; who from this time believe truly and are baptized will rejoice with Christ forever'. When he heard this the disbelieving prince, who had advanced to the font, withdrew his foot from it, saying that he could not deprive himself of the companionship of his predecessors, the Frisian princes, and dwell in the heavenly kingdom with a small number of the poor; nay indeed that he could not easily give his assent to new teachings but would rather continue in those which for a long time he had observed with all the Frisian nation.[20]

Some beliefs could not be reconciled with the new religion.[21] Once again, the failure of the monarch to accept baptism means the failure of the people to accept baptism, and the halting of the missionary's enterprise.

Difficulties with Radbod persuaded Willibrord to shift his attention to Denmark. In the early eighth century the mission-field there was virtually untouched by Christianity, whereas the area on the fringe of Frankia was: 'a demi-world of lapsed Christians, lost communities practising what had survived of Christian cultus in isolation'.[22] It is true that Christianity crossed borders by casual contacts, religious, commercial and military in nature, and may have taken root in Denmark before intentional missionary activity. In Scandinavia, Willibrord encountered Ongendus, king of the Danes, a 'man more savage than any wild beast and harder than stone',[23] and, being unable to convert him, purchased boys, intending that they should be trained as missionaries and return to convert their native lands.

Nothing came of this plan, however, and Scandinavia remained isolated from Christianity for another century, save for casual trading contacts. These trading contacts intensified with the growth of the Viking Age market towns, which depended to a large extent for their commercial viability on trade with Christian, and specifically Carolingian, Europe.[24] Failure to convert the king left Willibrord as unsuccessful among the Frisians as Amand and Eligius had been. Other English missionaries were persuaded by Willibrord's example to attempt missionary work on the continent. These included the two Hewalds, White and Black, who were both martyred by the Frisians.[25] The next significant figure was Wynfrith, who is better known as Boniface, Willibrord's assistant in his later years. Willibrord died in 739 aged eighty-one.[26]

Boniface

It is fortunate that Boniface's correspondence has been preserved and that an early *Vita* by Willibald also exists. Bede also offers useful commentary, making Boniface, along with Wilfrid of Hexham, one of the best-documented saints of the late seventh and early eighth centuries. Boniface was born in Wessex around 675, and died with fifty-two others at Dokkum in Holland in 754 or 755. His early education was in a monastery in Exeter, where he was a good student and developed a strong affection for the Rule of St Benedict.[27] He first left England in 716, in response to a call for aid from Willibrord, perhaps because of the Frisian revolt against the Franks led by Radbod in 714.[28] This trip was brief, and he left England a second time in 718.

Boniface is remembered as the 'Apostle of the Germans', which acknowledges his efforts in converting regions such as Thuringia, Bavaria and Hesse, which were substantially free from Christianity. But his work of conversion was far more than simply preaching the Gospel. It was political in two senses. Firstly, there was the desire of the Frankish monarchy (the Austrasian mayors of the palace, the Arnulfings, as the Merovingian monarchy had declined into powerlessness) to annex all the surrounding territory.[29] Conversion aided this policy. Wallace-Hadrill notes that this indicates a change of world-view: 'the conversion of the Germanic peoples bordering the Frankish world is something that could never have happened in Antiquity. The concept of a barbaric hinterland, essential to the thinking of the Later Empire, was gone: and in its place was born the conviction that those outside should be inside.'[30] In this case, conversion was hastened by the use of force. Instead of a slow process of absorption of Christian concepts and adjustment to the new faith, conquered groups had to reorganize themselves rapidly in order to retain their identity through forced political and religious transformations. This alliance of conversion with military conquest later became the basis of Charlemagne's policy of expansion.[31]

The second political aspect of Boniface's mission was his aim to organize the new converts into strong Churches and to bind those Churches to the Papacy. This is interesting when it is realized that Boniface was not sent to evangelize by any authority. Like Willibrord, he acquired the support of the Papacy after he had commenced missionary work.[32] The Frankish Church had never been as close to Rome as the Anglo-Saxon Church, and the Franks were just realizing that the approval of the Pope could legitimize many of their plans: a realization which ultimately led to the coronation of Charlemagne as Holy Roman Emperor in 800. This meant increased power for the Carolingian monarchy, and greater control over the activities of the Church, including missions.[33] Boniface's first communication with Charles Martel was an appeal for assistance in 719 due to aggression on the part of Radbod, the fierce old king of the Frisians. Radbod and Charles Martel were virtually at war, and Willibald's *Vita* states that: 'the greater part of the Christian churches, which previously had been subject to the Frankish Empire, were laid waste and brought to ruin. Moreover, the pagan shrines were rebuilt and, what is worse, the worship of idols was restored.'[34] The Church and the secular powers were in agreement here: Radbod must be stopped. He died later that year and the immediate threat to both Christianity and the Frankish empire abated. The death of Radbod enabled Boniface to proceed with conversion and the organization of the new Churches. Boniface's political acumen in forming an alliance with Charles Martel was considerable.[35] Fisher sees him primarily as the architect of the alliance between the Carolingians and the Papacy, and asserts that Boniface was 'a willing instrument of Carolingian policy', because their aims coincided with his own spiritual policies.[36] The rulers of the mission-field culture were cultivated in order to bring about conversion, and the rulers of neighbouring Christian cultures were cultivated to ensure adequate protection for the mission.

Boniface eventually broke away from Willibrord, preferring to use his own methods. These included the founding of monasteries, at Amoneburg, Ohrdruf, Fulda, and Fritzlar; and convents at Bischofsheim, Kitzingen and Ochsenfurt.[37] Like Willibrord and Anskar he recruited young men to be educated as missionaries. It is unfortunate that little evidence for Boniface's preaching techniques has been preserved by Willibald or in Boniface's own letters. It is not even known which language he preached in. Emerton, editor of Boniface's *Letters*, comments:

> we should like to know in what language he addressed the unconverted Frisians and Saxons or the nominally Christian Franks and Bavarians. ... As an Anglo-Saxon, acutely conscious of his Teutonic kinship, he would, in all probability,

have retained command at least of that dialect in which he had been reared ... doubtless all his formal intercourse was conducted in Latin; but it is hard to believe that so broadly human a nature should have lost the power to communicate freely with the people whom he especially desired to influence. How are we to explain the stories of him preaching to throngs ... if we suppose him to be using a language which none of them could understand? ... of [interpreters] there is no mention in the letters. More to the point is the undoubted fact that to the untutored mind religion was not so much a matter of individual conviction as of racial or tribal property.[38]

Institutionally, Boniface's methods are apparent. He had a large group of correspondents and they offered him support in spiritual and practical ways. However it does seem that on occasion he encountered crowds and was able to preach and perform grand gestures to impress the potential converts.

An example of a grand gesture is his destruction of a great oak tree dedicated to Jupiter Donar (Thor). This incident bears some resemblance to Columbanus' splitting of the barrel of beer intended as an offering to Woden.[39] Willibald recorded as follows:

> with the counsel and advice of the latter persons, Boniface in their presence attempted to cut down, at a place called Gaesmere, a certain oak of extraordinary size called by the pagans of olden times the oak of Jupiter. Taking his courage in his hands (for a great crowd of pagans stood by watching and bitterly cursing in their hearts the enemy of the gods), he cut the first notch. But when he had made a superficial cut, suddenly the oak's vast bulk, shaken by a mighty blast of wind from above, crashed to the ground shivering its topmost branches into fragments in its fall. As if by the express will of God (for the brethren had done nothing to cause it) the oak burst asunder into four parts, each part having a trunk of equal length. At the sight of this extraordinary spectacle the heathens who had been cursing ceased to revile and began, on the contrary, to believe and to bless the Lord.[40]

This incident demonstrates the importance of the theatrical in attracting the attention of an audience. Wallace-Hadrill suggested that 'the tradition of persuasion was a respectable one'.[41]

Boniface also employed more conventional techniques, such as the conversion of monarchs in order to win over their retainers as converts. An example is his conversion of the twin rulers Dettic and Devrulf, whose seat of government was at Amanburch.[42] Boniface's superior success (when compared to that of his predecessors) can be explained by the changed political context and by his attempts to connect his conversions and Church foundations with Rome, creating a safety net which helped preclude apostasy. Boniface's letters reveal his preoccupations with consolidation and his desire for support from distinguished Christians. He was constantly in contact with England and preferred to have English clergy working for him, believing the native clergy to be only imperfectly Christianized.[43] He corresponded with a number of women, including the Anglo-Saxon abbess Bugga and the nun Leoba, a woman of great learning as well as faith.[44] Her convent assisted by copying manuscripts, which Boniface used as holy objects to awe his audience. Boniface also founded bishoprics and monasteries as repositories of learning and prayer where monks laboured to produce books for the missionaries in the field and prayed for their success daily, and to which missionaries could retreat when tired and discouraged.[45] These monasteries and bishoprics (in the regions of Bavaria, Thuringia, and Hesse) were a significant contribution to the development of a Christian society, the creation of which was also an important motivation in the conversion of the peoples on the fringes of the Frankish Empire.[46]

Boniface had a regular correspondence: with the Pope, who encouraged his efforts;[47] with Anglo-Saxon monarchs who were interested in the mission because of its extension of English influence on the Continent;[48] and with fellow-clergy who provided him with practical suggestions and prayer. A letter from Bishop Daniel of Winchester offered advice as to how to present Christian theology to the Germans; it is of particular interest, especially when compared to the earlier letter of Pope Gregory the Great to Mellitus, and with Martin of Braga's sample sermon 'On the Castigation of Rustics'. Pope Gregory's letter advocated the inclusion of all pre-Christian customs which could possibly be harmonized with Christianity, while Bishop Daniel's letter stressed the importance of convincing potential converts by argument, as did Martin's sermon. So where Gregory suggested that the gods be dealt with by substituting saints' days for their festivals, Daniel advised Boniface:

> Do not begin by arguing with them about the origin of their gods, false as they are, but let them affirm that some of them were begotten by others through the intercourse of male with female, so that you may at least prove that gods and goddesses born after the manner of men are men and not gods and, since they did not exist before, must have had a beginning.[49]

Daniel's letter, nearly three pages in Emerton's edition, focused on simple theological arguments which can be used to confound the audience, rather than on practical matters of substitution of new for old. This may indicate an increased awareness on the part of eighth and ninth century missionaries of the risks of syncretism.

Boniface evangelized for nearly forty years, which enabled him to establish continuity for the Churches he founded, and he was assisted by companions who covered a vast area. He also revitalized the Frankish (now Carolingian) Church, by re-introducing the Church Council, which had been dormant since the early sixth century. Under Carloman two Councils were held in 742 and 743; and Pepin the Short held one the next year at Soissons. Talbot states that: 'to crown the work, a general Council of all the Frankish Empire was held in 745. These four councils brought order out of chaos, suppressed abuses, enforced discipline, and gave back to the Church a sense of respect and dignity.'[50] As Papal Legate, Boniface presided at all these Councils, which role was the apogee of his career in Germany. He was brutally martyred with fifty-two companions at Dokkum, in modern Holland, in 754 or 755. Ever aware of the power of the grand gesture in convincing even the most fervent opponent of Christianity, and aware that his death was not far off (he was over seventy), Boniface appears to have engineered the martyrdom deliberately. Willibald has him tell Lull, his successor in the mission field, 'an astonishing prophecy [of] the approaching day of his death and made known to him the manner in which he would meet his end'.[51] He then went deep into unconverted territory of Frisia and behaved in a highly provocative manner, destroying temples and images and aggressively declaring the Christian message. Willibald says of him and his companions: 'they had but one heart and one soul, and thus deserved to share in the same crown of martyrdom and the same final and eternal reward'.[52] They deserved their martyrdom for another reason: they had provoked the Frisians beyond endurance.

The conversion of the Saxons

After Boniface, missionaries such as Lull and Sturm consolidated his gains. It is known from a *Vita* written by Eigil, abbot of Fulda, that Sturm continued to work among the Saxons and also made missionary overtures to some of the Slavic tribes. He was given charge of Saxony after Charlemagne's armies had invaded and conquered the region. Eigil says of this:

> he [Charlemagne] gathered together a mighty army, placed it under the patronage of Christ, and, accompanied by bishops, abbots and priests and all true believers, set out for Saxony. His purpose was to bring this people, which had been fettered from the beginning with the devil's bonds, to accept the faith and to submit to the mild and sweet yoke of Christ. When the king reached Saxony he converted the majority of the people partly by conquest, partly by persuasion, partly even by bribes, and not long afterwards he divided the whole of the province into episcopal sees and handed it over to the servants of God to evangelise and baptise. The greater part of that territory with its people was entrusted to Sturm.[53]

Eigil is more interested in Sturm than in the conquest of the Saxons. This was a very violent and bloody affair, in which territorial imperatives were joined to Christian conversion. When Charlemagne came to the throne there were only two missionary centres in his territory, in Frisia and Bavaria. He began to campaign against the Saxons in 772 and from thereon brought about the 'conversion of the Saxons, the Frisians, and a large number of Slavs and Avars in the area of Pannonia and Carinthia'.[54]

Charlemagne was willing to use savage measures to effect the transition to Christianity, as Einhard's description of the conversion of the Saxons demonstrated:

> This war could have been brought to a more rapid conclusion, had it not been for the faithlessness of the Saxons. It is hard to say just how many times they were beaten and surrendered as suppliants to Charlemagne, promising to do all that was exacted from them, giving the hostages who were demanded, and this without delay, and receiving the ambassadors who were sent to them. Sometimes they were so cowed and reduced that they even promised to abandon their devil worship and submit willingly to the Christian faith; but, however ready they might seem from time to time to do all this, they were always prepared to break the promises they had made. . . . At long last this war, which had dragged on for so many years, came to an end on conditions imposed by the King and accepted by the Saxons. These last were to give up their devil worship and the malpractices inherited from their forefathers; and then, once they had adopted the sacraments of the Christian faith and religion, they were to be united with the Franks and become one people with them.[55]

This conquest spelled the end of Saxon resistance. The Saxon chieftain Widukind was baptized in 785, but the Saxons revolted again in 793. It may be that these revolts were occasioned by Charlemagne's *Capitulatio de Partibus Saxoniae*, promulgated between 755 and 790.[56] The substance of these legal documents was that the Franks were willing and able to enforce the conversion, and would actively prevent either civil rebellion or religious backsliding. The result of such draconian measures was that as late as 841 a rebellion arose in Saxony which 'the Franks claimed had religious motives'.[57] A document which deals directly with Saxon beliefs and practices, the *Indiculus Superstitionum et Paganiarum*, is brief and incomplete, but speaks of the sacrifice of animals to the old gods, tree worship, divination, funeral practices, and 'diabolical songs, dances and games'.[58] The reference to tree worship recalls Charlemagne's destruction of the Irminsul, a tree sacred to the Saxon god Irmin, a deity related to Woden, near Paderborn, as well as Boniface and the oak of Geisonar. The provisions of the Saxon capitularies were harsh. 'Henceforth, any unbaptised Saxon who conceals himself among his people and refuses to seek baptism but rather chooses to remain a pagan shall die.'[59] Other provisions made the payment of tithes to the Church and the baptism of children legal obligations, and the burial of people in the traditional fashion an offence. Wallace-Hadrill views Charlemagne's treatment of the Saxon conversion as purely politically motivated, but acknowledges that Charlemagne's contemporaries did not.

Charlemagne had become sole ruler of the Frankish Empire in 771 and spent his next three decades in warfare, expanding his territory and consolidating his power. He was crowned Holy Roman Emperor by Leo III on 25 December 800, and exercised great power over both Church and state. He saw Christianity as a means of overriding 'natural, linguistic and tribal differences',[60] and of creating one people. This was the eventual result of the dream of an ideal Christian society cherished by Caesarius of Arles and Gregory the Great centuries before.

The indigenization of Christianity

D. H. Green's *The Carolingian Lord* is a fascinating exploration of the 'view of God or Christ as Lord in Carolingian literature'.[61] The words *Balder, Fro, Truhtin,* and *Herro*, which were used to refer to the Christian God, all had pre-Christian connotations; Green traces their etymologies and shows how the terminology of the *comitatus* and of pre-Christian Germanic religion was adapted for the new deity. Poems like the *Heliand* portrayed God as a 'Germanic warrior-leader',[62] and the *comitatus* relationship, with elements of both reciprocity and hierarchy, expressed the relationship of the believer to God very well.[63] The vocabulary of the *comitatus* became the ethical language of the new faith, although the terms did not remain static. The institution of kingship showed the same type of continuation and expansion during the transition to Christianity. The Germanic king 'derives his authority from those who elected him and retains it for only as long as he is considered by them to be an effective channel for the transmission of divine *heil* to the tribe at large'.[64]

In the Christian world-view the king becomes elevated above the people, who are entrusted to his patriarchal care by God, and his dependence on his retainers is therefore reduced. Green argued that this change in attitude to the ruler occurred in the first half of the ninth century, which was when the gains of Charlemagne were being consolidated.

The *Heliand*, known as the 'Saxon Gospel', is a remarkable work which demonstrates more forcefully than any of the Anglo-Saxon literature discussed in Chapter 4 how the Germanic peoples indigenized Christianity. It is a re-telling of the Gospel story in the cultural mode of the Germanic peoples. Therefore, when Jesus leaves the wedding at Cana, it states that: 'Christ, most powerful of Kings, decided to go to Capharnaum, the great hill-fort, with his followers. His forces of good men, His happy warrior company assembled in front of him'.[65] Christ is a warrior, all the towns of the Gospels are hill-forts, the three wise men are warriors and thanes, John the Baptist is called a soothsayer, and the Lord's Prayer contains 'secret runes'.[66] Murphy argues that the author of the *Heliand* is theologically orthodox,[67] but the general effect is startling nonetheless. The Saxon author has completely indigenized the Gospels, in the manner proposed by James C. Russell (who, surprisingly, mentions the poem only in passing twice, and does not attempt a close analysis of its remarkable cultural qualities).

Ruth Karras proposed a different reading of the *Heliand* from that of Murphy. She noted that apostolic poverty was absent (Christ and his followers are always richly arrayed); that the injunction to 'turn the other cheek' is omitted; and the poem is explicitly about the nobility. Christ is a *sigidrohtin* (victory lord); Herod is a 'ring giver'; the disciples are the nobles of Judea; and Christ's teachings are 'spells' (Odin, god of kings and warriors, is also a powerful sorcerer).[68] It seems that the *Heliand* contains a good deal that is entirely Germanic, and represents an indigenization such as has already been discussed in the case of Gothic Arianism or Frankish Catholicism. The continuation of pre-Christian practices among the continental Germans is well attested in many of the sources for the period. In the case of the Saxons, conversion by force, rather than by a process of negotiation involving indigenous leaders, often produced no more than a shallow Christian overlay. The author of the *Heliand* was redressing this situation when he presented the Christ that the Saxons would have welcomed, in a cultural context that they could identify with.

Notes

1. Bede, *The Ecclesiastical History of the English People*, ed. and trans. Bertram Colgrave and R. A. B. Mynors, Oxford, 1969, p. 481. The Latin text is on p. 480.
2. Henry Mayr-Harting, 'St. Wilfrid in Sussex', in M. J. Kitch (ed.), *Studies in Sussex Church History*, 1981, pp. 8–9.
3. D. H. Farmer (ed.), *The Age of Bede*, Harmondsworth, 1983, p. 24.
4. Mayr-Harting, *op. cit.*, p. 3.
5. Farmer, *op. cit.*, p. 22.
6. Eleanor Shipley Duckett, *The Wandering Saints*, London, 1960, p. 177.
7. Daibhi Ó Croinin, 'Rath Melsigi, Willibrord, and the Earliest Echternach Manuscripts', *Peritia*, 3, 1984, p. 21.
8. Eddi, *Life of Wilfrid*, trans. J. F. Webb, in Farmer, *op. cit.*, ch. 26, p. 132. The Latin text is in Eddius Stephanus, *Vita Wilfridi*, in *MGH:SRM*, ed. B. Krusch and W. Levison, tom. VI, Hannover, 1913, p. 220.
9. Frank Merry Stenton, *Anglo-Saxon England*, Oxford, 1971, p. 136.

10. Mayr-Harting, *op. cit.*, pp. 8–9.

11. Alcuin, *Life of Saint Willibrord*, in C. H. Talbot (ed. and trans.), *The Anglo-Saxon Missionaries in Germany*, New York, 1954, p. 8.

12. Wilhelm Levison, *England and the Continent in the Eighth Century*, Oxford, 1946, p. 63.

13. Alcuin, Talbot, *op. cit.*, p. 11. The Latin text is in Alcuin, *Vita Willibrordi, in MGH:SRM*, ed. Bruno Krusch and Wilhelm Levison, tom. VII, par. I, Hannover, 1919, p. 126.

14. Bede, Colgrave and Mynors, *op. cit.*, p. 485.

15. Peter R. L. Brown, *Relics and Social Status in the Age of Gregory of Tours*, Reading, 1977, *passim*; also Carole Straw, *Gregory the Great*, Berkeley, CA, 1988, p. 57: 'In most instances, however, the faith of the petitioner and proximity to the body directly determine the power of the relic. The body of the saint is so potent that Romans do not dare to touch it. ... Relics worn as personal talismans put one into direct contact with the saint, and from these one gains a multitude of blessings: the saint's intercession, release from sin, cure of sickness, and protection from evil.'

16. Christopher Dawson, *Religion and the Rise of Western Culture*, London, 1950, p. 32.

17. Alcuin, Talbot, *op. cit.*, p. 10. The Latin is in Alcuin, *MGH:SRM, op. cit.*, p. 125.

18. Duckett, 1960, *op. cit.*, pp. 187–8.

19. J. A. Huisman, 'Christianity and Germanic Religion', in P. H. Vrijhof and J. Waardenburg (eds), *Official and Popular Religion*, Religion and Society 19, Mouten Publishers, 1979, p. 65.

20. *Life of St. Wulframn*, translated for this book by Andrew Gollan. The Latin text is in the *Vita Vulframni, in MGH:SRM*, ed. Bruno Krusch and Wilhelm Levison, tom. V, Hannover, 1910, p. 668.

21. It is possible that this is more an example of a culturally insensitive missionary. Compare Bishop Poppo's behaviour toward Harald Bluetooth in Chapter 6, section 'Missionary Activity in the Tenth Century'.

22. J. M. Wallace-Hadrill, *The Frankish Church*, Oxford, 1983, p. 143.

23. Alcuin, Talbot, *op. cit.*, p. 9. The Latin text is in Alcuin, *MGH:SRM, op. cit.*, p. 123.

24. Klaus Randsborg, 'Barbarians, Antiquity and Western Europe', *P&P*, 137, 1992, p. 23. Also Richard Hodges, *Dark Age Economics: The Origins of Towns and Trade, A.D. 600–1000*, London, 1982, *passim*.

25. Bede, Colgrave and Mynors, *op. cit.*, says 'they slew White Hewald quickly with a sword, but Black Hewald was put to lingering torture and was torn limb from limb in a horrible fashion', p. 483. The Latin text is on p. 482.

26. Eleanor Shipley Duckett, *Anglo-Saxon Saints and Scholars*, Hamden, 1967, pp. 369–70.

27. John Cyril Sladden, *Boniface of Devon*, Exeter, 1980, p. 19.

28. *Ibid.*, p. 35. Boniface is referred to in Adam of Bremen, *History of The Archbishops of Hamburg-Bremen*, ed. and trans. Francis J. Tschan, Bk One, section X (11), New York, 1959, p. 12.

29. Richard E. Sullivan, 'The Carolingian Missionary and the Pagan', *Speculum*, 28, 1953, pp. 705–40 *passim*, gives a good coverage of the various politicized missionary techniques which were employed, but his work is marred by aggressive and hostile terminology, and by uncritical Christian bias. For example, in speaking of Boniface, Sullivan says: 'he proceeded to free many pagans from the captivity of the devil by preaching', p. 707.

30. Wallace-Hadrill, 1983, *op. cit.*, p. 143. Sullivan, *op. cit.*, has as his opening line: 'A single ideal gave shape and meaning to much of Carolingian history. Men of that era were convinced that the City of God on earth was necessary, desirable, and attainable', p. 705.

31. Stephen Neill, *A History of Christian Missions*, Harmondsworth, 1964, p. 79, observed that 'once a German tribe had been conquered, its conversion was included in the terms of peace, as the price to be paid for enjoying the protection of the emperor and the good of the government that his arms ensured. But this meant the association of the new religion with the conquering power that could only be dangerous. Any spark of patriotism, any movement of resistance to the dominant race, could only take the form of equally violent opposition to the Christian faith'.

32. C. H. Talbot, 'St Boniface and the German Mission', in C. J. Cuming (ed.), *The Mission of the Church and the Propagation of the Faith*, Cambridge, 1970, p. 47.

33. Timothy Reuter, 'Saint Boniface the Monk', in T. Reuter (ed.), *The Greatest Englishman: Essays on St. Boniface and the Church at Crediton*, Exeter, 1980, pp. 75–6.

34. Willibald, *Life of Saint Boniface*, in Talbot, *op. cit.*, pp. 35–6. The Latin text is in Willibald, *Vita S. Bonifatii*, ch. 4, in *MGH:S*, ed. G.H. Pertz, tom. II, Hannover, 1829, p. 339.

35. Duckett, 1967, *op. cit.*, p. 368.

36. D. J. V. Fisher, *The Anglo-Saxon Age*, London, 1973, p. 187. Wallace-Hadrill in *Early Medieval History*, Oxford, 1975, suggests that Boniface was ambivalent about the situation his relations with the Carolingians placed him in: 'Research since the days of Levison has done nothing to dim the splendour of Boniface's achievement; it was greater than that of any other missionary of his time. What research has done is to reveal the complexity of the situation he faced, the varieties of Christian experience already available in the lands of his mission, and the difficulties of the men who supported him. These, and not hostility, were the forces to which he was a martyr', p. 150.

37. Talbot, 1970, *op. cit.*, pp. 50–1.

38. Ephraim Emerton (ed. and trans.), *The Letters of Saint Boniface*, New York, 1940, pp. 15–16.

39. See Chapter 3, section 'The Indigenization of Catholicism'.

40. Willibald, Talbot, *op. cit.*, pp. 45–6. The Latin text is in Willibald, *MGH:S*, *op. cit.*, ch. 8, pp. 343–4.

41. Wallace-Hadrill, 1975, *op. cit.*, p. 82.

42. Willibald, Talbot, *op. cit.*, ch. 7, p. 342.

43. J. N. Hillgarth (ed.), *The Conversion of Western Europe 350–750*, Englewood Cliffs, NJ, 1968, p. 169.
44. S. J. Crawford, *Anglo-Saxon Influence on Western Christendom 600–800*, Cambridge, 1933, p. 69.
45. Neill, *op. cit.*, pp. 73–4; Sullivan, *op. cit.*, pp. 708–9.
46. Talbot, 1970, *op. cit.*, pp. 53–4.
47. Emerton, *op. cit.*, letter LXXI (87), Pope Zacharias to Boniface, 4 November 751: 'You beg for advice as to whether it is permitted to flee from the persecution of the heathen or not. We give you this wholesome counsel: so long as it can be done, and you can find a suitable place, carry on your preaching; but if you cannot endure their assaults you have the Lord's authority to go into another city', p. 163. The Latin text is in Boniface, *Epistolae*, in *MGH:E*, ed. E. Dummler, tom. I, Berlin, 1957, p. 372.
48. Boniface, Emerton, *op. cit.*, letter LVII (73), Boniface to King Ethelbald of Mercia, 746–7: 'The Wends, who are the vilest and lowest race of men, have such high regard for the mutual bond of marriage that the wife refuses to survive her husband. Among them a woman is praised who dies by her own hand and is burned on the same pyre with her husband', p. 128. The Latin text is in Boniface, *Epistolae*, in *MGH:E*, *op. cit.*, p. 342.
49. Boniface, Emerton, *op. cit.*, p. 48. The Latin text is in Boniface, *MGH:E*, *op. cit.*, pp. 271–2.
50. Talbot, 1970, *op. cit.*, p. 55.
51. Willibald, Talbot, *op. cit.*, p. 54. The Latin text is in Willibald, *MGH:S*, *op. cit.*, p. 349.
52. *Ibid.*, p. 55. The Latin text is in Willibald, *MGH:S*, p. 350.
53. Eigil, *Life of Saint Sturm*, in Talbot, *op. cit.*, p. 200. The Latin text is in Eigil, *Vita S. Sturmii*, in J.-P. Migne (ed.), *PL*, tom. 105, Turnholt, n.d., pp. 441–2.
54. Richard E. Sullivan, 'The Papacy and Missionary Activity in the Early Middle Ages', in R. E. Sullivan, *Christian Missionary Activity in the Early Middle Ages*, III, Variorum, 1994, p. 80.
55. Einhard the Frank, *The Life of Charlemagne*, ed. and trans. Lewis Thorpe, London, 1970, pp. 36–9. The Latin text is in Einhard, *Vita Karoli Magni*, *MGH:SRG*, ed. G. H. Pertz and G. Waitz, Hannover, 1911, pp. 9–10.
56. Adam of Bremen, Tschan, *op. cit.*, pp. 14–15, says: 'Now, at the end of two years, that is in the eighteenth year of Charles, Widukind, the instigator of the rebellion, came into Charles' obedience and was baptized, he and other magnates of the Saxons', Bk One, section xi (12). The Latin text is in Adam of Bremen, *Gesta Hammaburgensis*, in *MGH:SRG*, ed. Bernhard Schmeidler, Hannover, 1917, p. 13.
57. Ruth Mazo Karras, 'Pagan Survivals and Syncretism in the Conversion of Saxony', *Catholic Historical Review*, LXXII, 4, October 1986, p. 558.
58. *Ibid.*, p. 564.
59. Wallace-Hadrill, 1983, *op. cit.*, p. 413.
60. Walter Ullmann, *The Carolingian Renaissance*, London, 1969, p. 8.
61. D. H. Green, *The Carolingian Lord*, Cambridge, 1965, p. x.
62. *Ibid.*, p. 60.

63.   *Ibid.*, p. 193.
64.   *Ibid.*, p. 223.
65.   *The Heliand*, ed. and trans. G. Ronald Murphy, London, 1992, p. 70.
66.   *Ibid.*, *passim*.
67.   Anton Wessels, *Europe: Was it ever Really Christian?*, trans. John Bowden, SCM Press, 1994, agrees that the poem is theologically orthodox and represents an incomplete indigenization, p. 141.
68.   Karras, *op. cit.*, pp. 568–9.

6 Christianity in the North

'The first time I set eyes on the king, I was so impressed by him that I realised at once that he was a man of outstanding qualities, and this has been confirmed on every occasion I have seen him since in public. But never have I been so impressed by him as I was today, and now I am sure that all our welfare depends on our believing that he whom the king proclaims is the true God. The king cannot be any the more eager for me to accept this faith than I am now to be baptised.'

Laxdaela Saga (trans. Magnusson and Pálsson)[1]

The Mission of Anskar

The missionary complex at Hamburg-Bremen, which developed as a result of the expansionist policies of Charlemagne, was essentially on the frontier with Denmark. Charlemagne received several requests for alliances from the Danish kings, but he would not agree: 'except in return for permission to pursue missionary work in Denmark; but what one Danish faction could allow might be nullified by the other'.[2] In 822 three bishops, Ebbo of Rheims, Halitgar of Cambrai and Willeric of Bremen penetrated Denmark with the support of the papal and Frankish courts, but the result was little more than the baptism of a few Danes.[3] One of the kings, Harald Klak, decided to seek baptism, possibly to ensure greater favour, as godson of Louis the Pious, than his rival king Godric. Adam of Bremen records that:

At that very time the king of the Danes, Harold, despoiled of his kingdom by the sons of Gotafrid, came to Louis a suppliant. And on being instructed thereupon in the Christian faith, he was baptised at Mainz with his wife and brother and a great multitude of Danes.[4]

This event is described by Ermoldus Nigellus, with more enthusiasm but less certainty about the multitude.[5] That Harald left a hostage with Louis when he went home indicates the true state of affairs. A missionary, Anskar of Corbie, accompanied Harald Klak on his return journey in 826.

Anskar (801–865) and his activities are described by both Adam of Bremen and Rimbert, his successor as bishop of Hamburg-Bremen, who wrote an account around 880. Both Rimbert and Adam of Bremen were concerned primarily with the diocese of Hamburg-Bremen, and this colours their material and occasionally results in manipulation of the evidence.[6] Rimbert's other focus is the monastery of Corbie, and he is concerned to establish that Anskar maintained monastic discipline and ascetic habits while evangelizing. Anskar had been placed in the monastery of Corbie at the age of five and become determined to spread the Gospel among the pagans. Rimbert's biography clearly presents the dangers which missionaries to Scandinavia faced, entering hostile territory on short missionary journeys, making a few converts and occasionally ransoming captives. Adam of Bremen states that Anskar was willing 'to go not only among the barbarians but also "both into prison and to death' for Christ'.[7] The support of the Carolingian emperors meant little when the missionaries were so far from their power bases, with the Scandinavian social and political climate so disturbed.[8] This willingness to face danger was not mere bravado.

When Anskar went with Harald Klak into Denmark, he and his companion Autbert set up a school in Harald's household and attempted to educate the new Danish converts in the faith. Rimbert states that:

> Harald, to whom they had been committed, was as yet ignorant and untaught in the faith, and was unaware of how God's servants ought to behave. Moreover, his companions who had been but recently converted and had been trained in a very different faith, paid them little attention.[9]

The argument of this book suggests that the baptism of the king and his retainers should have provided a strong basis for the establishment of the new religion. It seems, however, that Harald was more interested in appropriating the power of Louis the Pious and in securing protection for his family against his opponents than in being a Christian. Once he had returned to Scandinavia, outside the closed Christian society of central Europe, it is likely that his advisers persuaded him to return to the worship of the traditional gods.

This first venture not being particularly successful, in 829 Anskar was back at the court of Emperor Louis. That year Swedish ambassadors arrived to seek an audience with Louis and, allegedly, requested that missionaries be sent to Sweden, since there were 'many belonging to their nation who desired to embrace the Christian religion, and that their king so far favoured this suggestion that he would permit God's priests to reside there'.[10] Many scholars have questioned the likelihood of such a request,[11] and the reception of Anskar and his new companion Witmar, who were sent to Sweden, was not welcoming. The journey by sea had been perilous, with a viking attack resulting in the loss of their holy books, and they arrived at Birka on Lake Mälar on foot. The king, Björn, seems to have been unaware that he had 'asked' for missionaries, since Rimbert described his meeting with Anskar thus:

> they were kindly received by the king, who was called Biorn, whose messengers had informed him of the reason for which they came. When he understood the object of their mission, and had discussed the matter with his friends, with the approval and consent of all he granted them permission to remain there and to preach the gospel of Christ, and offered liberty to any who desired it to accept their teaching. Accordingly, the servants of God, when they saw that matters had turned out propitiously as they had desired, began eagerly to preach the word of salvation to the people of that place. There were many who were well-disposed towards their mission and who willingly listened to the teaching of the Lord. There were also many Christians who were held captive amongst them, and who rejoiced that now at last they were able to participate in the divine mysteries.[12]

Rimbert's language here is somewhat unclear. Although he speaks of many who listened to Anskar and Witmar, he does not mention any converts. It appears that Anskar made only one notable convert during this visit to Birka, Herigar (Hergeir), who was a prefect of the town. Most of Anskar's pastoral duties involved succouring Christian captives.

Björn's response to the mission is important because the Scandinavians held their kings in the same regard as the Anglo-Saxons and the continental Germans. Saxo Grammaticus, in the *Gesta Danorum*, links kingship to descent from the gods in his discussion of the origins of the Danes. Because of the late date of composition of this work (1185–1223), Saxo is inclined to downplay the power and status of the heathen gods. He describes Odin as consulting 'seers, soothsayers and others whom he had discovered strong in the finest arts of prediction. ... Divinity is not always so perfect that it can dispense with human aid.'[13]

Other evidence for the relationship between kings and gods in Scandinavia can be found in Snorri Sturluson's *Heimskringla*, composed in the thirteenth century.[14] This is a history of the kings of Norway which traces their ancestry to the god Frey, in the guise of Ing or Yngvi, their eponymous ancestor. Snorri was a medieval Christian and the heir of several hundred years resistance to monarchy, yet his work reflected traditional Germanic views of sacral kingship.[15] Ström has analysed the role of the Scandinavian king in ritual, and particularly sacrificial, life. He concludes that the king was the legitimate sacrificer, ensuring the stability of society, and was himself the sacrificed when the gods demanded.[16] Specifically the king is connected with Odin, whom the *Hávamál* depicts as sacrificed to himself, by himself (so he is the victim, the sacrificer, and the deity sacrificed to) in order to gain the power of the runes:

Odin said:
I know that I hung   on a high windy tree
for nine long nights;
pierced by a spear   – Odin's pledge –
given myself to myself.
No one can tell   about that tree,
from what deep root it rises.

They brought me no bread,   no horn to drink from,
I gazed toward the ground.
Crying aloud,   I caught up runes;
finally I fell.[17]

The *Eddas* date from the thirteenth century, and it has been argued that the Rune Poem and other sections of the *Poetic Edda* are influenced by Christian theology. There are similar difficulties involved in using genealogical material as evidence for divine kingship, and it has been noted that, in the case of *Heimskringla*, which contains pre-Christian material but which was composed when Iceland had been Christian for more than two centuries, these problems multiply. For example:

if genealogies were taken back to the gods in heathen times, they were presumably closely associated with the kind of legend that survives in the Eddic poems ... and may have implied that those who could claim such descent were different from ordinary mortals. But if the gods were only introduced into genealogies after the coming of Christianity, then the euhemeristic interpretation of the gods must have preceded the construction of the genealogies.[18]

Sometimes pre-Christian genealogies are interspersed with Christian ones; with lines of descent traced back to Adam (as in the Anglo-Saxon poem *Widsith*). Saxo, Snorri, and, earlier, Jordanes all have their kings achieve deification in their lifetime, not after death. Snorri, showing an awareness of Western intellectual history, traces the origins of the Scandinavian deities back to the Trojan War, thus linking barbarian and classical learning.

For a Germanic king descent from the gods was one of the prerequisites for rule.[19] Another was the support of a *comitatus* of retainers who had pledged their loyalty to him. The king depended on these men for his continued reign. Björn's consultations with his 'friends' suggest consultations with his retainers to see if they would support him in the decision to allow Anskar and Witmar to preach (a decision which Jones argues was made in order to retain the favour of Emperor Louis the Pious). In cases where the king converted (for example, Augustine's mission to Kent), his retainers and their retainers accepted baptism too. Björn's tolerance of the missionaries extended only to allowing them to preach, not to active support, and this explains the lack of converts to Christianity. Anskar continued his small scale missionary activities: 'he began also to buy Danish and Slav boys and to redeem some from captivity so that he might train them for God's service'.[20]

In 831 Anskar was consecrated archbishop of Hamburg, a new archdiocese. Pope Gregory IV also appointed him joint Papal Legate (with Ebbo of Rheims) to all the Scandinavian peoples. At Birka, however, there were problems. Bishop Gauzbert and his companion Nithard were persecuted and eventually Nithard was killed and the bishop expelled from Sweden. Herigar remained faithful to the new faith in the absence of any missionary presence. Adam of Bremen wrote: 'Anund at that time carried on a persecution of the Christians. Alone Hergeier, the prefect of Bjorko [Birka], upheld there the Christian religion.'[21] Other clerics, such as Bishop Willeric of Bremen, were also attempting to extend Christianity's sway in the North, but with a similar lack of success.

Wood noted that Rimbert says virtually nothing of Carolingian or Scandinavian politics in his analysis of Anskar's mission. In the 830s Louis the Pious and his son Lothar were locked in a struggle, with Louis allied to the Danish king Horic and Lothar to his rival Harald Klak.[22] These alliances may explain why Christianity fared poorly in Denmark under Harald Klak; the Emperor's power had been transferred from him to a rival. Under Horic, Christianity was tolerated and missionaries were active with his permission. The first half of the ninth century was a time of violent activity for the vikings, and the *Vita Anskarii* commented on their sacking of bishoprics such as Hamburg. Wood indicated that alliances with the Frankish rulers dictated policy for Horic: he probably organized the raid on Hamburg and sent a fleet against Louis the German in 845; yet he assured Louis the Pious that he disapproved of viking raids and had even executed a number of the raiders. It may be that Rimbert, knowing of Horic's friendship with Anskar, kept deliberately silent about his involvement in these anti-Christian activities.[23] The position of the Scandinavian missions was further undermined with the death of Louis in 840. His three sons, Lothar, Charles the Bald, and Louis the German, fought among themselves over their inheritance.

The Danes immediately intensified their attacks southward, sacking Hamburg in 845. Anskar escaped but the church, school and library were all destroyed.[24] In 847 Anskar was made archbishop of Bremen and the see of Bremen was merged with the sacked see of Hamburg, all according to Rimbert's chronology. This was brought about by the efforts of Archbishop Gunther of Cologne, Pope Nicholas, and Louis the German. Anskar's next significant missionary attempt was a meeting with Horic of Denmark in 849. Rimbert spoke of Horic's regard for Anskar:

his fidelity and goodness having been thus recognised, King Horic began to regard him with great affection and to make use of his advice and to treat him in every respect as a friend; so that he was allowed to share his secrets when with his fellow counsellors he was dealing with matters relating to the kingdom ... when Anskar had thus gained his friendship he began to urge him to become a Christian. The king listened ... and declared that it was both good and helpful ... and that he desired to earn the favour of Christ ... our good father suggested to him that he grant to the Lord Christ that which would be most pleasing to him, namely, permission to build a church in his kingdom.[25]

Rimbert's wording is interesting: it is not acceptance of Christianity by the Danish king which would be 'most pleasing' to Christ. The church was built at Hedeby in 850.

After this small success, Anskar became interested in Sweden again and sent a hermit, Ardgar, to Birka to see Herigar. Shortly after this, Herigar died and Ardgar returned to Anskar. Herigar had proved faithful to Christianity, which is significant because he was prefect of the town and thus a prominent citizen. St Saba had been killed by fellow villagers when he refused to worship with them,[26] but Herigar was merely harassed for his lack of social solidarity.[27] He coped with the isolation the new faith required of him, and continued to live in Birka. He may have been assisted in this by the fact that, whereas Saba lived in a village, a traditional conservative community, Birka was a thriving market town, a gateway community which saw many strangers and tolerated a variety of viewpoints. Anskar himself then travelled to Birka and encountered yet another Scandinavian king, Olaf. He proved friendly and eventually:

the king accordingly, with the goodwill and approval of all, determined that churches might be built among the people, and that priests might come to them and that whoever so desired might become a Christian ... to him the king granted permission to build a hall to serve as a place of prayer ... the king displayed further his affectionate regard for the lord bishop and promised that in every district he would show the utmost kindness to his companions who were concerned with the observance of the Christian religion.[28]

The later history of Adam of Bremen asserts that Olaf was baptized by Anskar, but it seems likely that Rimbert would have mentioned this if it were true. Rimbert's silence also argues against the baptisms of kings Björn, Horic I and Horic the Younger.

Horic I died in 854 and Denmark apostasized under the rule of his son Horic the Younger. It is doubtful whether Denmark had been substantially Christian at all, but the elder Horic had at least tolerated the new religion, which his son was not prepared to do. Rimbert records that Anskar was distressed by his loss of human aid, but had faith in divine assistance.[29] He lived to see the re-opening of the church at Hedeby (which had been closed in 853 by Horic the Younger) and the building of a second church at Ribe. But a bleak time resulted for Anskar when Bishop Gauzbert and his nephew, the priest Erimbert, died. In 865 he fell seriously ill with dysentery and died. His purpose, the conversion of the northern countries, was not achieved; indeed, it was as if his forty years' mission had never happened, so slight had been the influence of Christianity on Scandinavia.[30]

Pre-Christian religion and society

The institution of sacral kingship has been discussed previously. Among other factors in pre-Christian Scandinavian society which formed the intellectual background to the conversion (to use Horton's term), religious beliefs and social structure were primary. The Scandinavians had the same basic social organization as the other Germanic peoples; law-codes surviving from the viking period demonstrate that loyalty and obligation to the family were still regarded as central.[31] It has often been argued that the Viking Age was a period where individualism was dominant. While there were great individualists among the vikings, they tended to be opposed to the conventions of religion and society, and were often outlaws who had abandoned their families and lost faith in the gods and believed in their own 'might and main'.[32] For the overwhelming majority, the structure of society, with the three orders – the nobility, the peasants and the unfree – was divinely ordained.[33] The *Rigsthula* describes the fathering of the eponymous ancestors of the three classes by the god Heimdall, disguised as Rig.[34] Only in the case of Jarl and his family, the aristocrats, does the god show an interest in the education of his offspring. Jarl's son Konungr (the young king) is educated by Rig and given supernatural knowledge of the runes.[35] This accords well with records of Scandinavian religion and society; the warrior and priestly classes were not distinct as they were in many other Indo-European societies.

The message of Christianity may have appeared more positive than the pre-Christian beliefs of the Scandinavians, which were dominated by a conception of fate as over-arching, determining existence for gods as well as mortals. It is difficult to make generalizations about fate. Ringgren has commented:

> the belief in a personal determiner of destiny produces religious behaviour, while the belief in an impersonal Fate does not. But the problem is complicated by the fact that both of these attitudes seem to occur together in one and the same religion, even in one and the same person.[36]

Ström, in the same collection of essays, asserts that the Scandinavians never distinguished between individual destiny and impersonal Fate.[37] That even the gods were at the mercy of fate is clear from the *Poetic Edda*, where Odin, in the related poems *Völuspá* (The Sibyl's Prophecy) and *Baldrs Draumar* (Balder's Dream), seeks the advice of the *volva* (sibyl) in order to learn the fate of the world. Her vision culminates with *Ragnarok*, the doom of the gods, in which the world is dissolved in a final great conflagration.[38] Yet it was generally agreed that it was better not to know one's fate, and Bauschatz comments that the Fates (Norns) of Scandinavian mythology 'speak of what has been, of what is already known. Explicit mention of predestination or foreknowledge is absent'.[39]

Worship of the gods in pre-Christian Scandinavia was both public and private. Public worship included the nine-yearly sacrifices at the great temple of Uppsala, where images of Odin, Thor and Frey were displayed. Adam of Bremen provided an account biased by his Christianity, but quite probably accurate in its details. He wrote:

> the sacrifice is of this nature: of every living thing that is male, they offer nine heads, with the blood of which it is customary to placate the gods of this sort. The bodies they hang in the sacred grove that adjoins the temple. Now this grove is so sacred in the eyes of the heathen that each and every tree in it is believed divine because of the death or putrefaction of the victims. Even dogs and horses hang there with men.[40]

Smaller sacrifices were performed in buildings called 'hofs' and '*blót* houses' by the priests (godar) and by private individuals.

Fertility, both agricultural and sexual, was the preserve of the gods Frey and Thor and the goddess Freya, sister of Frey. The goddesses in general had fertility attributes. Some of the myths concerning these deities are humorous, and might suggest a lack of reverence for, or faith in, these deities. It has been argued that the Scandinavians accepted Christianity because their society was fragmenting and people no longer believed in the gods. Gurevich argued against this:

> but even if the Christian God is the absolute incarnation of goodness, grace, justice, and purity, we are not obliged to think that the beliefs of pagan religion were formed on the same model. ... The description of faults typical of the gods *in itself* does not permit us the inference that people lost faith in them, or in their power and role in the structure of the universe.[41]

Another factor which must have made the Scandinavians receptive to Christianity was the prior existence of concepts of salvation. Sharpe has suggested that there was 'an element of salvation in Germanic religion in the sense of a belief in the protection afforded by a god or gods from other destructive powers'.[42] Scandinavian courtly religion had its own profile, centred on strength and manhood and the family bond. Some of the skalds (court poets) were converted, and it is possible by studying their writings to get some picture of the function of religion, and of the image of Christianity in their society. It can be argued from skaldic writings that Christianity was not primarily understood as a soteriology which released the individual from sin, but as an ideology of *Christus victor* – an element which some have claimed to be primary in Christian theology, but which does not really correspond to the theology of the Church in the tenth and eleventh centuries.[43] Sharpe claimed that there:

> is a great deal of evidence to show that amid these experiences of conversion, some traumatic, some less so, one image in particular retained all its old power: the image of salvation as resulting from a cosmic conflict between the forces of good (law) and evil (chaos). Previously Thor had been the victor; now he in his turn had been overthrown by the White Christ, and all Christ's symbols became symbols of victory.[44]

These contests of power were also apparent in public demonstrations of the power of the new god by the priests and missionaries, such as the incidents when pagan sacrifices were interrupted by Christians. The *Vita Anskarii* contains such an account, as does the section of the *Heimskringla* which recounts the life of St Olaf. These contests are highly stylized pieces of literature where the 'Christian and heathen gods are matched against each other, the Christian god triumphs (by a real or mock miracle), and the leader of the Christian party draws the obvious conclusion for the benefit of the astonished pagans'.[45]

Missionary activity in the tenth century

An English bishop, Sigfrid, came to Norway around 960, at the time King Hákon Haraldsson (the foster-son of Athelstan of Wessex) died. Hákon had adopted Christianity while he was in England, and upon his return to Norway intended to introduce the new religion, but his subjects proved reluctant and he reverted to his old beliefs.[46] It seems that his exile to England had broken the bonds with his retainers and he was unable to persuade the nobility to accept Christianity, so he had to revert to the old religion in order to remain king. The dominance of the anti-Christian Sigurd, Jarl of Hlad, in the Trondelag area supports this hypothesis.[47] Hákon's rejection of Christianity was complete; when he died in battle, the skald Eyvindr composed *Hákonármal*, a heroic elegy which celebrates his reception into Valhalla.[48]

Sigfrid is a shadowy figure, lacking a superb biography such as Rimbert's of Anskar, but Oppermann argues that he did more for the conversion of Sweden than any other individual.[49] This is disputed by Birgit Sawyer, whose sifting of the evidence suggests that the connection between Sigfrid and Olaf Eriksson (called Skötkonung, 'the Lapp king'), whom Sigfrid is supposed to have baptized at Husaby in Västergötland around 1000, is probably unhistorical.[50] Adam of Bremen mentions Sigfrid and says that he came to Scandinavia as one of Olaf Haraldsson's missionary bishops and died during Adam's own lifetime.[51] It has been suggested that the story of Olaf Skötkonung's baptism was vengeful propaganda by Olaf Tryggvason, who had been defeated by the Swedish king: the bishop of Olaf Tryggvason could triumph where the king, by military means, could not.[52] The slow progress made by Christianity in Sweden is also evidence against Olaf Skötkonung's baptism. The great temple of Uppsala continued to be a powerful centre of the old religion.[53]

In Denmark in 935 or 936, Harald Bluetooth (Gormsson) was listening to the preaching of Unni, the first effective missionary to Denmark since Anskar. He did not accept baptism, but permitted preaching of the new faith, unlike his father Gorm, who had violently opposed it.[54] Peter Sawyer advises caution when dealing with Adam's account of the treatment of Unni by Gorm and Harald. Adam has an interest in demonstrating the greatness of the German Henry I and the archbishopric of Hamburg-Bremen.[55] Adam describes Henry I's defeat of Gorm and imposition of the terms of peace, and then says of Unni:

> When our most blessed archbishop Unni saw that the door of the faith had been opened to the gentiles, he gave thanks to God for the salvation of the pagans, and more especially because the mission of the Church of Hamburg, long neglected on account of adverse times, had with the help of God's mercy and through the valor of King Henry been given occasion and opportunity for its work.[56]

That this is propaganda is clear. After visiting Denmark, Unni went to Birka, where he found that Anskar's missionary work had almost been forgotten:

> the Northmen [had] indeed entirely forgotten the Christian religion and could by no means be easily persuaded to believe, because they had lived through the period of barbarian invasion when in a few years many kings had held bloody sway over them.[57]

During his visit to Birka in 936 Unni died and his body was brought home to Bremen. In the same year Otto the Great became emperor of Germany; he was to rule until 973.

Harald Bluetooth was finally baptized around 965 by the priest Poppo. Widukind of Corvei's *Saxon History*, first completed in 968, describes the encounter between the missionary and the king. At a feast in Denmark a quarrel broke out between Poppo and some Danes about the gods, and Harald challenged Poppo to prove that Christ was the only God.[58] Understanding the value of grand gestures, and having a captive audience, Poppo declared that he would answer the challenge:

> the next day the king had a large piece of iron heated and ordered Poppo to carry the glowing iron for the sake of the Catholic Faith. Poppo took the iron and carried it as far as the king determined. He then showed his undamaged hand and demonstrated to all the truth of the Catholic Faith. Consequently the king converted, resolved that Christ alone should be worshipped as God, ordered the people subject to him to reject idols and thereafter gave due honour to priests and God's servants.[59]

Sawyer notes that the Danes accepted that Christ was a god before the king's conversion; they were just not convinced that he was the only God.[60] This supports the view that casual contacts had, by the mid-tenth century, created awareness of Christianity among the Danes. Poppo's ordeal is more problematic: is it to be interpreted literally? It has some of the atmosphere of the destruction of the temple at Yeavering by Coifi or the exploits of Columbanus and Boniface; in each case there was a demonstration of the power of the new God and the audience were convinced. Whatever methods Poppo used to persuade Harald Bluetooth, they were effective.[61]

Harald built a church at the old sacred royal site of Jelling, in between the burial mounds of his parents, whom he disinterred and reburied in the church.[62] Where Radbod refused baptism to be with his ancestors,[63] Harald Bluetooth transferred his dead parents from the old universe to the new. It may be that Poppo foresaw the problem of insisting that Christianity separated the convert from the family. Harald claimed that during his reign he had made the Danes Christians, a claim which is inscribed on the great Jelling rune stone: 'King Harald had this monument made in memory of his father Gorm and his mother Thyri: this was the Harald who won for himself all Denmark and Norway and made the Danes Christians'.[64] Foote and Wilson note that this sort of formula is found elsewhere: as an example, a mid-eleventh century rune stone from Östersundsbro, Frösö, reads 'Ostman, son of Gudfast, had this stone set up and this causeway to be made and he caused Jämtland to become Christian'.[65] The usurpation of the throne in 986 by Harald's son Svein Forkbeard threw the Christians of Denmark into confusion. Svein had won the support of those whom Harald Bluetooth had pressured into Christianity, and 'in that deplorable and worse than civil war the party of Harald was vanquished. Wounded, Harald fled from the conflict, boarded ship, and escaped.'[66] Nonetheless, Christianity had made significant inroads into Denmark, and the return to the old religion was short-lived.

The reign of Olaf Tryggvason

Olaf Tryggvason became king of Norway in 995 and during his reign Christianity became the official religion of that country. Olaf had become acquainted with Christianity while in exile in England. Several accounts of his life exist, and even the most cautious of them, that of Snorri Sturluson in the *Heimskringla*, suggests that his acceptance of the new religion was the result of a decisive encounter with a hermit in the Isles of Scilly.[67] Snorri's account was dependent on that of Oddr Snorrason, but is considerably shorter, since Snorri omitted much material involving magic and miracle stories, topics which were notably distasteful to him. He also omitted information about the spread of Christianity, including:

> accounts of Olaf's *prima signatio* in Greece, his conversion of the Russian king Valdimarr, his participation in Emperor Otto's conversion attempt in Denmark, and a general hymn on Olaf's proselytizing in Norway. The elimination of Olaf's early missionary activity prior to his arrival in Norway stems no doubt from Snorri's reasonable suspicion that [it] was apocryphal. ... Snorri's changes are therefore not dictated by any lukewarm interest in the fortunes of the Church, but ... an adherence to common verisimilitude.[68]

A reliable account of Olaf Tryggvason's baptism is not available. The encounter with the hermit, although picturesque, is probably fictional. Jones has demonstrated that the structure and content of the episode are literary constructs.[69] The only contemporary evidence, the *Anglo-Saxon Chronicle*, records his confirmation in England in 994, with King Æthelred as his sponsor:

> then the king sent Bishop Ælfheah and ealdorman Æthelweard to seek king Anlaf (Olaf), hostages being sent meanwhile to the ships, and king Anlaf was conducted with great ceremony to the king at Andover. The king stood sponsor for him at confirmation, and gave him royal gifts, and Anlaf then promised and also kept his word, that he would never come again to England with warlike intent.[70]

This incident has the ring of truth. Olaf, homeless and in exile, almost certainly fought in the battle of Maldon, after which a treaty was concluded with King Æthelred. One of the conditions of this treaty may have been baptism: certainly Olaf had acquired a debt of loyalty to King Æthelred.[71]

The Scandinavian kings who adopted the new religion were all seeking to unify and consolidate their kingdoms, an aim which had been influential since the reign of Harald Fairhair.[72] Olaf's approach to Christianity was enthusiastic once he had committed himself. He married Christianity to his territorial ambitions. Snorri says that Olaf

> invited every man to accept Christianity; and those who opposed him he punished severely, killing some, mutilating others, and driving others into banishment. At length he brought it so far, that all the kingdom which his father King Trygve had ruled over, and also that of his relation Harald Graenske, accepted of Christianity; and during that summer and the following winter all Viken was made Christian.[73]

It is clear that such force on Olaf Tryggvason's part would have created resentment. However, he was a man of great personal power who was usually able to compel those around him to accept his views. Opposition to Christianity by the powerful jarls of Hlad was probably linked to their desire to resist centralized government under one king.[74]

It is interesting that Adam of Bremen was uncertain as to whether Olaf Tryggvason died a Christian.[75] Adam wrote around 1080 and Snorri in the mid-thirteenth century, so it may be that Adam's view is more accurate. It is more likely, however, that Adam was simply unaware of the English sources for the king's Christianity. It is even possible he suppressed them, because they linked Scandinavian Christianity to the English Church rather than to Hamburg-Bremen. The English missionary influence in the Scandinavian conversion period is very interesting: Oddr Snorrason records that the ecclesiastical complex at Selja, which dates from the reign of Olaf Tryggvason, had a church dedicated to St Alban, although the origins of the Alban cult are shrouded in mystery.[76]

Adam's view of Olaf was consistently negative: he stated that Olaf was much interested in divination and was called *Craccaben* ('crowbone') due to his attention to bird omens, and alleged that he practised magic.[77] Adam even claims that it was Svein, Olaf's successor, who made Norway accept Christianity.[78] This negative view of Olaf is directly contradicted by Norwegian and Icelandic sources, which are careful to state that Christianity came from England,[79] and are likely to be correct. As Jones notes:

> on the most favourable witness [Olaf] appears little touched by ... spiritual values. But ... he was alive to the advantages of being part of the Christian community of Europe; and like other travelled vikings he had observed first hand the dignity, wealth, and ceremonial of the Church in other countries.[80]

In 999/1000 Olaf Tryggvason sent emissaries to the Althing, Iceland's annual assembly and they effected the conversion of all Iceland. Jones is of the opinion that the conversion of Iceland would have happened with or without the intervention of Olaf, because there were casual contacts between Iceland and Christianity due to English and German influences.[81] Olaf died in the battle of Svolder in September 1000[82] – 'he was fighting then against Svein Haraldsson, king of the Danes, and Olaf the Swede, son of Eirik king of the Swedes at Uppsala, and Eirik Hákonarmál who was later earl of Norway'.[83]

Adam reports his death as suicide: Olaf leapt from his ship, the 'Long Serpent', into the sea when his enemies were upon him. Snorri captures the disbelief that people felt when they heard that Olaf was dead, quoting Hallfredr's poem which expressed people's hopes that the king still lived:

> Some swains still say
> To the poet, that the king
> Was wounded or came
> Safely east from the stormy clash.
> But truthfully told from the south
> Is the Sikling's death in that
> Great battle (I cannot trust
> The uncertain tales of men).[84]

The king's men

Laxdaela Saga has an account of a conversion at Trondheim in Norway in 999 which illustrates some of the key issues involved in Scandinavian conversions.[85] Kjartan, his kinsman Bolli, and their men, had travelled from Iceland to Norway. Upon arrival they were informed that Hákon had fallen and that the new king, Olaf Tryggvason, was advocating a change of faith. The people were uncertain, fearing that neglect of the old gods would lead to catastrophe. The weather was bad, with an early and very cold winter, and they murmured 'it's all because of the king's innovations and this new faith of his that the gods are angry'.[86] Unsurprisingly, given the Icelanders' lack of respect for kings of any kind, they decided to refuse the new religion. Olaf was aware of this dissent, and kept them there throughout the summer and would not let them set sail. The resulting stalemate was unsettled by a swimming competition in which Olaf and Kjartan raced against each other. Olaf was very impressed with Kjartan and gave him a cloak as a gift. This upset all the other Icelanders, who believed that Kjartan had become loyal to Olaf, because accepting gifts brought one under the king's power.

The notion of the king's power was important: at one meeting Olaf preached the new faith and scorned those who clung to the old, and many of the Icelanders lost heart and capitulated to his power, accepting baptism. Christianity does not appear to have had much appeal itself; Bolli considered that it was feeble and unfit for warriors, although it might be acceptable for women, since the priests who officiated dressed like women.[87] But Olaf Tryggvason was a different matter entirely. Bolli recognized his power, and said of him 'the king is a man of great luck and good fortune ...'.[88] Therefore, the God whom such a ruler worships must be worthy of respect.

The Icelanders were put under pressure, but Olaf did not attempt to persuade them by more violent means. Kjartan offered a compromise to Olaf, suggesting '... I shall only accept this new faith in Norway to the extent that I shall have little reverence for Thor next year when I go back to Iceland'.[89] Olaf's response to this suggestion is interesting: his reply suggests that Kjartan places more faith in his own strength than in any of the old gods.[90] Kjartan admitted that it was the king who impressed him. Not to go along with the king's wishes could be a serious matter. At the very least he could be stuck in Norway indefinitely. So he and Bolli were baptized with their crews. The Scandinavian sources contain several such accounts, where the adoption of Christianity is dependent on the assurance of the king's protection.[91]

There is a Christian tendency to portray the hearers of the message as being ripe for conversion, but in this case it may be accurate: outlaws had usually ceased participation in community sacrifices, and were therefore cut off from the ritual life of the people. This may have made them more inclined to accept a new religion, but they had to be convinced of its power.[92] This concern with power was not so much psychological as practical: if adopting the new faith led to emasculation, what use would it be to a man who had to live by the strength of his sword arm? There is material which suggests that the vikings were fascinated by Christian ritual, but this may have just been curiosity about a rite alleged to contain power.

Another instructive conversion was that of Hallfredr Ottarsson Vandraedskáld (the Troublesome Poet). He lived through the conversion period and was baptized at the command of Olaf, who stood as his godfather, and so he is a personal example of Olaf's commitment to Christianity and its furtherance.[93] Hallfredr's poetry expressed a belief in the equal reality of Odin and Christ, and an understanding of his choice as one based on the power of the two gods and his allegiance to Olaf.

One poem says:

Every race of men has made songs to honour Odin; I remember the excellent poetry of our father's day. I do not willingly hate Frigg's mighty husband because I serve Christ — for the power of Vidrir (Odin) served the poet well.[94]

These words were written in 997 shortly after his baptism. Hallfreðr used traditional themes in his poetry before his conversion, and afterwards incorporated Christian ones, but his attitude to his change of faith was ambivalent:

> Olaf had trouble enough with his 'difficult skald', partly because he expressed his dislike of leaving his old friends, Odin, Thor and the rest, behind; partly because he felt that his verses, which Olaf wouldn't listen to, were at least as poetic as the holy teaching he would listen to.[95]

The gods endowed individual people (especially kings) with power. The decision to convert was often a decision that one form of power outweighed another. Any given individual or people may have a soteriology of their own which causes them to look with suspicion, fear or contempt on the soteriologies of others. For Hallfreðr, the king was his salvation.[96]

A Scandinavian saint

Olaf Haraldsson, who was to become St Olaf, was another great-grandson of Harald Fairhair (like Olaf Tryggvason). He had been a very successful viking chieftain and had been 'baptised in Rouen, France, in 1013 or 1014 by Archbishop Robert'.[97] At twenty he returned to Norway with two ships and 140 men, among them priests and bishops. He travelled around and secured the support of some of the local kings, and was eventually acclaimed sole king by the Thing in 1015. Snorri portrays the minor kings as desiring centralized rule: '... this man Olaf [that] his fate and luck must determine whether he is to obtain the kingdom or not; and if he succeed in making himself supreme king, then he will be best off who has best deserved his friendship'.[98] Olaf Haraldsson took as his model Charlemagne, a hero of the eleventh century, who had shown no hesitation in conquering and forcibly converting pagans. He named his son Magnus, after Charlemagne. Adam of Bremen wholeheartedly endorses Olaf Haraldsson: 'Olaf governed his realm with judgement and justice. They say that among other virtuous characteristics of his was a great zeal for God, so that he routed the magicians from the land.'[99] Olaf used brutal methods to further the Gospel, being literally a 'viking for Christ'. He had no qualms about the measures he took to effect conversion. He 'executed the recalcitrant, blinded or maimed them, drove them from their homes, cast down their images and marred their sacred places.'[100] Undset suggests that those who were forced into Christianity by the king frequently identified with him as their lord, and consequently 'often became fanatical in their beliefs',[101] and compelled their own families and followers to accept Christianity. This represents a case of the mission-field culture indigenizing Christianity in the manner suggested by Trompf and Russell, where the mores of the microcosmic culture completely rework the macrocosmic religion, so that its character changes.

The reasons for the acceptance of the new faith were more complex than mere fear, however. Many scholars have stressed that the old religion had many problems, including lack of a centralized organization, a theology which presented gods which were fallible and untrustworthy, and a lack of power. Hassing commented that Christianity was prestigious because of the wealth and political might of Europe; its ritual was magnificent and impressive; its theology was sophisticated and uniform (suggesting the eternal unchanging God); and 'in the missionary preaching Jesus was portrayed as the Lord, the Chief, strong and powerful, and the liberator from death and destruction, the final judge'.[102]

Olaf Haraldsson died in 1030 at the battle of Stiklestad. He was declared a saint in 1031 by Bishop Grimkjell, (the nephew of Sigurd, Olaf Tryggvason's bishop), and his tomb at Trondheim became the centre of a cult. Adam of Bremen wrote that 'the miracles that take place every day at that king's tomb in Trondhjem testify to his extraordinary merits'.[103] Snorri cited the contemporary testimony of the *Glaelognskviða* of Thorarin Loftunga, written about 1032, which shows the very early growth of the Olaf cult:

> There he lies whole and pure
> The high-praised king, with his body
> And there may hair and nails
> Grow on him as when he lived.[104]

At the death of Olaf Haraldsson Christianity was the official religion of Norway. Sweden was the last Scandinavian country to hold out against the new religion and, although Olaf Skötkonung was baptized in 1008, it was not till approximately one hundred years later that the great temple of Uppsala was demolished.

Scandinavia received Christianity late, when it was already powerful on the continent of Europe. It is not always easy to tell how the tribes and their rulers in Scandinavia reacted to the pressures of the new Christian faith, if one refers only to the sources written by and about the missionaries. There is a fair amount of alternative evidence from various parts of Scandinavia. Some of this evidence is contained in the Icelandic saga literature, which although late (twelfth to thirteenth centuries) preserves some authentic traditions. The pattern which emerges is very similar to that in England, although not in every respect. One important difference is the presence in England of papally-authorized missions staffed by monks. Monks and priests there always were: but in Scandinavia the initiative was that of the local rulers, such as the three Olafs.

It has been argued that conversion to Christianity did not alter the traditional materials for poetry, and that centuries after the conversion of Scandinavia Christian poets (possibly clergy) continued to use the old mythology. This is analogous to the debate over *Beowulf* in the Anglo-Saxon context. This literature was written by Christian poets for Christian audiences, but conversion did not eradicate the desire for traditional forms of literature among the Scandinavians.[105] It was only in the mid-thirteenth century that Snorri Sturluson perceived that the knowledge of how to compose traditional poetry was disappearing and wrote the *Prose Edda* to rectify the situation. This is understandable if a continuity is perceived between paganism and Christianity in Scandinavia. Sharpe's research is relevant here:

> religiously, however, the Germanic mind was very far indeed from being a *tabula rasa* on which the first words of salvation were to be written by the Christian Church. The presentation of Christ as the cosmic victor and the symbolism in which that act of salvation was depicted fell into prepared soil ... they understood the drama, the mythos, of salvation; and they understood the power of the risen and ascended Christ, the judge of all men. To this end they took and reshaped their ancient symbols and their ancient concepts, conscious that they were now part of a greater Empire, but conscious equally of their own distinctive heritage.[106]

Notes

1. *Laxdaela Saga*, ed. and trans. Magnus Magnusson and Hermann Pálsson, Harmondsworth, 1969, p. 148. The Icelandic text is in Gudni Jónsson (ed.), Íslendinga Sögur, vol. IV, Odds Björnssonar, 1968, p. 123.
2. J. M. Wallace-Hadrill, *The Frankish Church*, Oxford, 1983, pp. 414–15.
3. Peter R. McKeon, 'Archbishop Ebbo of Rheims (816–835): A Study in the Carolingian Empire and Church', *CH*, XLIII, 1974, p. 439.
4. Adam of Bremen, *History of the Archbishops of Hamburg-Bremen*, ed. and trans. Francis J. Tschan, New York, 1959, p. 21. The Latin text is in Adam of Bremen, *Gesta Hammaburgensis*, in *MGH:SRG*, ed. Bernhard Schmeidler, Hannover, 1917, p. 21.
5. Gwyn Jones, *A History of the Vikings*, Oxford, 1973, p. 106, says 'in 826 Harald Klak and four hundred of his followers were, in the picturesque phrase of the *Vita Hludovici*, "drenched in the wave of holy baptism" at Ingelheim, near Mainz'.
6. Ian Wood, 'Christians and Pagans in Ninth Century Scandinavia', in B. Sawyer, P. Sawyer and I. Wood (eds), *The Christianization of Scandinavia*, Alingsås, 1987, p. 38. Wood noted that Rimbert places Pope Nicolas I's approval of the amalgamation of the dioceses of Hamburg and Bremen at

half-way through the *Vita*, which is approximately fifteen years too early.

7. Adam of Bremen, Tschan, *op. cit.*, p. 22. The Latin text is in Adam of Bremen, *MGH:SRG*, *op. cit.*
8. Wallace-Hadrill, 1983, *op. cit.*, p. 416.
9. Rimbert, *Anskar Apostle of the North*, ed. and trans. Charles H. Robinson, London, 1921, p. 43. The Latin text is in Rimbert, *Vita S. Anskarii, MGH:S*, ed. G. H. Pertz, tom. II, Hannover, 1829, p. 695.
10. Robinson, *ibid.*, p. 45. The Latin text is in Rimbert, *MGH:S, ibid.*, p. 696.
11. Jones, 1973, *op. cit.*, p. 78 comments that 'few things are less believable' than king Björn's request.
12. Rimbert, Robinson, *op. cit.*, pp. 48–9. The Latin text is in Rimbert, *MGH:S, op. cit.*, p. 697.
13. Saxo Grammaticus, *The History of the Danes*, ed. Hilda Ellis Davidson and trans. Peter Fisher, Cambridge, 1979, p. 76.
14. Diana Whaley, *Heimskringla: An Introduction*, London, 1991, pp. 123–6.
15. John Stanley Martin, 'Some Aspects of Snorri Sturluson's View of Kingship', *Parergon*, 15, August 1976, pp. 43–55.
16. Åke V. Ström, 'The King God and his Connection with Sacrifice in Old Norse Religion', in *The Sacral Kingship*, VIIIth International Congress for the History of Religions, Rome, 1955, Leiden, 1959, pp. 702–15.
17. Patricia Terry (trans.), *Poems of the Elder Edda*, Philadelphia, 1990, Hávamál, p. 31. The Icelandic text is in Finnur Jónsson (ed.), *Saemundar-Edda*, Reykjavík, 1926, pp. 49–50.
18. Anthony Faulkes, 'Descent from the Gods', *MS*, 11, 1978–9, p. 95.
19. See Chapter 2, section 'The Germans and the Roman Empire'.
20. Rimbert, Robinson, *op. cit.*, p. 56. The Latin text is in Rimbert, *MGH:S, op. cit.*, p. 700.
21. Adam of Bremen, Tschan, *op. cit.*, p. 27. The Latin text is in Adam of Bremen, *MGH:SRG*, *op. cit.*, p. 27.
22. Wood, *op. cit.*, p. 46.
23. *Ibid.*, pp. 48–9. Wood comments that Rimbert's descriptions of the Horics are 'so favourable that Adam of Bremen was able to depict the elder as a Christian and to imply that the younger was also converted', *op. cit.*, p. 52.
24. Jones, 1973, *op. cit.*, p. 107.
25. Rimbert, Robinson, *op. cit.*, p. 83. The Latin text is in Rimbert, *MGH:S, op. cit.*, p. 709.
26. See Chapter 2, section 'Christianity and the Goths'.
27. Wood, *op. cit.*, p. 53.
28. Rimbert, Robinson, *op. cit.*, p. 95. The Latin text is in Rimbert, *MGH:S, op. cit.*, p. 713.
29. *Ibid.*, p. 102. Adam of Bremen claims that Horic the Younger became a Christian. Tschan commented that Adam used the *Vita Anskarii* but altered statements: 'thus, Horic II did not become a Christian, Ansgar placed Rimbert in charge of the Swedish mission and not of the church at Ribe, Hamburg was still in ruins and remained so for another half century,

Ansgar's reproval of the Frisians preceded that of the Nordalbigingians', Adam of Bremen, Tschan, *op. cit.*, note 91, p. 32.

30. Fridjov Birkeli, 'The Earliest Missionary Activities from England to Norway', *NMS*, 16, 1972, comments that Anskar was only an 'episode', having had little effect in Sweden and Denmark and never having reached Norway.

31. Peter Foote and David Wilson, *The Viking Achievement*, London, 1984, observe that 'to be a legal man one needed to be free, to belong to a family and to have a residence ... and general legal responsibility rested with the next-of-kin', p. 370.

32. Sven Ulric Palme, *Kristendomens genombrott i Sverige*, Stockholm, 1959, p. 46. See Chapter 7, section 'The individual and the family'.

33. Jónsson, *op. cit.*, pp. 177–90.

34. Hilda Ellis Davidson, *Myths and symbols in pagan Europe*, Manchester, 1988, p. 211, discussed the identification of 'Rig' with the god Heimdall.

35. *Ibid.*, p. 126.

36. Helmer Ringgren, 'The Problem of Fatalism', in H. Ringgren (ed.), *Fatalistic Beliefs*, Stockholm, 1967, p. 8. H. R. Ellis commented, somewhat acidly, that 'there are no thirty nine articles of heathen belief lurking behind the obscurities of Norse mythology or the welter of strange practices recorded in the sagas', *The Road to Hel*, New York, 1968, p. 3.

37. Åke V. Ström, 'Scandinavian Belief in Fate', in Ringgren, *op. cit.*, pp. 77–8.

38. *Poems of the Elder Edda*, Terry, *op. cit.*, pp. 4–7. See also Snorri Sturluson, *Edda*, ed. and trans. Anthony Faulkes, London, 1987, pp. 52–8.

39. Paul Bauschatz, *The Well and the Tree*, Amherst, 1982, p. 7.

40. Adam of Bremen, *op. cit.*, ch. xxvii (27), p. 208. The Latin text is in Adam of Bremen, *MGH:SRG*, *op. cit.*, pp. 259–60. See also Jacqueline Simpson, 'Some Scandinavian Sacrifices', *Folklore*, 78, 1967, pp. 190–202, *passim*.

41. Aron J. Gurevich, 'On Heroes, Things, Gods and Laughter in Germanic Poetry', *Studies in Medieval and Renaissance History*, vol. V, o.s. vol. XV, 1982, p. 161.

42. E. J. Sharpe, 'Salvation, Germanic and Christian', in E. J. Sharpe and J. R. Hinnells (eds), *Man and His Salvation*, Manchester, 1973, p. 249.

43. G. Aulén, *Christus Victor*, London, 1950, pp. 97–116.

44. Sharpe, *op. cit.*, p. 257.

45. Theodore M. Andersson, 'Heathen Sacrifice in *Beowulf* and Rimbert's *Life of Ansgar*', *Medievalia et Humanistica*, n.s. 13, 1985, p. 71.

46. Jones, 1973, *op. cit.*, p. 119.

47. P. Sawyer, in Sawyer, Sawyer and Wood (eds), *op. cit.*, p. 71.

48. Foote and Wilson, *op. cit.*, pp. 361–2. See also John Lindow, 'Mythology and Mythography', in Carol J. Clover and John Lindow (eds), *Old Norse-Icelandic Literature*, Ithaca, NY, 1985, pp. 24–9.

49. C. J. A. Oppermann, *The English Missionaries in Sweden and Finland*, London, 1937, p. 90.

50. B. Sawyer, 'Scandinavian Conversion Histories', in Sawyer, Sawyer and Wood (eds), *op. cit.*, pp. 88–110.

51. *Ibid.*, pp. 101–2.

52. *Ibid.*, p. 103.
53. Finn Fuglestad, 'Earth-Priests, "Priest-Chiefs" and sacred Kings in Ancient Norway, Iceland and West Africa', *Scandinavian Journal of History*, 4, 1979, p. 67.
54. Adam of Bremen, Tschan, *op. cit.*, p. 51.
55. Boyd H. Hill Jr, *Medieval Monarchy in Action*, London, 1972, pp. 22–4.
56. Adam of Bremen, Tschan, *op. cit.*, bk I, lviii (60), p. 50. The Latin text is in Adam of Bremen, *MGH:SGR, op. cit.*, p. 57.
57. Tschan, *ibid.*, p. 52. The Latin text is in Adam of Bremen, *ibid.*, p. 59.
58. P. Sawyer, *op. cit.*, p. 69.
59. Widukind of Corvei, *Saxon History*, bk III, 65. Quoted in P. Sawyer, *op. cit.* The Latin text is in Widukind of Corvei, *Res Gestae Saxoniae*, in *MGH:SRG*, ed. H.-E. Lohmann and P. Hirsch, Hannover, 1935, pp. 140–1.
60. P. Sawyer, *op. cit.*
61. Lene Demidoff, 'The Poppo Legend', *MS*, 6, 1973, pp. 39–67, traces the development of the cult of Poppo, and attempts to identify him with a historical prototype, either Bishop Folkmar of Cologne (965–969) who was also called Poppo, or Bishop Poppo of Würzburg (961–984).
62. P. Sawyer, *op. cit.*, p. 70.
63. See Chapter 5, section 'Willibrord'.
64. P. H. Sawyer, *Kings and Vikings*, London, 1982, p. 138.
65. Foote and Wilson, *op. cit.*, p. 131.
66. Adam of Bremen, *op. cit.*, p. 72. The Latin text is in Adam of Bremen, *MGH:SRG, op. cit.*, p. 87.
67. Theodore M. Andersson, 'The Conversion of Norway according to Oddr Snorrason and Snorri Sturluson', *MS*, 10, 1977, p. 84.
68. *Ibid.*, pp. 84–5.
69. Gwyn Jones, *The Legendary History of Olaf Tryggvason*, Glasgow, 1968, p. 19.
70. G. N. Garmonsway, ed. and trans., *The Anglo-Saxon Chronicle*, The Canterbury Chronicle (F), 994, London, 1960, p. 128. The Anglo-Saxon text is in Plummer and Earle, *op. cit.*, The Canterbury MS, p. 128.
71. Peter Sawyer, 'Ethelred II, Olaf Tryggvason, and the Conversion of Norway', *Scandinavian Studies*, 59, 1987, p. 300.
72. B. Sawyer, in Sawyer, Sawyer and Wood (eds), *op. cit.*, p. 108.
73. Snorri Sturluson, *Heimskringla: The Olaf Sagas*, trans. Samuel Laing, ed. Jacqueline Simpson, London, 1964, ch. LIX, p. 53. The Icelandic text is in Snorri Sturluson, *Heimskringla*, ed. B. S. Kristjánsdóttir *et al.*, vol. 1, Reykjavík 1991, p. 204.
74. Per Hassing, 'Religious Change in Eleventh Century Norway', *Missiology*, III, (4), October 1975, p. 474.
75. Adam of Bremen, Tschan, *op. cit.*, p. 82, says 'some relate that Olaf had been a Christian, some that he had forsaken Christianity'. The Latin text is in Adam of Bremen, *MGH:SRG, op. cit.*, pp. 100–1. However, Adam also comments in Book Two that 'Olaf, the son of Tryggve, when expelled from Norway, went to England and there embraced Christianity, which he was

the first to bring back into his fatherland', p. 80. The Latin text is in Adam of Bremen, *MGH:SRG, op. cit.*, p. 98.

76. Lesley Abrams, 'The Anglo-Saxons and the Christianization of Scandinavia', *A-SE*, 24, p. 241.

77. Adam of Bremen, Tschan, *op. cit.*, p. 82.

78. *Ibid.*, p. 83.

79. Geraldine Barnes, 'The medieval Anglophile: England its rulers in Old Norse history and saga', *Parergon*, n.s. 10, (2), pp. 11–26, *passim*.

80. Jones, 1973, *op. cit.*, p. 134.

81. *Ibid.*, p. 285.

82. Hassing, *op. cit.*, p. 472.

83. Ari the Learned, *The Book of the Icelanders*, ed. and trans. Jones, in *The Norse Atlantic Saga*, Oxford, 1986, p. 150. The Icelandic text is in Ari the Learned, *Íslendingabók*, in Guðni Jónsson (ed.), *Íslendinga Sögur*, vol. I, Odds Björnssonar, 1968, pp. 11–12.

84. Snorri Sturluson, *Heimskringla*, ed. E. Monsen and trans. A. H. Smith, Cambridge, 1932. The Icelandic text is in Snorri Sturluson, Kristjánsdóttir *et al.*, *op. cit.*, p. 250.

85. *Laxdaela Saga*, Magnusson and Pálsson, *op. cit.*, pp. 141–9.

86. *Ibid.*, p. 145. The Icelandic text is in *Laxdaela Saga*, Jónsson, *op. cit.*, p. 119.

87. *Ibid.*, p. 146.

88. *Ibid.* The Icelandic text is in *Laxdaela Saga*, Jónsson, *op. cit.*, p. 120.

89. *Ibid.*, pp. 147–8. The Icelandic text is in *Laxdaela Saga*, Jónsson, *op. cit.*, p. 122.

90. This attitude is to be found in other texts, such as *Finboga Saga*, in which Finboga asserts his belief in himself.

91. Georg Sverdrup, *Da Norge ble Kristnet*, Oslo, 1942, p. 161 ff.

92. I am grateful to Prof. E. J. Sharpe for some of the material and perspectives in this section.

93. Fredrik Paasche, *Kristendom og Kvad*, Kristiania, 1914, pp. 8–10.

94. Sharpe, 1973, *op. cit.*, pp. 253–4. The Icelandic text is in Bjarni Einarsson (ed.), *Hallfreðar Saga*, Reykjavík, 1977, p. 47.

95. Eric J. Sharpe, unpublished manuscript referring to Finnur Jónsson, *Den islandske litterature historie*, Copenhagen, 1907, pp. 124–7.

96. Dag Strömbäck, *The Conversion of Iceland*, trans. Peter Foote, London, 1975, p. 81.

97. Hassing, *op. cit.*

98. Snorri Sturluson, Laing, *op. cit.*, p. 143. The Icelandic text is in Snorri Sturluson, Kristjánsdóttir *et al.*, *op. cit.*, p. 282.

99. Adam of Bremen, Tschan, *op. cit.*, p. 94. The Latin text is in Adam of Bremen, *MGH:SRG, op. cit.*, p. 117.

100. Jones, 1973, *op. cit.*, p. 377.

101. Sigrid Undset, *Saga of Saints*, trans. E. C. Ramsden, London, 1934, p. 31.

102. Hassing, *op. cit.*, p. 478.

103. Adam of Bremen, Tschan, *op. cit.*, p. 128. The Latin text is in Adam of Bremen, *MGH:SRG, op. cit.*, p. 159.

104. Snorri Sturluson, Monsen, *op. cit.*, p. 390. The Icelandic text is in Snorri Sturluson, Kristjánsdóttir, *op. cit.*, vol. 2, p. 550.
105. John Simpson, 'Comparative structural analysis of three ethical questions', *JIS*, 3, (3), 1975, p. 239.
106. Sharpe, *op. cit.*, p. 261.

7   The conversion of Iceland

> To this country he sent a priest whose name was Thangbrand, who taught men
> Christianity and baptized all who embraced the faith.
>
> Ari the Learned[1]

The sources

The chief sources for the settlement and conversion of Iceland are: Ari the
Learned's (1067–1148) *Libellus Islandorum*, which is an abridged version of
a longer, lost *Íslendingabók*, probably written between 1122 and 1133;[2] the
anonymous *Landnámabók* (Book of the Settlements), which records the
names of those who settled Iceland from Norway in the late ninth century;
Snorri Sturluson's *Saga of Olaf Tryggvason*; and some of the 'Sagas of the
Icelanders'. Other sources include the *Historia de antiquitate regum
Norwagensium* by the Norwegian monk Theodoricus and Oddr Snorrason's
Olaf's Saga. Ari's account is the earliest (written *c.* 1122–33), and his
evidence came mostly from informants born before 1050. Theodoricus
wrote around 1180, and Oddr Snorrason around 1190.

The original *Landnámabók* is thought to have been written in the late
eleventh or early twelfth centuries, but it has been lost, and the
Landnámabók as it is now known exists in five versions dating from the
middle thirteenth to the early seventeenth centuries. It has never been
doubted that Ari the Learned was a strong influence on the writer of the
Landnámabók and some scholars even argue that Ari was its author.[3] This
affects the historiography of the conversion: if the *Landnámabók* was an
early composition which influenced the later family sagas of the thirteenth
century, then it can be treated as reliable, and the sagas are therefore also
valuable as sources; if *Landnámabók* was itself only put together from oral
sources in the thirteenth century, and may even have been influenced by
the composition of the sagas, then it is of much less value historically.

The most important of the sagas are *Laxdaela Saga*, *Njál's Saga*, *Kristni
Saga*, and *Hallfreðar Saga*. All of these texts are relatively late compositions;
Iceland accepted Christianity in 999/1000, but the saga is a literary form
which developed in the twelfth and thirteenth centuries. Since the sagas

have been variously interpreted as reliable history and total fiction, they must clearly be treated very carefully as sources.[4] Nevertheless, they potentially provide information on both the arrival of Christianity in Iceland and its subsequent progress.

Since all the written sources postdate the official conversion and the introduction of Christian scholarship, the presence of Christian bias in them is inevitable. The culture of Iceland also influenced Christianity, however, and elements of pre-Christian Icelandic society are visible through the Christian filter. For Christian beliefs being moulded by Icelandic cultural preconceptions, the *Skarðsárbók* (a collection of apocryphal lives of the apostles) is an example of 'the Icelanders [adapting] these lives of spiritual adventure to their own standards of aristocratic idealism. St. Paul, for instance, is depicted not so much as the apostle who would become "all things to all men" as an old saga hero of distinguished family.'[5] This is the sort of adaptation that the Saxon author of the *Heliand* was engaged in.

The saga writers may have all been Christians, but the terms of the adoption of Christianity by Iceland had been generous. Ari the Learned indicated that while public acts of sacrifice were prohibited, private *blót* (sacrifice) was permitted.[6] That the saga writers had not reconciled their past with their Christian present is obvious. Some of the saga heroes exemplified Christian virtues, even though they were not Christians themselves: Njál is a faithful husband, a devoted father, a hard working farmer, and a loyal friend unto death. Many, however, inhabit a world completely foreign to Christianity, where life is a perpetual struggle against hostile supernatural forces and human treachery. Clunies-Ross mused that:

> most scholars … would agree that saga-writers found certain aspects of their forefathers' beliefs and customs embarrassing to the extent that they felt a need to justify the past and bring it into accordance with the Christian values of their own times. Thus many of Egill's character traits and beliefs are usually accorded a morally negative value in Icelandic saga literature: his acknowledged paganism, his violence, moodiness and lack of moderation, his avarice and delight in litigation. His physical appearance, too, as a dark, ugly, bald and troll-like figure, usually signals a writer's moral disapprobation to the saga-audience. How, then, does this author reconcile the expectations of conventional Christian morality of the thirteenth century with his anti-hero's wild, demonic qualities in such a way that our sympathy is not lost and Egill not depicted as a thorough reprobate?[7]

Questions like this cannot be answered here, but they must be kept in mind when interpreting evidence from the sagas.

Pre-Christian society and religion

Iceland was settled in 870 from Norway and the Norwegian colonies. The original settlement appears to have been partly a response to the political ambitions of Harald Fairhair, who was actively unifying Norway under a centralized monarchy. The settlers from Norway were accustomed to a society in which the monarch was an essential part of the religious life of the country. Therefore it is interesting that they avoided establishing a monarchy in the new colony, preferring an annual national assembly, called the Althing, at which all the regions of the country were represented.[8] 'Things', or assemblies of free men, had been present in Germanic societies throughout history, but the system of government which developed in Iceland was peculiar given the great religious significance of sacral kingship.[9]

In place of centralized loyalty to a king the Icelanders substituted loyalty to a code of law, commissioning Úlfljót to study lawcodes in Norway and to compose an Icelandic code.[10] The Icelandic landowners of influence were organized into *goðorðs*, bands of neighbours united under a *goði*, a chieftain who officiated as priest at the local temple. They accepted Úlfljót's Law and elected him the first *Lögsögumaðr*, or Lawspeaker.[11] The Lawspeaker presided over the Althing, which met annually at Thingvellir, and proclaimed the law of Iceland each year. In the conversion of Iceland it was the decision of the Lawspeaker which was decisive, rather than that of the king as in the other cases studied. Later settlers to Iceland responded to the attraction of being able to claim large estates in a land where all were equal.[12] It was this attitude in part which led Jones to assert that: 'by definition the [Icelandic] Republic was an anachronism, pagan and anti-monarchic'.[13]

In other ways Iceland conformed to the religious norms of Scandinavia: the settlers constructed temples, and images of the gods have been found by archaeologists.[14] The significance of the *goðar* is hard to assess, but their existence suggests that the Icelanders considered officiating priests a necessity, even if the priesthood was essentially part-time.[15] They also had some of the qualities and powers of the Scandinavian kings; while the role of the kings was much broader, the *goðar* served essentially the same local religious and judicial functions.[16] Both presided over assemblies and officiated at sacrifices.

The pre-Christian religion of Iceland receives considerable attention in the sagas, but it is not easy to interpret many of the references. Eddic and skaldic verse speaks of cultic activities, but gives no descriptions of them. Other accounts of pre-Christian rituals are also of dubious value: Adam of Bremen's account of the Uppsala Festival is hearsay, and the Rus funeral Ibn Fadlan witnessed in 922 takes place outside Scandinavia. The importance of folk religion is evidenced by the great devotion to the cult of the *landvaettir* in the sources. These were the guardian spirits of the country.[17] The cult of the spirits stood alongside *goðatru* or *asatru*, faith in the gods. Place-names including the elements *hof* and *horgar* indicate sites where sacrifices were offered.[18] There is no place-name evidence to suggest that Odin was worshipped in Iceland, and among the devout the chief god seems to have been Thor. Thor's cult is represented by the 'high-seat pillars' which many settlers erected. Devotion to other deities is less easy to substantiate, although the poets are assumed to have worshipped Odin, as evidenced by the case of Hallfredr Vandraedaskáld.[19] Evidence for this is found in both *Landnámabók* and *Eyrbyggja Saga*.[20] There is also evidence in *Viga-Glum's Saga* for worship of Freyr.

Landnámabók also speaks of the mixed religious allegiances of the earliest settlers. One notable example was Helgi the Lean, who 'believed in Christ but invoked Thor when it came to voyages and difficult times'.[21] Another is the father and son Helgi and Hall, both surnamed 'the Godless'; father and son believed in their own strength and refused to hold sacrifices.[22]

Christianity had been in Iceland from the start: Ari tells of Irish hermits (*papar*) who were there when the settlers arrived,[23] and *Landnámabók* gives the names of Christian settlers, including the influential woman, Aud the Deep-Minded. It is said that she 'used to say her prayers at Cross Hills; she had crosses erected there, for she'd been baptized and was a devout Christian. Her kinsmen later worshipped these hills, and then when sacrifices began a pagan temple was built there.'[24] This suggests that any Christianity brought by the settlers in the late ninth century was not of long duration, but Iceland had clearly been in contact with Christianity since its foundation.

We do not know how many Christians there were in Iceland at the time of the Althing of 999/1000, but it is likely that there were a sizeable number. There is evidence of casual contact and bottom-up influence of Christianity prior to the Althing.[25] That many of the early converts to Christianity had high status as members of the *goðorð* is significant. (It must be supposed that their households and retainers adopted the new faith along with them.) However, as Adalsteinsson points out, Christianity was a minority position, and adherence to the old religion was strong.[26]

The individual and the family

It appears that the deities which received the most devotion from the Icelanders were those who encouraged self-reliance. Thor was, after all, the god of those who believed in their own power and strength. The sagas tell of many actions of individual resourcefulness, bravery, and cowardice. One of the most famous of the saga heroes, Egil Skallagrímsson, exemplifies the individualist cut adrift from the stabilizing bonds of society. *Egil's Saga* is anonymous, but there are good reasons for attributing it to Snorri Sturluson.[27] Despite the author's Christianity, Egil has many qualities incompatible with Christian heroic expectations; he was a violent man, a killer, and passionately devoted to that most ambiguous of the pre-Christian gods, Odin. His poem 'Lament for my Sons' (*Sonatorrek*), composed after the death of his son by drowning, shows Egil coming to terms with his grief by understanding that while Odin has taken his son, he has given the gift of poetic inspiration in return. Egil concludes resignedly that he will continue to offer sacrifices to Odin:

> I'll make offerings to Odin,   Though not in eagerness,
> I'll make my soul's sacrifice,   Not to suffer silently:
> Though this friend has failed me,   Fellow of gods,
> To his credit he comforts me   With compensation.[28]

Egil's devotion to Odin is logical, because Odin is the god of poetic inspiration, the god of the dark side of power.

None of this should be interpreted as evidence that the Scandinavians in general were great individualists. It remains vitally important to keep in mind that no individual was expected to live a life separated from others, and particularly from those to whom he or she was related by ties of blood.[29] The saga heroes were the exception rather than the rule. Indeed there is much evidence to suggest that the family unit was as strong in Iceland as in other Germanic societies. Recent archaeology has unearthed many house-complexes in the north, buildings in which an entire family, perhaps as many as thirty individuals, might live, presided over by the head of the family.[30] One such family head was the celebrated 'Burnt Njál', who ruled a family of three generations within which his word was undisputed law.

Within such a social complex – to which one belonged whether one liked it or not – ethical values were of the strictest. An injury done to one was done to all (hence the elaborate feuds of which the sagas bear such frequent witness) and a good turn done to one placed an obligation on all.[31] Ulfila's Gothic translation of the Bible rendered the words 'unlawful' and 'godless' (amounting to more or less the same thing) with the word *unsibjis* – literally that which is not done in the sib, or family. Family members enjoyed the rights of the family, the protection of the family, and the luck of the family. They could call on not only the might of the living, but also the infinitely more powerful influence of the dead, since no distinction was drawn between the two. The dead usually found their final resting place on or near the family property and at certain times of the year were welcomed back to their old places at the family table. They were consulted whenever occasion arose and great pains were taken not to do anything which might arouse their disapproval.[32]

Where the family functioned as such a homogeneous unit and focus of power and influence, it is clear that the worst thing that could happen to the individual was exclusion from hearth and home. If this happened the individual would be rootless and powerless, separated from all those customs, rituals, symbols and beliefs which made life meaningful.

> The full irredeemable outlaw 'is as if he were dead', said the Eidsivathing Law. It was criminal to feed him, harbour him, help him on his way. He lost all goods and all his rights – his children illegitimate, his body buried in unconsecrated ground. In its full rigour the sentence of outlaw required the rejection of the condemned man not only by indifferent society but also by his own family.[33]

The prelude to the conversion

There were two early, shadowy attempts to bring Christianity to Iceland: the mission of Bishop Frederick of Saxony and the Icelander Thorvaldr, from 981 to 986; and that of Stefnir Thorgilsson, sent by Olaf Tryggvason in 996.[34] These earlier missions are referred to in both *Kristni Saga* and *The Saga of Olaf Tryggvason*. Stefnir was found guilty of blasphemy and forced to leave the country. The impetus for the conversion of Iceland lay with Olaf Tryggvason, whose dedication to spreading Christianity has been discussed earlier.[35] Ari the Learned records that he sent the German priest Thangbrandr to Iceland as a missionary around 998. Thangbrandr succeeded in baptizing three influential chieftains, Sidu-Hallr, Gizurr Teitsson (the White) and Hjalti Skeggjason (Theodoricus records a fourth, Thorgils). He then returned to Norway 'having been the death of two or three men who had lampooned him'.[36] These lampoons have survived in later saga literature, and explicitly present Thangbrandr as being in conflict with Thor.[37]

Under Icelandic law the killings were justifiable, and Jóhannesson believes they probably enhanced Thangbrandr's reputation as a man protected by a powerful deity.[38] He reported to Olaf that the conversion of the Icelanders was most unlikely. Ari's sources for this mission are impressive: his foster-father was Hallr Thorarinsson of Haukadalur, who had been baptized by Thangbrandr in 999 at the age of three; and his teacher at Haukadalur was Teit Ísleifsson, Gizurr the White's grandson.[39]

Olaf Tryggvason was angered by this and wished to kill or maim all Icelanders then in Norway.[40] Olaf's rage was diverted by the arrival from Iceland of Gizurr and Hjalti, who had been sentenced for blasphemy against Freya. Together with Kjartan, whose baptism has been discussed,[41] they persuaded Olaf that Iceland could be persuaded to accept Christianity.[42] Gizurr would have had some influence with Olaf, since they were quite closely related and Hjalti was Gizurr's son-in-law. Snorri speaks of other influential Icelandic Christians at the Norwegian court on the eve of the conversion. The next year (999) Gizurr and Hjalti returned to Iceland, with a priest named Thórmodr in place of Thangbrandr, in order to attend the Althing.

The Althing of 999/1000

In preparation for the Althing, Gizurr summoned his supporters, fearing that he would be barred from the assembly, and he was joined by Hjalti and his supporters. According to Ari, they were armed, but a battle was avoided. Jóhannesson suggests three reasons for this: there were more Christians than expected; there were those in both groups who were anxious to keep the peace; and it was likely that those attending knew that Olaf Tryggvason held Icelanders as hostages (Ari does not mention this, but Oddr Snorrason does).[43] It would have been clear to all present that Olaf Tryggvason was intent on expanding his power in Iceland through the agency of Christianity. The Icelanders had resisted kingly domination for over a century and it was not at all clear how they would evade Olaf's imperialism. Gizurr and Hjalti went to the Law Rock, and spoke effectively. The content of Hjalti's and Gizurr's message is unknown, as is why Hjalti, an outlaw, was permitted to address the meeting. It seems likely, however, that they gained more credibility and attention as secular emissaries of Olaf Tryggvason than as exponents of a new religion. Ari says: 'what followed from this was that one man after another, Christian and heathen, called witnesses, each swearing that he would not live under the same laws as the other, after which they left the Law Rock'.[44] The scene resembled the council of Edwin of Northumbria, where Paulinus presented the new faith and the high priest, Coifi, responded by accepting the change. The calling of witnesses makes it clear that the issue of social stability was uppermost in most minds.

That the Icelandic Christians swore oaths, declaring themselves outside the law of the Icelandic Commonwealth, is probably due to the existence of a law dating from the earlier mission of Stefni:

> in that summer a law was passed at the General Assembly that every man should be convicted and made an outlaw who reviled the gods or did them any damage or dishonour. The relatives of the person accused, second or third cousins or between these degrees, should be the ones to prosecute them because the heathens called Christianity a shame to one's kinsmen.[45]

Jóhannesson notes that the Christian *goðar* were therefore unable to perform their traditional legal and religious duties.[46] Adalsteinsson speculates that the Christians may have been willing to throw off the community of laws because they felt capable of founding their own state with the help of Olaf Tryggvason.[47] The non-Christian Icelanders had already disowned the Christian element in their society; their oath-taking merely confirmed their position.

At this point Ari's account becomes quite frustrating. The role of Sidu-Hallr is puzzling. He was called on by the Christians to proclaim the Christian law, and is supposed to have paid the non-Christian Lawspeaker, Thorgeir, to proclaim the law. Thorgeir then lay down under his cloak for a day and a night without speaking. The next morning he emerged from under his cloak and went to the Law Rock to announce his decision.[48] It is interesting to speculate on how the two groups of his audience felt at that moment. Were the supporters of the old religion sure that the Lawspeaker would find in favour of the ancient law? Were the Christians confident that Thorgeir would support their cause? At the Law Rock, he counselled the assembly in this way:

> 'I think it policy that we do not let those prevail who are most anxious to be at each others' throats, but reach such a compromise in these matters that each shall win part of his case, and let all have one law and one faith. It will prove true, if we break the law in pieces, that we break the peace in pieces too.' And so he concluded his speech that both sides agreed that all should have that one law which he would proclaim.[49]

After stressing the value of having one law for all, Thorgeir went on to proclaim that: 'all men should be Christians, and be baptized, those who so far were unbaptized here in Iceland. But as for the exposure of infants the old laws should stand, and for the eating of horse-flesh too. Men might sacrifice in secret if they so wished.'[50]

The account of events at the Althing has many puzzling elements. What is the significance of the 'payment' which Sidu-Hallr made to Thorgeir? *Njál's Saga* records that this payment was three silver marks and suggests that this sum could not have influenced the outcome, observing 'that was most hazardous counsel, since he [Thorgeir] was an heathen'.[51] Strömbäck interprets the fee as a bribe, but Adalsteinsson believes it was not.[52] Several scholars have speculated on the initial exchange between Thorgeir and Sidu-Hallr. This presumably pertained to the proclamation of the law to come, but there is no evidence.[53] There have also been several explanations of what Thorgeir was doing under the cloak; most scholars consider that he was formulating an acceptable speech.[54]

Adalsteinsson thinks the real question is why the non-Christians accepted Thorgeir's pronouncement. He sees Thorgeir's sojourn under his cloak as a clue, and cites instances of similar practices which suggest that this was a soothsaying or prophesying ritual: 'Thorgeir did not stay under the cloak to think but to carry out an ancient soothsaying ritual, the outcome of which he proclaimed at the Logberg the following day. All those present were well aware of this.'[55] There is no direct evidence to support this interpretation.[56] Adalsteinsson countered the assertion that the Icelanders had lost interest in matters of religion by noting that it had been sufficient motivation for evicting Stefni's mission and outlawing Hjalti Skeggjason. He explains the absence of further detail in Ari's account as a result of his work being written for two Icelandic bishops, Thorlakr and Ketill, and being checked by his learned contemporary Saemundr the Priest. Such a text would not preserve references to the old religion, as they were not edifying. But there is plentiful evidence that Scandinavians were interested in and practised divination, Adalsteinsson's hypothesis remains in the realm of speculation.

Other scholars have concluded that the Icelanders were really concerned with preserving their Commonwealth at all costs, and that therefore 'their acceptance of the new faith around the year A.D. 1000, while the rest of Europe was frantically anticipating the Apocalypse, was decidedly cool and businesslike'.[57]

Dag Strömbäck also supports a 'political decision' hypothesis. He believes that 'the high-born Icelandic chiefs were afraid that the king would not hesitate to subjugate their country by force, if Christianity was not accepted'.[58] Olaf Tryggvason was a powerful ruler, with almost imperial ambitions, but the sources nowhere state that this was his intention or that the Icelanders were aware of this possibility. There is oblique evidence that the decision of the Icelanders was not primarily motivated by political concerns. Olaf Tryggvason died shortly after the Althing, but, despite this release from their political foe, Iceland did not apostasize, suggesting a deeper reason for the acceptance of the new faith. It is not clear why all the Icelanders accepted Thorgeir's decision.

The consequences of the conversion

After the official conversion, Iceland's contacts with Europe quickly became more intimate and more extensive. European Christian learning and the use of the Latin alphabet spread in Iceland through the foreign priests who arrived to service the fledgeling Churchmen who introduced Roman script to Iceland. After one generation native clergy emerged in Iceland, 'the most famous of them Ísleif, son of the chieftain Gizurr the White'.[59] Ísleif Gizursson was bishop from 1056 to 1080, and, with his younger contemporaries, Ari the Learned (1067–1148) and Saemundr the Wise

(1056–1133), founded the Icelandic historical tradition. Looking back to Horton's stress on the leading role played by the old religious and secular leaders in the transition, it is interesting that the *goðorð* often become priests and bishops after conversion, retaining their influence despite the change of religion.[60] The great power wielded by Ísleif Gizursson, son of Gizurr the White and his third wife Thordis, is evidence for this. He was the first bishop consecrated to work in Iceland and, from 1057 to his death in 1080, was bishop of Skalholt. He instituted a system of tithes which made the Icelandic church financially independent and strengthened the position of Christianity.[61]

The corporate acceptance of Christianity by the Althing was critical, because many individuals would have found it difficult, if not impossible, to change allegiance without it. Whether or not individuals had the opportunity to respond to the Christian message, they scarcely ever did so *as individuals*. It not true that the individual never had a mind of his own in matters of religion, but certainly to go against the customs of the family was a step which few ever even contemplated making. To abandon the old religion without communal sanction would have been seen as *aettarspillar* and *fraendaskomm* – both Icelandic words denoting the destruction of the family and dishonour to its members.

Those people who had made a commitment to Christianity before the Althing were all high-born, people with a strong sense of personal identity. If such a person felt that Christ and God (close distinctions were not drawn and the Holy Spirit remained virtually unknown) would serve them well, providing them with the supernatural power they so much needed in order to remain alive and well, then they would become Christian. And because Christ was henceforth their God, so too would he become the God of their people; an illustration of the 'principle of association' which so governed Germanic society, and which has been discussed in detail in earlier chapters. Monks and missionaries might portray the joys of heaven and the miseries of hell with great eloquence,[62] but they could only succeed if they were able to ensure that the entire social unit responded at the same time. This meant that they had first to convince the leader of the social unit, whether king, Lawspeaker, or family head.

To the present-day Christian, moral conduct tends to be the major focus of the faith, on the grounds that: all human beings are equally the children of one God; God desires the good of all without distinction or exception, and the chief of all the commandments is the commandment to love. In the world of the Germanic tribes this was not so. It was not that they had no standards of ethical conduct – merely that whatever standards there were applied only within the community of law.[63] To break the laws of the tribe or family meant instant expulsion and the life of an outlaw. Enemies and strangers, on the other hand, could not be expected to conform to the laws of the tribe, and might be dealt with in accordance with the needs of the moment — territory, trade, revenge or malice.

In its way, this was as much of a religious attitude as the ethical universalism of the twentieth century. It was based on the firm belief that the writ of the gods did not extend outside the tribal frontiers. On the 'other side' there would be other gods and therefore other standards. This attitude is comparable to that of the Hebrews in the Old Testament: let these gods protect their people.[64] Conversion to Christianity in the north did not alter this basic perspective. The Christian law was a new law, but it was no different in its *modus operandi*.

The early Christianity of the Icelanders was syncretistic, like that of the other Germanic groups. Officially the old religion ceased with Thorgeir's pronouncement, but private sacrifices continued for some time. Thorgeir's provision for the preservation of exposure of infants and the eating of horse-meat makes this clear. Peter Foote, in a study of twelfth century Iceland, comments that: 'there was no strong centralised authority in the country, neither secular nor religious; there was much contact with foreign parts and a multiplicity of intellectual influences from abroad; and all this seems to have made for an easy-going acceptance of diversity'.[65] The very nature of pre-Christian Scandinavian beliefs, where there were no creeds or articles of faith which made the old religion a definite whole, encouraged its survival and subtle interpenetration with Christianity.[66] *Eyrbyggja Saga* depicts a series of events which include the dismantling of a pagan temple in Norway and its reassembly in Iceland, a series of sacrifices and hauntings, and a final Christian solution to these problems of supernatural origin. Martin has argued that:

> an official change of religion on the theological-social level does not affect drastically the complex of ritual acts which play such a large role in peasant life. They exist on as a substratum, just as in Israel a substratum of the older Canaanite religion existed on in later Jahwism. The sagas depict a world rich in concepts of the supernatural and demonic forces and we find magic, taboo, witchcraft and prophecy used as protection against the powers of darkness.[67]

Some examples of this syncretism include the collection of pre-Christian mythical and legendary poems in the thirteenth-century *Poetic Edda*. This collection is anonymous and it is not obvious (as it would have been elsewhere) that the writer was a priest, since Iceland in the thirteenth century had its share of educated laypeople. A notable example was Snorri Sturluson, whose *Prose Edda*, written at about the same time, was a manual for poets. Snorri's *Edda* is evidence of considerable interest in, and tolerance of, pre-Christian religion.

Several of the Eddic poems contain syncretistic elements. The *Hávamál* refers to Odin's search for the power of the runes, and the sacrifice he is prepared to make in order to receive that power. Scholars have pointed out similarities to the crucified Jesus in the depiction of a god sacrificed to himself by hanging on a gallows.[68] A similar relationship between Jesus and another (superficially more appropriate) deity, Balder, god of goodness and light, can also be detected. As with the debate surrounding *Beowulf*, it seems unlikely that the extent of Christian influence in *Hávamál* will ever be determined. Foote's article refers to the frequently made connection between Odin (in his role of Bolverkr, the mischief maker) and Satan, which is similarly found in Anglo-Saxon England (for example, Wansdyke [Woden's Dyke] being referred to as the Devil's Ditch).[69]

Another Eddic poem which reflects a possible Christian influence is *Völuspá*, which is also the most informative poem regarding pre-Christian Scandinavian beliefs, providing what is almost a systematic theology, beginning with the creation of the world and ending with its destruction in Ragnarok. That structure may itself reflect a biblical influence, and the potential of forms and structures for encoding meaning has been recognized by many scholars.[70] At the close of *Völuspá* a vision of a new heaven and a new earth emerging from the destruction of Ragnarok is described:

> She sees the earth   rising again
> out of the waters,   green once more;
> ...
> She sees a hall,   fairer than the sun,
> thatched with gold;   it stands at Gimle.
> There shall deserving   people dwell
> to the end of time   and enjoy their happiness.[71]

There is not much in this description which resembles the dark and grim spirit of Scandinavian pre-Christian beliefs as they are known from other sources, but it does resemble the 'new heaven and new earth' of the New Testament, and the Celestial City after the Second Coming.

The mixture of Christian and pre-Christian values and attitudes which pervade the sagas has been skilfully analysed by Carol Clover.[72] It has already been demonstrated that such syncretism was a natural consequence of the type of conversion undergone by the various Germanic peoples, and that this is the result of the appropriation by a microcosmic society of the faith of a macrocosmic society, while retaining its own world-view.

Notes

1. Ari the Learned, *The Book of the Icelanders*, ch. 7, ed. and trans. Gwyn Jones, in *The Norse Atlantic Saga*, Oxford, 1986, p. 148.
2. E. Turville-Petre, *The Origins of Icelandic Literature*, Oxford, 1953, p. 93.
3. *Ibid.*, p. 105.
4. Jesse L. Byock, *Medieval Iceland*, Berkeley, CA, 1988, has as its dedication the following quotation: 'In 1956 Jón Jóhannesson published a work on Iceland's early history in which he ... mentioned almost none of the events recounted in the *Íslendinga Sögur* [family sagas], just as if they had never taken place. Yet, Jón Jóhannesson was far from being extreme in his views. Shortly after his *History* appeared, I asked him whether he believed that the sagas were pure fiction. "No, not at all," he answered, "I just don't know what to do with them." – And this is still the situation today. Jonas Kristjánsson (1986)', p. v.
5. Carig Davis, 'Icelandic Sagas, Eddas and Art', *Scandinavian Review*, 71, 1, 1983, p. 18.
6. John Stanley Martin, 'Some Comments on the Perception of Heathen Religious Customs in the Sagas', *Parergon*, 6, 1973.
7. Margaret Clunies-Ross, 'The Art of Poetry and the Figure of the Poet in Egils Saga', *Parergon*, 22, 1978, p. 3.
8. Jón Jóhannesson, *A History of the Old Icelandic Commonwealth*, trans. Haraldur Bessason, University of Manitoba Press, 1974, pp. 37–40.
9. See Chapter 6, section 'The king's men'.
10. Jóhannesson, *op. cit.*, p. 38.
11. Johannes Brøndsted, *The Vikings*, Harmondsworth, 1960, p. 84.
12. T. D. Kendrick, *A History of the Vikings*, London, 1968, pp. 340–1.
13. Jones, 1986, *op. cit.*, p. 69.
14. Björn Björnsson, 'Icelandic Art of the Middle Ages', *The American Scandinavian Review*, LV, (4), 1967, p. 345.
15. Kendrick, *op. cit.*, pp. 342–3 discusses the goðorð briefly. John Kennedy, *The Goðar*, unpublished doctoral thesis, University of Sydney, Department of English, 1985, pp. 36–47.
16. P. G. Foote and D. M. Wilson, *The Viking Achievements*, London, 1984, pp. 132–5.
17. Jóhannesson, *op. cit.*, p. 118.
18. *Ibid.*, p. 121.
19. See Chapter 6, section 'The king's men'.
20. Jón Hnefill Aðalsteinsson, *Under the Cloak*, Uppsala, 1978, p. 40.
21. *The Book of Settlements*, ed. and trans. Hermann Pálsson and Paul Edwards, University of Manitoba Press, 1972, ch. 218, p. 97. The Icelandic is in Finnur Jónsson (ed.), *Landnámabók Islands*, Copenhagen, 1925, p. 112.
22. *The Book of the Settlements, op. cit.*, ch. 12, p. 22. The Icelandic text is in *Landnámabók, Íslands, op. cit.*, p. 31.
23. Brøndsted, *op. cit.*, p. 62.
24. *The Book of Settlements, op. cit.*, ch. 97, p. 52. The Icelandic text is in *Landnámabók Íslands, op. cit.*, p. 64.

25. Aðalsteinsson, *op. cit.*, p. 31, comments on the supposed presence of a substantial number of Celtic slaves brought by the settlers, who were all probably Christian.
26. *Ibid.*, p. 78.
27. *Egil's Saga*, ed. and trans. Hermann Pálsson and Paul Edwards, Harmondsworth, 1988, p. 7.
28. *Egil's Saga*, Pálsson and Edwards, *op. cit.*, p. 209. The Icelandic text is as in *Egils Saga Skallagrímssonar*, Jónsson, *op. cit.*, p. 307.
29. Kirsten Hastrup, *Culture and History in Medieval Iceland*, Oxford, 1985, pp. 136–45.
30. Foote and Wilson, *op. cit.*, pp. 154–8, discusses the Icelandic farmsteads of Thjorsardalur and Stong.
31. *Ibid.*, pp. 4–7.
32. Saxo Grammaticus, *The First Nine Books of the Danish History*, trans. Oliver Elton, ed. Frederick York Powell, Liechtenstein, 1967: York Powell's introduction catalogues the barrows referred to by Saxo, and comments upon their peculiar features, pp. lxvi–lxvii. See also Hilda Ellis Davidson, *Myths and Symbols in Pagan Europe*, Manchester, 1988, p. 127.
33. Foote and Wilson, *op. cit.*, p. 382.
34. Jóhannesson, *op. cit.*, pp. 125–8. Thorvaldr and Frederick's activities are detailed in *Thorvalds thattr ens vidforla*, see Hastrup, *op. cit.*, p. 180.
35. See Chapter 6, section 'The reign of Olaf Tryggvason'.
36. Ari the Learned, Jones, *op. cit.*, p. 148. The Icelandic text is in *Íslendingabók*, in Guðni Jónsson (ed.), *Íslendinga Sögur*, vol. I, Odds Björnssonar, 1968, p. 9.
37. Aðalsteinsson, *op. cit.*, quotes the verses of Steinunn, mother of Skaldrefr, 'Thor moved Thangbrand's ship from its place; he shook it and smashed it and struck it against the land: the ship will not after that be fit to sail, for the storm which he [Thor] is said to have made broke it to splinters', p. 39.
38. Jóhannesson, *op. cit.*, p. 130.
39. *Ibid.*, p. 128.
40. Snorri Sturluson, *Heimskringla: The Olaf Sagas*, ed. Jacqueline Simpson, trans. Samuel Laing, London, 1970, ch. XCL, p. 74.
41. See Chapter 6, section 'The king's men'.
42. Snorri Sturluson, *op. cit.*, p. 75.
43. Jóhannesson, *op. cit.*, pp. 161ff.
44. Ari the Learned, Jones, *op. cit.*, p. 149. The Icelandic text is in *Íslendingabók*, Jónsson, *op. cit.*, p. 10.
45. Aðalsteinsson, *op. cit.*, p. 74.
46. Jóhannesson, *op. cit.*, p. 131.
47. Aðalsteinsson, *op. cit.*, p. 134.
48. Hastrup, *op. cit.*, p. 184.
49. Ari the Learned, Jones, *op. cit.*, p. 150. The Icelandic text is in *Íslendingabók*, Jónsson, *op. cit.*, p. 11.
50. Ari the Learned, Jones, *op. cit.* The Icelandic text is in *Íslendingabók*, Jónsson, *op. cit.*

51. *The Story of Burnt Njál*, ed. and trans. George Webbe Dasent, London, 1911, p. 184.

52. Dag Strömbäck, *The Conversion of Iceland*, London, vol. VI, 1975, pp. 30–1.

53. Björn M. Olsen jokingly suggested that he was composing *Völuspá*!

54. Eric J. Sharpe in conversation has suggested that 'going under his cloak' is merely a figure of speech, like 'putting his thinking cap on'.

55. Aðalsteinsson, *op. cit.*, p. 123. Hilda Ellis Davidson, *Myths and Symbols in Pagan Europe*, Manchester, 1988, pp. 157–8, sympathizes with Aðalsteinsson's views, in that she concluded that: 'The answer to the problem came to Thorgeir, according to this account, when he kept silence and opened his mind to receive wisdom, following traditional practice'.

56. One obvious problem is that most of the Scandinavian sources which Aðalsteinsson cites relating this practice are later than Ari the Learned, and the practice may have gained credence through Thorgeir's use of it rather than his use deriving authority from earlier pagan uses.

57. Davis, *op. cit.*, p. 17. The mention of the Apocalypse is really quite irrelevant. The Icelanders were not (in the main) Christians, and therefore would not have been expecting the Second Coming, as they would have been quite unaware of the significance of the millennium.

58. Strömbäck, *op. cit.*, p. 36.

59. Jones, 1973, *op. cit.*, p. 287.

60. Birgit Sawyer, Peter Sawyer and Ian Wood (eds), *The Christianization of Scandinavia*, Alingsås, 1987, pp. 16–17.

61. Jóhannesson, *op. cit.*, pp. 144–8.

62. Fredrik Paasche, *Møtet mellom hedendom og kristendom i Norden*, Oslo, 1958, p. 83.

63. Foote and Wilson, *op. cit.*, p. 371.

64. 'You see,' said Naomi, 'your sister-in-law has gone back to her people and her gods; go back with her.' 'Do not urge me to go back and desert you', Ruth answered. 'Where you go, I will go, and where you stay, I will stay. Your people shall be my people, and your God my God.' *Ruth*, 1:15–17, in Godfrey Driver (ed.), *The New English Bible*, Oxford, 1970, p. 298.

65. Peter Foote, 'Secular Attitudes in Early Iceland', *MS*, 7, 1974, p. 32.

66. Hilda Roderick Ellis, *The Road to Hel*, New York, 1968, p. 3.

67. Martin, *op. cit.*, p. 49.

68. See Chapter 6, section 'Pre-Christian religion and society'.

69. Foote, *op. cit.*

70. Roland Robertson, 'The Sociology of Religion: Problems and Desiderata', *Religion*, 1, 1971, p. 116.

71. Patricia Terry (trans.), *Poems of the Elder Edda*, Philadelphia, 1990, *Völuspá*, p. 31. The Icelandic text is in Finnur Jónsson (ed.), *Saemundar-Edda*, Reykjavík, 1926, pp. 17–18.

72. Carol J. Clover, 'Icelandic Family Sagas (*Íslendinga Sögur*)', in Carol J. Clover and John Lindow (eds), *Old Norse-Icelandic Literature*, Ithaca, NY, 1985, pp. 263–71.

8 Conclusion

While the day of Pentecost was running its course they were all together in one place, when suddenly there came from the sky a noise like that of a strong driving wind, which filled the whole house where they were sitting. And there appeared to them tongues like flames of fire, dispersed among them and resting on each one. And they were filled with the Holy Spirit and began to talk in other tongues, as the Spirit gave them power of utterance.

Now there were living in Jerusalem devout Jews drawn from every nation under heaven; and at this sound the crowd gathered, all bewildered because each one heard his own language spoken. They were amazed and in their astonishment exclaimed, 'Why, they are all Galileans, are they not, these men who are speaking? How is it then that we hear them, each of us in his own native language? ...'[1]

Towards a new theory of conversion

Until the nineteenth century the study of conversion to Christianity concentrated on the triumph of the Holy Spirit, with Christianity's success in converting peoples throughout the ages being attributed to its being true. Converts were convinced by Christianity and were glad and grateful for admission to the fold. This Christian bias is evident in many studies:

the onset against deities feathered and scaly, deities adulterous and infested with vice, and on the other hand against idols of wood and stone, formed the most impressive and effective factor in Christian preaching for wide circles, circles in which all ranks in society down to the lowest classes (where indeed they were most numerous) had, owing to experience and circumstances, reached a point at which the burning denunciations of the abomination of idolatry could not fail to arrest them and bring them nearer to monotheism.[2]

Harnack acknowledged Christianity's borrowings from the culture of the Greeks, and was aware of parallels such as the portrayal of Jesus as a physician, which would be comprehensible to those who were familiar with Aesculapius, but he never engaged fully with the idea that these cultural factors may have influenced people in their adoption of the new faith.[3]

The twentieth century saw the development theories of conversion which were based on the insights of William James' *The Varieties of Religious Experience*. Pioneering scholars such as Arthur Darby Nock and A. C. Underwood analysed the conversion experience, and argued that conversion was an individual and interior phenomenon. Nock's famous definition of conversion: 'the reorientation of the soul of an individual, his deliberate turning from indifference or from an earlier form of piety to another, a turning which implies a consciousness that a great change is involved, that the old was wrong and the new is right',[4] influenced a generation of scholars of conversion. The presuppositions they held were that the consciousness of the individual was the arena in which conversion occurred, and that valuable data could be collected if religious people were able to speak for themselves, as what they have to say 'is worth taking seriously, particularly in respect of ... "religious experiences" – conversion, prayer, experience of the transcendent, and so on'.[5]

Conservative Christian theories of conversion combined the interior approach with the conviction that Christianity was true to produce an extremely narrow definition of conversion as individual, interior and cognitive.[6] However, a survey of the history of Christianity reveals that these theories cannot be applied to group or national conversions. If these theories are correct, the only possible conclusion is that these conversions were inauthentic or never actually happened.

In response to this realization twentieth-century scholarly theories of conversion developed along broadly sociological and anthropological lines. The process was often referred to as 'Christianization', 'religious transition', or 'acceptance of baptism', all terms which are less emotionally charged than 'conversion'. The emphasis was on factors which were relevant to the culture of the society in question.[7] Important work by J. W. Pickett, Robin Horton, and Garry Trompf (among others) convincingly linked Christian missionary activity with the expansion of political entities and culture which were macrocosmic, which had the effect in microcosmic mission-field cultures of dislocating previously held views of reality, and creating a climate which facilitated change.[8] Pickett emphasized the authenticity of mass movements, demonstrating that social units which preserved their identity through group conversion did not lack sincerity. Horton also stressed the importance of pre-existing intellectual structures which facilitate the adoption of Christianity and the role of indigenous religious and secular leaders. Trompf contributed insights into the processes of indigenization, where the mission-field culture adapts and changes Christianity to meet its needs.

Lewis Rambo's *Understanding Religious Conversion* proposed a theory which identified seven equally important factors which will be present in any conversion, although differing in intensity and decisiveness according to the particular case. These factors are context, quest, crisis, encounter, interaction, commitment and consequences.[9] This sequential stage model is very broad and accommodating, and many of its stages resemble methodological concerns already raised in the work of other scholars. For example, Rambo's 'context' is similar to Horton's 'intellectual background' and Rambo's 'consequences' can be harmonized with Trompf's concept of 'indigenization'. Other insights have been found in the work of scholars who are not primarily involved in the development of theories of conversion. These include Michael Richter's analysis of the place of hospitality in pre-Christian Germanic society and J. T. Addison's identification of the significance of kings in the conversion of Germanic societies.[10]

The work of other scholars makes a substantial contribution to this thesis, but the model developed for the conversion of the Germanic peoples is an original construction. The model has three components. The first is an analysis of pre-Christian Germanic society, identifying social and cognitive structures which created a receptive environment for conversion, and the extent to which casual (bottom-up) contacts had brought knowledge of Christianity. The second is an examination of the encounters between agents of conversion and the kings and priests of the traditional society, focusing on the element of power and identifying the motivations for the decision to change. The third is consideration of the type of Christianity which emerges in the newly converted society, with an emphasis on the level of indigenization which occurs as a result of the preservation of the unity of the society and the development of a native clergy.

Save for James C. Russell's *The Germanization of Early Medieval Christianity*, no attempt has yet been made to apply a primarily anthropological model to the conversion of a late Roman or early medieval people, although anthropology and sociology have contributed to the understanding of medieval Germanic culture in general.[11] Also, while excellent studies of the conversion process in particular Germanic societies exist, no general survey (with the possible exception of Russell, who excludes Scandinavia and Iceland) which attempts to identify parallels and convergences across the whole range of Germanic peoples over an extended time-frame has yet been attempted.[12] The existing studies are also somewhat dated, as new material has emerged and new methodological approaches have developed since they were written.

The pattern of conversion

The processes involved may have been complex, but the conversions of the Germanic peoples followed a standard pattern: agents of mission would approach a ruler, and if he converted, his people would follow suit.

Understanding this pattern is not so easy, however; many different factors have to be taken into account.

Perhaps the most important are the tight bonds between king and people which were a common feature of German social organization. The king was maintained by a group of retainers (a *comitatus*), who in their turn were owed oaths of loyalty by their followers.[13] Information about these social ties has been traced from the first century through to the thirteenth and the evidence shows that the ethnographic context remained remarkably constant.[14] This societal context, to use Rambo's term, explains why leaders of one kind or another played an important role in almost every example of conversion considered.

Because the allegiance of the people was owed to a monarch, when a Christian king died and his heir was a believer in the old religion it was customary for a whole people to apostasize, and in binding themselves to the new king to re-commit themselves to the old gods. This process is most clearly observed in Anglo-Saxon England, and particularly in the case of Christian kings who were killed on the battlefield by non-Christian enemies. The king was the 'luck' of the people, and any sign that his new god was not as powerful as believed was taken as a motive for returning to old allegiances.[15] It is important not to think of these conversions as individual, interior decisions, however. Approaches to conversion which focus on the interior dimension of the conversion experience are simply inapplicable to the conversions examined. Case studies of the various Germanic groups indicate that this interior element was almost entirely lacking in their acceptance of Christianity. Social ties, while manifestly asymmetrical, held in both directions. Leaders had to retain (or obtain) the support of their followers, and this constrained their decisions; conversion had to be negotiated, at least with the aristocracy and warriors, and was a group action rather than an individual one.[16] Mass conversion was the norm rather than the exception, and it is easy to list the few examples of individual conversions – St Saba the Goth, Herigar of Birka, and perhaps Edwin of Northumbria.

A key element in the negotiations between missionaries and kings was access to and control of power: both supernatural and this-worldly. This is the underlying factor in the encounter between the representatives of the two world views. External political forces were influential in the decisions of rulers. The desire for support from other (Christian) rulers – whether gifts of money, imperial sanction, or armed support – was often the primary motivation for conversion. There was a close correlation between the level of political support and the degree of mission success. This process was ongoing: once a new leader adopted Christianity it was often in his interests to support further missionary activity.

Pre-existing intellectual structures did much to assist conversion, providing analogies which made the doctrines of the new religion comprehensible. Horton may have exaggerated the role of the Supreme Being in the conversion of the Yoruba, but his ideas work well in understanding the crucial importance of sacral kingship in the Germanic conversions. It must be stressed that there was no clash between systematic philosophies, between Christianity and paganism, involved in the Germanic conversions. Christianity itself was only gradually systematized, and variant forms – some of which were declared heretical fairly quickly (like Gnosticism), some of which were more or less acceptable for a long time (like Arianism), and some which were eventually incorporated into the mainstream (like Celtic Christianity) – were present. The growth in the secular power of the Papacy was far more important than the development of Christian theology. Paganism is a Christian construct:

> to start with, there was no such thing as 'paganism', as a creed. The word can be used in a negative sense only, to indicate what a man did not believe, not what he did. In fact the word pagan means simply one who lives in a village, just as the word heathen means one who dwells on a heath; that is, remote from civilisation, at a time when that had been assimilated to the Christian Church.[17]

There was significant religious variation even among the German peoples; some were in contact with Celtic and Roman religions as well as with Christianity.

Given the paucity of historical ethnographic data, the importance of bottom-up conversion and cultural diffusion of Christianity is almost impossible to assess; a full treatment would be a major work of comparative anthropology, and is outside the scope of this book. Some of the case studies present evidence that familiarity with Christianity from such low-level influences had paved the way for the later, formal conversion.

While an individualist view of conversion is not useful, the personal agency of individuals was sometimes important, but only of individuals who had personal or institutional power. St Saba was a person of small consequence in his village and therefore played no role in the spread of Christianity among the Goths.[18] Monarchs like Edwin of Northumbria, Æthelberht of Kent, Clovis of the Franks and Harald Bluetooth of Denmark were probably the only members of their societies who might be credited with a sense of individual identity: they who were descended from gods, and were the representatives of the gods on earth.

Missionaries represented a certain type of power: early on the Christian Church was allied with the continuing Roman Empire through the conversion of Emperor Constantine in 312, and later the Church represented the interests of European monarchs such as Clovis and Charlemagne, who allied the process of Christianization with territorial imperatives. Other agents of conversion (such as Christian queens) also influenced decision-making processes. The textual accounts of the conversions are not always reliable, but it cannot be doubted that the presence of a well-connected royal woman who was a Christian, such as Clotild in Frankia or Bertha in Kent, was a powerful image of the high status of Christianity in European culture.

The contextualization of Christianity

The quotation from *The Acts of the Apostles* at the beginning of this chapter suggests a model of evangelism where the sender and the receptor of the message understand each other perfectly. The possibility that the message may be altered by imperfect understanding, whether due to simple translation from one language to another or to differing cultural pre-suppositions, is not acknowledged. Little is known about the problems of language barriers — Augustine's lack of knowledge of Old English is the most notable instance — but problems of cross-cultural communication are evident.[19]

The Christianity which resulted from the conversion of the German peoples was a broadly syncretistic fusion of pre-Christian and Christian ideas. There were several reasons for this. The conversions were not motivated by theological conviction, and nuances of doctrine were unknown. The very cultural parallels which had assisted adoption of Christian ideas also assisted incorporation of pre-Christian ideas into Christianity. Missionaries, in their desire to present Christianity in a form acceptable to the mission-field culture, often consciously modified it. On occasion it was even stated policy that everything that was acceptable in the old religion should be retained in the transition to Christianity. Pope Gregory wrote to Abbot Mellitus in 601:

> However, when Almighty God has brought you to our most reverend brother Bishop Augustine, tell him what I have decided after long deliberation about the English people, namely that the idol temples of that race should by no means be destroyed, but only the idols in them. Take holy water and sprinkle it in these shrines, build altars and place relics in them. For if the shrines are well built, it is essential that they should be changed from the worship of devils to the service of the true God. When the people see that their shrines are not destroyed they will be able to banish error from their hearts and be more ready to come to the places they are familiar with, but now recognizing and worshipping the true God. And because they are in the habit of slaughtering much cattle as sacrifices to devils, some solemnity ought to be given them in exchange for this. So on the day of the dedication or the festivals of the holy martyrs, whose relics are deposited there, let them make themselves huts from the branches of trees around the churches which have been converted out of

shrines, and let them celebrate the solemnity with religious feasts. Do not let them sacrifice animals to the devil, but let them slaughter animals for their own food to the praise of God, and let them give thanks to the Giver of all things for his bountiful provision. Thus while some outward rejoicings are preserved, they will be able more easily to share in inward rejoicings. It is doubtless impossible to cut out everything at once from their stubborn minds: just as the man who is attempting to climb to the highest place, rises by steps and degrees and not by leaps.[20]

Such a programme ensured that the Christianity which took root in Anglo-Saxon England was distinctively Germanic in character, as was the case in all the Germanic conversions. Doubtless Pope Gregory did not intend that the doctrines of the two religions become intermingled, only that the externals be utilized to facilitate a smooth transition. Form and content are not so easily separable, however, and form sometimes determines content.

Another factor which encouraged syncretism was that Christianity often entered at the top level of the social pyramid, and then seeped downwards. Those who lived in remote places and were socially insignificant were able to preserve their old beliefs for a long time. Finally, it is a common phenomenon that after the destruction of high-level beliefs, there are low-level survivals which continue in the form of folk-beliefs.[21]

The research for this book began, at least partly, with the conviction that the 'king converts and the people follow' model was crude and inadequate and failed to account for the nuances in late antique and early medieval mass conversions. At the conclusion of the study it remains to be said that this model, when applied judiciously and in the light of crucial religio-political factors, is extraordinarily illuminating. The conversion of the Germanic peoples was effected through the institution of kingship, not understood primarily as a governmental institution, but as a sacral office in which the king was the channel of power for the gods.

Notes

1. *New English Bible*, Godfrey Driver (ed.), Cambridge, 1970, *Acts* 2:1–9, p. 148. The Greek text is in *The Greek New Testament*, ed. Kurt Aland *et al.*, London, 1966, pp. 419–20.
2. Adolf Harnack, *The Mission and Expansion of Christianity in the First Three Centuries*, Harper Torchbooks, 1962, p. 26.
3. *Ibid.*, pp. 118–19.
4. A. D. Nock, *Conversion*, Oxford, 1933, p. 7.
5. Eric J. Sharpe, *Comparative Religion*, London, 1975, p. 100.
6. F. Peter Cotterell, 'The Conversion Crux', *Missiology*, II, (2) p. 185.
7. Louis J. Luzbetak, 'Unity in Diversity: Ethnotheological Sensitivity in Cross-Cultural Evangelism', *Missiology*, IV, (2), pp. 207–15.

8. Robin Horton and Garry Trompf, as discussed in Chapter 1, section 'Anthropological Approaches to Conversion'; J. W. Pickett as discussed in Chapter 1, section 'Conversion, Christianization and Religious Change'.

9. Lewis Rambo, *Understanding Religious Conversion*, New Haven, CT, 1993, p. 17.

10. Michael Richter, 'Practical Aspects of the Conversion of the Anglo-Saxons', in Próinséas Ní Chatháin and Michael Richter (eds), *Irland und die Christenheit*, Stuttgart, 1987, p. 364; and J. T. Addison, *The Medieval Missionary*, London, 1936, p. 22.

11. James C. Russell, *The Germanization of Early Medieval Christianity*, London, 1944. See also Kirsten Hastrup, *Culture and History in Medieval Iceland*, Oxford, 1985, and Jesse Byock, *Medieval Iceland*, Berkeley, CA, 1988, which are examples of an anthropological approach to medieval societies.

12. For example, Dag Strömbäck's *The Conversion of Iceland*, London, 1975, and Henry Mayr-Harting's *The Coming of Christianity to Anglo-Saxon England*, London, 1972.

13. For example, Tacitus, *The Agricola and the Germania*, ed. and trans. H. Mattingly, Harmondsworth, 1970, p. 113.

14. This material is in chapters 2 to 7. See E. A. Thompson, *The Early Germans*, Oxford, 1965, Dorothy Whitelock, *The Beginnings of English Society*, Harmondsworth, 1952, and Peter Foote and David Wilson, *The Viking Achievement*, London, 1984, for further information.

15. This is discussed in Chapter 4, section 'Christianity Advances'. Bede, *The Ecclesiastical History of the English People*, ed. and trans. Bertram, Colgave and R. A. B. Mynors, Oxford, 1969, provides the source materials.

16. Jón Hnefill Aðalsteinsson, *Under the Cloak*, Uppsala, 1978.

17. Stuart Perowne, *Caesars and Saints*, London, 1962, p. 53.

18. *The Passion of Saint Saba*, in Peter Heather and John Matthews, ed. and trans., *The Goths in the Fourth Century*, Liverpool, 1991, p. 113.

19. Wulframn's failure to convert Raðbod is one example. See Chapter 5, section 'Willibrord'.

20. Bede, Colgrave and Mynors, *op. cit.*, pp. 107–9. The Latin text is on pp. 106–8.

21. Jón Hnefill Aðalsteinsson, *Under the Cloak*, Uppsala, 1978, p. 21.

Bibliography

Primary sources

Adam of Bremen, *History of the Archbishops of Hamburg-Bremen*, ed. and trans. Francis J. Tschan, New York, 1959.

Adam of Bremen, *Gesta Hammaburgensis*, in *MGH:SRG*, ed. Bernhard Schmeidler, Hannover, 1917.

Adamnan, *Life of Columba*, ed. Alan Orr Anderson and Marjorie Ogilvie Anderson, Edinburgh, 1961.

Kurt Aland *et al.* (eds), *The Greek New Testament*, London, 1966.

Alcuin, *Alcuini Epistolae*, ed. E. Dummler, *MGH:SRM*, Ep. Sel. Karolini Aevi, II.

Alcuin, *Life of Saint Willibrord*, in C. H. Talbot (ed. and trans), *The Anglo-Saxon Missionaries in Germany*, New York, 1954.

Alcuin, *Vita Willibrordi*, in *MGH:SRM*, ed. Bruno Krusch and Wilhelm Levison, tom. VII, par. I, Hannover, 1919.

Alexander, M. (ed.), *The Earliest Anglo-Saxon Poems*, Harmondsworth, 1966.

Ammianus Marcellinus, *Histories*, ed. and trans. John C. Rolfe, London, 1939.

Anon., *The Anglo-Saxon Chronicle*, ed. and trans. G. N. Garmonsway, London, 1972.

Anon., *The Book of Settlements*, ed. and trans. Hermann Pálsson and Paul Edwards, University of Manitoba Press, 1972.

Anon., *Egil's Saga*, ed. and trans. Hermann Pálsson and Paul Edwards, Harmondsworth, 1988.

Anon., *Egils Saga Skallagrímssonar*, ed. Finnur Jónsson, Halle, 1924.

Anon., *The Elder Edda*, ed. and trans. Paul B. Taylor and W. H. Auden, London, 1969.

Anon., *The Gospel of Nicodemus*, ed. H. C. Kim, Toronto, 1973.

Anon., *Hallfreðar Saga*, ed. Bjarni Einarsson, Reykjavík, 1977.

Anon., *The Heliand*, ed. and trans. by G. Ronald Murphy, Oxford University Press, 1992.

Anon., *Landnámabók Íslands*, ed. Finnur Jónsson, København, 1925.

Anon., *Laxdaela Saga*, ed. and trans. Magnus Magnusson and Hermann Pálsson, Harmondsworth, 1969.

Anon., *Laxdaela Saga*, in Guðni Jónsson (ed.), *Íslendinga Sögur*, vol. IV, Odds Björnssonar, 1968.

Anon., *Liber Historiae Francorum*, ed. and trans. Bernard S. Bachrach, Coronado Press, 1973.

Anon., *Poems of the Elder Edda*, trans. Patricia Terry, Philadelphia, 1990.

Anon., *Saemundar-Edda*, ed. Finnur Jónsson, Reykjavík, 1926.

Anon., *The Story of Burnt Njál*, ed. and trans. George Webbe Dasent, London, 1911.

Anon., *Vita Caesarii*, in *MGH:SRM*, ed. Bruno Krusch, tom. III, Hannover, 1896.

Anon., *Vita Vulframni*, in *MGH:SRM*, ed. Bruno Krusch and Wilhelm Levison, tom. V, Hannover, 1910.

Apuleius, *The Golden Ass*, ed. and trans. Robert Graves, Harmondsworth, 1951.

Apuleius, *The Golden Ass*, ed. and trans. W. Adlington, revised S. Gaselee, London, 1965.

Ari the Learned, *Íslendingabók*, in Guðni Jónsson (ed.), *Íslendinga Sögur*, vol. I, Odds Björnssonar, 1968.

Ari the Learned, *The Book of the Icelanders*, ed. and trans. Gwyn Jones, in *The Norse Atlantic Saga*, Oxford, 1986.

Augustine, *Confessions*, ed. and trans. R. S. Pine-Coffin, Harmondsworth, 1961.

Avitus of Vienne, *Epistolae*, in *MGH:AA*, ed. Rudolfus Peiper, tom. VI, Berlin, 1883.

Bede, *The Ecclesiastical History of the English People*, ed. and trans. Bertram Colgrave and R. A. B. Mynors, Oxford, 1969.

Bede, *A History of the English Church and People*, ed. and trans. Leo Sherley-Price, Harmondsworth, 1975.

Boniface, *The Letters of Saint Boniface*, ed. and trans. Ephraim Emerton, New York, 1940.

Boniface, *Epistolae*, in *MGH:E*, ed. E. Dummler, tom. I, Berlin, 1957, pp. 215–433.

Caesarius of Arles, *Sermons*, ed. and trans. Sr Mary Magdaleine Muller, New York, 1956.

Coleman-Norton, P. (ed.), *Roman State and Christian Church: A Collection of Legal Documents to A.D. 535*, 3 vols, London, 1966.

Columbanus, *Sancti Columbani Opera*, ed. and trans. G. S. M. Walker, Dublin, 1970.

Constantius of Lyons, *The Life of Saint Germanus*, in F. H. Hoare, ed. and trans., *The Western Fathers*, London, 1954.

Constantius, *Vita Germani Episcopi*, in *MGH:SRM*, ed. B. Krusch and W. Levison, tom. VII, par. I, Hannover, 1919.

Delehaye, Hippolyte (ed.), *Passio S. Sabae Gothi*, in AB, XXXI, 1912, pp. 216–24.

Driver, Godfrey (ed.), *New English Bible*, Cambridge, 1970.

Eddi, *Life of Wilfrid*, trans. J. F. Webb in D. H. Farmer (ed.), *The Age of Bede*, Harmondsworth, 1983.

Eddius Stephanus, *Vita Wilfridi*, in *MGH:SRM*, ed. B. Krusch and W. Levison, tom. VI, Hannover, 1913.

Eigil, *Life of Saint Sturm*, in C. H. Talbot (ed. and trans.), *The Anglo-Saxon Missionaries in Germany*, New York, 1954.

Eigil, *Vita S. Sturmii*, in J.-P. Migne (ed.), *PL*, tom. 105, Turnholt, n.d.

Einhard the Frank, *Life of Charlemagne.*, ed. and trans. Lewis Thorpe, London, 1970.

Einhard, *Vita Karoli Magni*, ed. G. H. Pertz and G. Waitz, *MGH:SRG*, Hannover, 1911.

Eugippius, *Life of Saint Severin*, ed. and trans. Ludwig Bieler and Ludmilla Krestan, Washington, 1965.

Eusebius, *The Ecclesiastical History*, ed. H. J. Lawlor, trans. J. E. L. Oulton, vol. II, London, 1938.

Evagrius, *History of the Church*, ed. and trans. anon, London, 1864.

Farmer, D. H. (ed.), *The Age of Bede*, Harmondsworth, 1983.

Fredegar, *The Fourth Book of the Chronicle of Fredegar with its continuations*, ed. and trans. J. M. Wallace-Hadrill, London, 1960.

Gildas, *The Ruin of Britain and Other Works*, ed. and trans. Michael Winterbottom, Phillimore, 1978.

Gordon, R. K. (ed.), *Anglo-Saxon Poetry*, London, 1977.

Gregory the Great, *The Book of Pastoral Rule and Selected Epistles*, trans. Rev. James Barmby, NP-NF, vol. XII, Grand Rapids, 1979.

Gregory the Great, *Opera Omnia*, in J.-P. Migne (ed.), *PL*, tom. LXXVII, Paris, 1896, pp. 931–2.

Gregory the Great, *Selected Epistles*, trans. Rev. James Barmby, NP-NF, vol. XIII, Grand Rapids, 1979.

Gregory of Tours, *The History of the Franks*, ed. and trans. Lewis Thorpe, Harmondsworth, 1974.

Gregory of Tours, *Libri Historiarum*, in *MGH:SRM*, ed. Bruno Krusch, tom. I, par. I, fasc. I, Hannover, 1937.

Gregory of Tours, *Lives of the Fathers*, ed. and trans. Edward James, Liverpool, 1985.

Heather, P. and Matthews, J. (eds), *The Goths in the Fourth Century*, Liverpool, 1991.

Herodotus, *The Histories*, ed. and trans. Aubrey de Selincourt, Harmondsworth, 1954.

Hillgarth, J. N. (ed.), *The Conversion of Western Europe 350–750*, Englewood Cliffs, NJ, 1968.

Hillgarth, J. N. (ed.), *Christianity and Paganism 350–750*, University of Pennsylvania Press, 1986.

Hoare, F. H. (ed. and trans.), *The Western Fathers*, London, 1954.

Hydatius, *The Chronicle of Hydatius and the Consularia Constantinopolitana*, ed. and trans. R. W. Burgess, Oxford, 1993.

Isidore of Seville, *History of the Kings of the Goths, Vandals and Suevi*, ed. and trans. Guido Donini and Gordon B. Ford Jnr., Leiden, 1966.

Isidore of Seville, *Historia Gothorum*, in *MGH:AA*, ed. Theodore Mommsen, tom. XI, vol. II, Berlin, 1894.

Jonas, *Life of Saint Columban*, ed. and trans. Dana Carleton Munro, Philadelphia, 1895.

Jonas, *Vita Columbani*, in *MGH:SRM*, ed. Bruno Krusch, tom. IV, Hannover, 1902.

Jones, Alexander (ed.), *The Jerusalem Bible*, London, 1968.

Jordanes, *The Gothic History of Jordanes*, ed. and trans. Charles Christopher Mierow, Cambridge, 1915.

Jordanes, *Getica*, in *MGH:AA*, ed. Theodore Mommsen, tom. V, Berlin, 1882.

Lactantius, *The Minor Works*, ed. and trans. Sr Mary Francis McDonald, Washington, 1965.

Levine, James, ed. and trans., *France Before Charlemagne: A Translation from the Grandes Chroniques*, Studies in French Civilization, vol. 3, Lampeter, 1990.

Lucan, *Pharsalia*, ed. and trans. J. D. Duff, London, 1969.

Martin of Braga, 'On the Castigation of Rustics', in J. N. Hillgarth (ed.), *Christianity and Paganism 350–750*, University of Pennsylvania Press, 1986.

Nennius, *British History and the Welsh Annals*, ed. and trans. John Morris, Phillimore, 1980.

Nicetius of Trier, *Epistolae Duae*, in J.-P. Migne (ed.), *PL*, tom. 68, Turnholt, n.d.

Origen, *Against Celsus*, ed. and trans. H. Chadwick, Cambridge, 1953.

Patrick, *St. Patrick*, ed. and trans. A. B. E. Hood, Phillimore and Co. Ltd., 1978.

Paulinus of Pella, 'Thanksgiving', in Ausonius, *Works*, ed. and trans. H. G. Evelyn White, London, 1921, pp. 295–351.

Philostorgios, *The Ecclesiastical History of Sozomen and the Ecclesiastical History of Philostorgios*, ed. and trans. Edward Walford, London, 1855.

Plato, *The Republic*, ed. and trans. Desmond Lee, Harmondsworth, 1974.

Pliny the Younger, *The Letters of the Younger Pliny*, ed. and trans. Betty Radice, Harmondsworth, 1963.

Pliny the Younger, *Selected Letters*, ed. Elmer Truesdell Merrill, London, 1903.

Plummer, C., and Earle, J. (eds), *Two of the Saxon Chronicles Parallel*, 2 vols, Oxford, 1972.

Procopius, *Gothic War*, in *History of the Wars*, ed. and trans. H. B. Dewing, London, 1928, vol. V.

Propertius, *The Poems of Propertius*, ed. and trans. A. E. Watts, Harmondsworth, 1961.

Propertius, *The Elegies of Sextus Propertius*, ed. and trans. G. P. Goold, London, 1990.

Rimbert, *Anskar Apostle of the North*, ed. and trans. Charles H. Robinson, London, 1921.

Rimbert, *Vita S. Anskarii, MGH:S*, ed. G. H. Pertz, tom. II, Hannover, 1829.

Saxo Grammaticus, *The First Nine Books of the Danish History*, trans. Oliver Elton, ed. Frederick York Powell, Liechtenstein, 1967.

Saxo Grammaticus, *The History of the Danes*, ed. H. Ellis Davidson and trans. Peter Fisher, Cambridge, 1979.

Sidonius Apollinaris, *Poems and Letters*, 2 vols, ed. and trans. W. B. Andersen, London, 1965.

Socrates Scholasticus, *The Ecclesiastical History of Socrates*, ed. and trans. unknown, London, 1880.

Socrates Scholasticus, *Ecclesiastical History*, ed. William Bright, Oxford, 1893.

Sozomen, *Ecclesiastical History*, ed. and trans. Edward Walford, London, 1855.

Sozomen, *Kirchengeschichte*, ed. Joseph Bidez, Berlin, 1960.

Sturluson, Snorri, *Edda*, ed. and trans. Anthony Faulkes, London, 1987.

Sturluson, Snorri, *Heimskringla*, ed. B. S. Kristjánsdóttir *et al.*, vol. 1, Reykjavík, 1991.

Sturluson, Snorri, *Heimskringla*, ed. Erling Monsem, trans A. H. Smith, Cambridge, 1932.

Sturluson, Snorri, *Heimskringla: The Olaf Sagas*, ed. Jacqueline Simpson, trans. Samuel Laing, London, 1970, ch. XCL.

Sulpicius Severus, *The Life of Saint Martin*, in F. H. Hoare, ed. and trans., *The Western Fathers*, London, 1954.

Tacitus, *The Agricola and the Germania*, ed. and trans. H. Mattingly, Harmondsworth, 1970.

Tacitus, *Agricola and Germania*, ed. H. M. Stephenson, Cambridge, 1894.

Tacitus, *The Dialogues of Publius Cornelius Tactitus*, ed. and trans. William Peterson, London, 1932.

Tacitus, *Germania, Agricola, and First Book of the Annals*, ed. and trans. William Smith, London, 1840.

Talbot, C. H. (ed.), *The Anglo-Saxon Missionaries in Germany*, New York, 1954.

Tertullian, *Adversus Judaeos*, in A. W. Haddan and W. Stubbs (eds), *Councils and Ecclesiastical Documents Relating to Britain and Ireland*, vol. 1, Oxford, 1869, p. 3.

Theodoret, *History of the Church from AD 322 to AD 427*, ed. and trans. unknown, London, 1864.

Victor of Vita, *History of the Vandal Persecution*, ed. and trans. John Moorhead, Liverpool University Press, 1992.

Willibald, *Life of Saint Boniface*, in C. H. Talbot (ed. and trans.), *The Anglo-Saxon Missionaries in Germany*, New York, 1954.

Willibald, *Vita S. Bonifatii, MGH:S*, ed. G. H. Pertz, tom. II, Hannover, 1829.

Secondary sources

Aberg, Nils, *The Anglo-Saxons in England*, Uppsala, 1926.

Abrams, Lesley, 'The Anglo-Saxons and the Christianization of Scandinavia', *A-SE*, 24, pp. 213-49.

Abrams, Philip, 'Sociology and History', *P&P*, 52, August 1971, pp. 118–26.

Abrams, Philip, 'History, Sociology, Historical Sociology', *P&P*, 89, May 1980, pp. 3–17.

Adalsteinsson, Jón Hnefill, *Under the Cloak*, Uppsala, 1978.

Addison, James Thayer, *The Medieval Missionary*, London, 1936.

af Edholm, Erik, 'Ideology and Social Reality', *Temenos*, 13, 1977, pp. 43-55.

Alcock, Leslie, *Arthur's Britain*, Harmondsworth, 1971.

Alföldi, Andrew, *The Conversion of Constantine and Pagan Rome*, Oxford, 1948.

Allardt, Erik, 'Approaches to the Sociology of Religion', *Temenos*, 6, 1970, pp. 9-19.

Almond, Philip, *Mystical Experience and Religious Doctrine*, Berlin, 1982.

Alroe, Michael, 'A Pygmalion Complex Among Missionaries: the Catholic Case in the Kimberley', in T. Swain and D. Rose (eds), *Aboriginal Australians and Christian Missions*, AASR, 1988, pp. 30–44.

Anderson, Perry, *Passages from Antiquity to Feudalism*, London, 1974.

Anderson, Theodore, 'The Conversion of Norway according to Oddr Snorrason and Snorri Sturluson', *MS*, 10, 1977, pp. 83–95.

Anderson, Theodore, 'Heathen Sacrifice in *Beowulf* and Rimbert's *Life of Ansgar*', *M&H*, n.s. 13, 1985, pp. 65–74.

Audin, Pierre, 'Césaire d'Arles et le Maintien de Pratiques Païennes Dans la Provence du VIe Siècle', in *La Patrie Gauloise d'Agrippa au VIème Siècle*, Lyon, 1983, pp. 327–40.

Auerbach, Erich, *Mimesis*, trans. Willard R. Trask, Princeton, NJ, 1953.

Auerbach, Erich, *Literary Language and its Public in Late Latin Antiquity and in the Middle Ages*, trans. Ralph Manheim, London, 1965.

Barlau, Stephen, 'An Outline of Germanic Kinship', *JIS*, 4, 1976, pp. 97–130.

Barley, M. W. and Hanson, R. (eds), *Christianity in Britain 300–700*, Leicester, 1968.

Barnes, Geraldine, 'The medieval Anglophile: England and its rulers in Old Norse history and saga', *Parergon*, n.s. 10, (2) pp. 11–26.

Barnes, T. D., *Constantine and Eusebius*, Cambridge, MA, 1981.

Barnes, T. D., *Early Christianity and the Roman Empire*, Variorum Reprints, London, 1984.

Barnes, T. D., 'Emperor and Bishops, A.D. 324–344: Some Problems', in T. D. Barnes, *Early Christianity and the Roman Empire*, Variorum Reprints, London, 1984, XVIII.

Barnes, T. D., 'Lactantius and Constantine', in T. D. Barnes, *Early Christianity and the Roman Empire*, Variorum Reprints, London, 1984, VI.

Barraclough, Geoffrey, *The Medieval Papacy*, London, 1968.

Bartlett, Robert, 'The Conversion of a Pagan Society in the Middle Ages', *History*, 70, (229), 1985, pp. 185–201.

Bauschatz, Paul, *The Well and the Tree*, Amherst, 1982.

Bayly, Susan, *Saints, Goddesses and Kings*, Cambridge, 1989.

Baynes, Norman H., *Constantine the Great and the Christian Church*, London, 1931.

Bellah, Robert, *Beyond Belief*, New York, 1970.

Berger, Peter L., *The Sacred Canopy*, New York, 1967.

Bieler, Ludwig, 'The Christianization of the Insular Celts during the Sub-Roman Period and its Repercussions on the Continent', *Celtica*, 8, 1968, pp. 112–25.

Bieler, Ludwig, 'The Mission of Palladius: A Comparative Study of Sources', *Traditio*, 6, 1948, pp. 1–32.

Birkeli, Fridjov, 'The Earliest Missionary Activities from England to Norway', *NMS*, 16, 1972, pp. 27–37.

Björnsson, Björn, 'Icelandic Art of the Middle Ages', *The American Scandinavian Review*, LV, (4), December 1967, pp. 345–59.

Blair, John, 'Minster Churches in the Landscape', in Della Hooke (ed.), *Anglo-Saxon Settlements*, Oxford, 1988, pp. 35–58.

Bloch, Marc, *Feudal Society*, trans. L. A. Manyon, London, 1961.

Bloomfield, Morton W., 'Beowulf, Byrtnoth and the Judgement of God: Trial by Combat in Anglo-Saxon England', *Speculum*, XLIV, (4), October 1969, pp. 545–59.

Blount, Ben G. (ed.), *Language, Culture and Society*, Cambridge, MA, 1974.

Bonner, Gerald, *Famulus Christi*, London, 1976.

Bosch, David J., 'Crosscurrents in Modern Mission', *Missionalia*, 4, (2), August 1976, pp. 54–84.

Bossy, John, 'Some Elementary Forms of Durkheim', *P&P*, 95, 1982, pp. 3–19.

Bradley, Henry, *The Goths*, London, 1888.

Branston, Brian, *Gods of the North*, London, 1955.

Branston, Brian, *The Lost Gods of England*, London, 1957.

Braswell, Bruce K., 'The *Dream of the Rood* and Aldhelm on Sacred Prosopopoeia', *Medieval Studies*, 40, 1978, pp. 461–7.

Brøgger, Jan, 'Socio-Economic Structures and the Form of Religion', *Temenos*, 13, 1977, pp. 7–30.

Brøndsted, Johannes, *The Vikings*, Harmondsworth, 1960.

Brooke, Christopher, 'The Cathedral in Medieval Society', in Wim Swaan, *The Gothic Cathedral*, Paul Elek, 1969, pp. 13–22.

Brown, Peter, 'Religious Dissent in the Later Roman Empire: The Case of North Africa', *History*, 46, 1961, pp. 83–101.

Brown, Peter, 'Religious Coercion in the Later Roman Empire: The Case of North Africa', *History*, 48, 1963, pp. 283–305.

Brown, Peter, 'The Diffusion of Manichaeism in the Roman Empire', in P. Brown, *Religion and Society in the Age of Saint Augustine*, Harper and Row, 1972, pp. 94–118.

Brown, Peter, 'The Later Roman Empire', in Peter Brown, *Religion and Society in the Age of Saint Augustine*, Harper and Row, 1972, pp. 46–73.

Brown, Peter, 'The Patrons of Pelagius: The Roman Aristocracy between East and West', in P. Brown, *Religion and Society in the Age of Saint Augustine*, Harper and Row, 1972, pp. 208–26.

Brown, Peter, 'Pelagius and his Supporters: Aims and Environment', in P. Brown, *Religion and Society in the Age of Saint Augustine*, Harper and Row, 1972, pp. 183–207.

Brown, Peter, *Religion and Society in the Age of Saint Augustine*, Harper and Row, 1972.

Brown, Peter, 'The Religious Crisis of the Third Century AD', in Peter Brown (ed.), *Religion and Society in the Age of Saint Augustine*, Harper and Row, 1972, pp. 74–93.

Brown, Peter, *Relics and Social Status in the Age of Gregory of Tours*, Reading, 1977.

Brown, Peter, 'Gibbon's Views', in P. Brown, *Society and the Holy in Late Antiquity*, University of California Press, 1982, pp. 22–48.

Brown, Peter, 'The Last Pagan Emperor: Robert Browning's The Emperor Julian', in P. Brown, *Society and the Holy in Late Antiquity*, University of California Press, 1982, pp. 83–102.

Brown, Peter, *Society and the Holy in Late Antiquity*, University of California Press, 1982.

Browne, G. F., *The Conversion of the Heptarchy*, London, 1896.

Browne, G. F., *The Church in These Islands Before Augustine*, London, 1899.

Bruce, F. F., *The Spreading Flame*, The Paternoster Press, 1958.

Bruce, Steve, 'Born Again: Conversion, Crusades and Brainwashing', *The Scottish Journal of Religious Studies*, III, (2), pp. 107–21.

Bruce-Mitford, R., *The Sutton Hoo Ship Burial: A Handbook*, London, 1972.

Buchholz, Peter, 'The Religious Geography of Pagan Scandinavia: A New Research Project', *MS*, 5, 1972, pp. 89–91.

Bulliet, Richard, *Conversion to Islam in the Medieval Period*, London, 1979.

Bullough, D. A., 'Early Medieval Social Groupings: the Terminology of Kinship', *P&P*, 45, November 1969, pp. 3–19.

Burch, Vacher, *Myth and Constantine the Great*, Oxford University Press, 1927.

Burckhardt, Jacob, *The Age of Constantine the Great*, New York, 1949.

Byock, Jesse, *Medieval Iceland*, Berkeley, CA, 1988.

Campbell, James, 'Bede I', in J. Campbell, *Essays in Anglo-Saxon History*, London, 1986, pp. 1–28.

Campbell, James, 'Bede II', in J. Campbell, *Essays in Anglo-Saxon History*, London, 1986, pp. 29–48.

Campbell, James, 'The Church in Anglo-Saxon Towns', in J. Campbell, *Essays in Anglo-Saxon History*, London, 1986, pp. 139–54.

Campbell, James, *Essays in Anglo-Saxon History*, London, 1986.

Campbell, James, 'The First Century of Christianity in England', in J. Campbell, *Essays in Anglo-Saxon History*, London, 1986, pp. 49–68.

Campbell, James, 'Observations on the Conversion of England', in J. Campbell, *Essays in Anglo-Saxon History*, London, 1986, pp. 69–84.

Campbell, J., John, E. and Wormald, P., *The Anglo-Saxons*, Phaidon Press, 1982.

Chadwick, Henry, 'The Circle and the Ellipse: Rival Concepts of Authority in the Early Church', in H. Chadwick, *History and Thought of the Early Church*, Variorum Reprints, London, 1982, pp. 3–17.

Chadwick, N. K., *Poetry and Letters in Early Christian Gaul*, London, 1955.

Chadwick, N. K. (ed.), *Celt and Saxon*, Cambridge, 1964.

Chadwick, N. K., 'The Conversion of Northumbria: A Comparison of Sources', in N. K. Chadwick (ed.), *Celt and Saxon*, Cambridge, 1964, pp. 138–66.

Chaney, William A., 'Paganism to Christianity in Anglo-Saxon England', *Harvard Theological Review*, LIII, 1960, pp. 197–217.

Chaney, William A., 'Paganism to Christianity in Anglo-Saxon England', in Sylvia L. Thrupp (ed.), *Early Medieval Society*, New York, 1967, pp. 67–83.

Chaney, William A., *The Cult of Kingship in Anglo-Saxon England*, Manchester, 1970.

Cherniss, Michael, 'The Cross as Christ's Weapon: the Influence of Heroic Literary Tradition on *The Dream of the Rood*', *A-SE*, 2, pp. 241–52.

Chesnut, Glenn F., *The First Christian Histories*, Paris, 1977.

Chevallier, Raymond, 'Des Dieux Gaulois et Gallo-Romains aux Saints du Christianisme. Recherches sur la Christianisation des Cultes de la Gaule', in *La Patrie Gauloise d'Agrippa au VIème Siècle*, Lyon, 1983, pp. 283–326.

Chroust, A.-H., 'A Note on the Persecutions of the Christians in the Early Roman Empire', *Classica et Medievalia*, XXVIII, 1967, pp. 321–9.

Clarke, H. B. and Brennan, Mary (eds), *Columbanus and Merovingian Monasticism*, BAR International Series 113, 1981.

Clover, Carol J., 'Icelandic Family Sagas (*Íslendinga Sögur*)', in Carol J. Clover and John Lindow (eds), *Old Norse-Icelandic Literature*, Ithaca, NY, 1985, pp. 239–315.

Clover, Carol J., and Lindow, John, (eds), *Old Norse-Icelandic Literature*, Ithaca, NY, 1985, pp. 239–315.

Clunies-Ross, M., 'A Suggested Interpretation of the Scene Depicted on the Right-Hand side of the Franks Casket', *Medieval Archaeology*, 14, 1970, pp. 148–52.

Clunies-Ross, M., 'The Art of Poetry and the Figure of the Poet in *Egils Saga*', *Parergon*, 22, December 1978, pp. 3–12.

Clunies-Ross, M., 'Concubinage in Anglo-Saxon England', *P&P*, 108, August 1985, pp. 3–35.

Cooke, J. D., 'Euhemerism: A Medieval Interpretation of Classical Paganism', *Speculum*, II, (4), October 1927, pp. 396–410.

Cooper, Kate, 'Insinuations of Womanly Influence: An Aspect of the Christianization of the Roman Aristocracy', *The Journal of Roman Studies*, LXXXII, 1992, pp. 150–64.

Cotterell, F. Peter, 'The Conversion Crux', *Missiology*, II, (2), April 1974, pp. 183–9.

Cowdrey, H. E. J., 'Bede and the 'English People', *JRH*, 11, (4), pp. 501–23.

Cramp, Rosemary J., '*Beowulf* and Archaeology', *Medieval Archaeology*, 1, 1957, pp. 57–77.

Crawford, S. J., *Anglo-Saxon Influence on Western Christendom 600–800*, Cambridge, 1933.

Cross, J. E., *The Literate Anglo-Saxon – On Sources and Disseminations*, Oxford, 1972.

Daly, William M., 'Caesarius of Arles, A Precursor of Medieval Christendom', *Traditio*, XXVI, 1970, pp. 1–28.

Daly, William M., 'Clovis: How Barbaric, How Pagan?', *Speculum*, 69, (3), 1994, pp. 619–64.

Dando, Marcel, 'The *Moralia in Job* of Gregory the Great as a Source for the Old Saxon *Genesis B*', *Classica et Medievalia*, XXX, 1969, pp. 420–39.

Davis, Craig, 'Icelandic Sagas, Eddas, and Art', *Scandinavian Review*, 71, (1), 1983, pp. 16–24.

Dawson, Christopher, *Religion and the Rise of Western Culture*, London, 1950.

Dawson, Christopher, *Medieval Essays*, London, 1953.

Dawson, Christopher, *The Making of Europe*, New York, 1956.

Deanesly, Margaret, 'Canterbury and Paris in the Reign of Æthelberht', *History*, n.s. XXVI, 1941–2, pp. 97–104.

Deanesly, Margaret, *Augustine of Canterbury*, London, 1964.

Deer, Donald S., 'The Missionary Language Learning Problem', *Missiology*, III, (1), January 1975, pp. 87–102.

Demidoff, Lene, 'The Poppo Legend', *MS*, 6, 1973, pp. 39–67.

Dierks, Friedrich, 'Communication and World View', *Missionalia*, II, (2), August 1983, pp. 43–56.

Dodds, E. R., *Pagan and Christian in an Age of Anxiety*, Cambridge, 1968.

Doerries, Hermann, *Constantine the Great*, trans. Roland H. Bainton, New York, 1972.

Donaldson, C., *Martin of Tours*, London, 1980.

Drake, H. A., *In Praise of Constantine*, University of California Press, 1976.

Drew, Kathryn Fisher, 'The Barbarian Kings as Lawgivers and Judges', in Robert S. Hoyt (ed.), *Life and Thought in the Early Middle Ages*, Minneapolis, 1967, pp. 7–29.

Duckett, Eleanor Shipley, *The Wandering Saints*, London, 1960.

Duckett, Eleanor Shipley, *Anglo-Saxon Saints and Scholars*, Hamden, 1967.

Dumville, David, 'Kingship, Genealogies and Regnal Lists', in Peter H. Sawyer and Ian N. Wood (eds), *Early Medieval Kingship*, Leeds, 1977, pp. 72–104.

Dumville, David, 'Sub-Roman Britain: History and Legend', *History*, 62, 1977, pp. 173–92.

Duncan, A. A. M., 'Bede, Iona and the Picts', in J. M. Wallace-Hadrill and R. H. C. Davis (eds), *The Writing of History in the Middle Ages*, Oxford, 1981, pp. 1–42.

Eadie, John W. (ed.), *The Conversion of Constantine*, Holt, Rinehart, and Winston, 1971.

Edsman, C.-M., 'Opening Address', in Tore Ahlback (ed.), *Old Norse and Finnish Religions and Cultic Place-Names*, Stockholm, 1990, pp. 9–34.

Elliott, R. V., 'Runes, Yews and Magic', *Speculum*, XXXII, (2), April 1957, pp. 250–61.

Elliott, R. V., *Runes*, Manchester, 1959.

Elliott, Thomas G., 'Constantine's Early Religious Development', *JRH*, 15, (3), pp. 283–91.

Elliott-Binns, L. E., *The Beginnings of Western Christendom*, London, 1948.

Ellis, Hilda R., *The Road to Hel*, New York, 1968.

Ellis Davidson, H., *Gods and Myths of Northern Europe*, Harmondsworth, 1964.

Ellis Davidson, Hilda, *Scandinavian Mythology*, Feltham, 1969.

Ellis Davidson, Hilda, *Myths and Symbols in Pagan Europe*, Manchester, 1988.

Esposito, Mario, 'Notes on a Latin Life of Saint Patrick', *Classica et Medievalia*, XIII, 1952, pp. 59–72.

Ettlinger, Ellen, 'The Mythological Relief of the Oseberg Wagon found in Southern Norway', *Folklore*, 87, 1976, pp. 81–8.

Farrell, R. T. (ed.), *Bede and Anglo-Saxon England*, BAR 46, 1978.

Faulkes, Anthony, 'Descent From the Gods', *MS*, 11, 1978–9, pp. 92–125.

Faulkes, Anthony, 'Pagan Sympathy: Attitudes to Heathendom in the Prologue to *Snorri Edda*', in Robert Glendinning and Haraldur Bessason (eds), *Edda*, University of Manitoba Press, 1983, pp. 283–314.

Finberg, H. P. R., *The Formation of England 550–1042*, London, 1974.

Fisher, D. J. V., *The Anglo-Saxon Age*, London, 1973.

Foote, Peter, 'Secular Attitudes in Early Iceland', *MS*, 7, 1974, pp. 31–44.

Foote, Peter G. and Wilson, David M., *The Viking Achievement*, London, 1984.

Fox, Robin Lane, *Pagans and Christians*, Harmondsworth, 1986.

Frank, Roberta, 'The Ideal of Men Dying With Their Lord in *The Battle of Maldon*: Anachronism or *Nouvelle Vague*', in I. Wood and N. Lund (eds), *Peoples and Places in Northern Europe 500–1600*, Woolbridge, 1991, pp. 95–106.

Frend, W. H. C., 'The Christianization of Roman Britain', in M. W. Barley and R. P. C. Hanson (eds), *Christianity in Britain 300–700*, Leicester, 1968, pp. 37–50.

Frend, W. H. C., 'The Missions of the Early Church 180–700', in W. H. C. Frend, *Religion Popular and Unpopular in the Early Christian Centuries*, London, 1976.

Frend, W. H. C., 'Religion and Social Change in the Late Roman Empire', in W. H. C. Frend, *Religion Popular and Unpopular in the Early Christian Centuries*, London, 1976.

Frend, W. H. C., *Religion Popular and Unpopular in the Early Christian Centuries*, London, 1976.

Frend, W. H. C., *Town and Country in the Early Christian Centuries*, London, 1980.

Frend, W. H. C., 'Town and Countryside in Early Christianity', in W. H. C. Frend, *Town and Country in the Early Christian Centuries*, London, 1980, section I, pp. 25–42.

Frend, W. H. C., 'The Winning of the Countryside', in W. H. C. Frend, *Town and Country in the Early Christian Centuries*, London, 1980, section II, pp. 1–14.

Frend, W. H. C., *The Early Church*, 2nd edn, SCM Press Ltd, 1982.

Frend, W. H. C., 'Romano-British Christianity and the West: Comparison and Contrast', in Susan M. Pearce (ed.), *The Early Church in Western Britain and Ireland*, British Archaeological Reports, British Series 102, 1982, pp. 5–16.

Frend, W. H. C., *Saints and Sinners in the Early Church*, London, 1985.

Fritz, Donald W., 'Caedmon: A Traditional Christian Poet', *Medieval Studies*, XXXI, 1969, pp. 334–7.

Frye, David, 'Aegidius, Childeric, Odovacer and Paul', *NMS*, XXXVI, 1992, pp. 1–14.

Frye, David, 'Transformation and Transition in the Merovingian Civitas', *NMS*, XXXIX, 1995, pp. 1–11.

Fuglestad, Finn, 'Earth-Priests, "Priest-Chiefs" and Sacred Kings in Ancient Norway, Iceland and West Africa: A Comparative Essay', *Scandinavian Journal of History*, 4, 1979, pp. 47–74.

Gager, John G., 'Introduction: The Dodds Hypothesis', in Robert C. Smith and John Lounibos (eds), *Pagan and Christian Anxiety*, University Press of America, 1983, pp. 1–11.

Gallyon, Margaret, *The Early Church in Wessex and Mercia*, Lavenham, 1980.

Geary, Patrick J., *Before France and Germany*, Oxford, 1988.

Gillespie, George, *A Catalogue of Persons Named in Germanic Heroic Literature 700–1600*, Oxford, 1973.

Glendinning, Robert and Bessason, Haraldur (eds), *Edda: A Collection of Essays*, University of Manitoba Press, 1983.

Goffart, Walter, *The Narrators of Barbarian History*, Princeton, NJ, 1988.

Gonda, J., 'The Sacred Character of Ancient Indian Kingship', in *The Sacral Kingship*, VIIIth International Congress for the History of Religions, supplement to Numen, Leiden, 1959, pp. 172–80.

Goodenough, Erwin R., *The Church in the Roman Empire*, New York, 1970.

Graham-Campbell, J., 'The Other Side of the Coin', *Scandinavian Review*, 68, (3), 1980, pp. 6–19.

Gransden, Antonia, *Historical Writing in England c. 550 to c. 1307*, New York, 1974.

Graves, Robert, *The Greek Myths*, 2 vols, Harmondsworth, 1955.

Green, Brian, 'Gregory's *Moralia* as an inspirational source for the Old English poem *Exodus*', *Classica et Medievalia*, XXXII, pp. 251–62.

Green, D. H., *The Carolingian Lord*, Cambridge, 1965.

Greenaway, George, 'Saint Boniface as a Man of Letters', in Timothy Reuter (ed.), *The Greatest Englishman: Essays on St. Boniface and the Church at Crediton*, Exeter, 1980, pp. 31–46.

Griggs, Charles W., *The History of Christianity in Egypt to 451 AD*, University Microfilms International, Ann Arbor, 1982.

Gurevich, Aron J., 'On Heroes, Things, Gods and Laughter in Germanic Poetry', *Studies in Medieval and Renaissance History*, V, o.s. XV, 1982, pp. 107–72.

Hald, Kristian, 'Angles and Vandals', *Classica et Medievalia*, IV, 1942, pp. 62–78.

Hanning, Robert W., '*Beowulf* as Heroic History', *M&H*, n.s., (5), 1974, pp. 77–102.

Hanson, R. P. C., 'The Mission of St Patrick', in James P. Mackey (ed.), *An Introduction to Celtic Christianity*, Edinburgh, 1989.

Harnack, Adolf, *The Mission and Expansion of Christianity in the First Three Centuries*, Harper Torchbooks, 1962.

Harrison, Kenneth, 'Woden', in Gerald Bonner (ed.), *Famulus Christi*, London, 1976.

Hassing, Per, 'Religious Change in Eleventh Century Norway', *Missiology*, III, (4), October 1975, pp. 469–85.

Hastrup, Kirsten, *Culture and History in Medieval Iceland*, Oxford, 1985.

Haugen, Einar, 'The *Edda* as Ritual: Odin and his Masks', in Robert Glendinning and Haraldur Bessason, *Edda*, University of Manitoba Press, 1983.

Heather, Peter, 'The Crossing of the Danube and the Gothic Conversion', *GRBS*, 27, (3), 1986, pp. 289–318.

Heather, Peter, *Goths and Romans 332–489*, Oxford, 1991.

Helgeland, John, 'Christians and the Roman Army AD 173–337', *CH*, 43, (2), 1974, pp. 149–63.

Helm, Karl, *Woden*, Giessen, 1946.

Hermannson, Halldor, *Icelandic Manuscripts*, Ithaca, NY, 1929.

Hesselgrave, David J., 'The Missionary of Tomorrow – Identity Crisis Extraordinary', *Missiology*, III, (2), April 1975, pp. 225–39.

Hill, Boyd H. Jr, *Medieval Monarchy in Action*, London, 1972.

Hill, John M., 'Beowulf and the Danish Succession: Gift Giving as an Occasion for Complex Gesture', *M&H*, n.s., (11), 1982, pp. 177–98.

Hill, Peter, *Whithorn II*, Whithorn Trust, 1988.

Hill, Rosalind, 'Bede and the Boors', in Gerald Bonner (ed.), *Famulus Christi*, London, 1976.

Hillgarth, J. N., 'Modes of Evangelization of Western Europe in the Seventh Century', in Próinséas Ní Chatháin and Michael Richter (eds), *Irland und die Christenheit*, Stuttgart, 1987, pp. 311–31.

Hillman, Eugene, 'Pluriformity in Ethics: A Modern Missionary Problem', *Missiology*, I, (1), January 1973, pp. 59–72.

Hills, Catherine, 'The Archaeology of Anglo-Saxon England in the Pagan Period: A Review', *A-SE*, 8, 1979, pp. 297–329.

Hodges, Richard, *Dark Age Economics: The Origins of Towns and Trade, A.D. 600–1000*, London, 1982.

Hoijer, Harry, 'The Sapir-Whorf Hypothesis', in Ben G. Blount (ed.), *Language, Culture and Society*, Cambridge, MA, 1974, pp. 120–31.

Holdsworth, C., 'Saint Boniface the Monk', in T. Reuter (ed.), *The Greatest Englishman: Essays on St. Boniface and the Church at Crediton*, Exeter, 1980, pp. 47–68.

Holm, Nils G., 'Pentecostalism: Conversion and Charismata', *International Journal for the Psychology of Religion*, I, (3), pp. 135–51.

Hooke, Della (ed.), *Anglo-Saxon Settlements*, Oxford, 1988.

Hope-Taylor, Brian, *Yeavering: An Anglo-British Centre of Early Northumbria*, Department of the Environment Archaeological Reports 7, London, 1977.

Horowitz, Sylvia, 'Beowulf, Samson, David and Christ', in *Studies in Medieval Culture*, XII, 1978, pp. 19—23.

Horton, Robin, 'African Conversion', *Africa*, 41, (2), 1971, pp. 85—108.

Horton, Robin, 'On the Rationality of Conversion Part I', *Africa*, 45, (3), 1975, pp. 219—235.

Horton, Robin, 'On the Rationality of Conversion Part II', *Africa*, 45, (4), 1975, pp. 373—99.

Hoyt, Robert S. (ed.), *Life and Thought in the Early Middle Ages*, Minneapolis, 1967.

Huelin, Gordon, *Saint Willibrord and His Society*, Westminster, 1960.

Hull, Eleanor, 'Pagan Baptism in the West', *Folklore*, XLIX, 1932, pp. 410—19.

Hunter, Michael, 'Germanic and Roman Antiquity and the Sense of the Past in Anglo-Saxon England', *A-SE*, 3, 1974, pp. 29—50.

Hunter Blair, Peter, *Roman Britain and Early England*, London, 1969.

Hunter Blair, Peter, *An Introduction to Anglo-Saxon England*, Cambridge, 1970.

Hunter Blair, Peter, *The World of Bede*, London, 1970.

Hunter Blair, Peter, 'The Letters of Pope Boniface V and the Mission of Paulinus to Northumbria', in Peter Clemoes and Kathleen Hughes (eds), *England Before the Conquest*, Cambridge, 1971, pp. 5—14.

Hunter Blair, Peter, *Anglo-Saxon Northumbria*, London, 1984.

Hvidtfeldt, Arild, 'History of Religion, Sociology and Sociology of Religion', *Temenos*, 7, 1971, pp. 75—89.

Irving, Edward J., 'The Nature of Christianity in Beowulf', *A-SE*, 13, 1984, pp. 7—21.

Jacobs, Donald and Loewen, Jacob A., 'Anthropologists and Missionaries Face to Face', *Missiology*, II, (2), April 1974, pp. 161—74.

James, Edward, *The Merovingian Archaeology of South-West Gaul*, part 1, BAR, Supplementary Series 25 (i), 1977.

James, Edward, *The Origins of France*, London, 1982.

James, Edward, *The Franks*, Oxford, 1988.

Jóhanneson, Jón, *A History of the Old Icelandic Commonwealth*, University of Manitoba Press, 1974.

John, Eric, 'The Social and Political Problems of the Early English Church', in Joan Thirsk (ed.), *Land, Church and People*, Reading, 1970, pp. 39—64.

Jolly, Karen L., 'Anglo-Saxon Charms in the Context of a Christian World View', *JMH*, 11, (4), December 1985, pp. 279—93.

Jones, A. H. M., 'Were Ancient Heresies National or Social Movements in Disguise?', *Journal of Theological Studies*, n.s. X, 1959, pp. 280—98.

Jones, A. H. M., *Constantine and the Conversion of Europe*, London, 1965.

Jones, A. H. M., *The Decline of the Ancient World*, London, 1966.

Jones, Charles W., 'Bede as Early Medieval Historian', *M&H*, 4, June 1946, pp. 26—36.

Jones, Gwyn, *The Legendary History of Olaf Tryggvason*, Glasgow, 1968.

Jones, Gwyn, *A History of the Vikings*, Oxford, 1973.

Jones, Gwyn, *The Norse Atlantic Saga*, Oxford, 1986.

Jones, P. F., 'The Gregorian Mission and English Education', *Speculum*, III, (3), July 1928, pp. 335–48.

Jordan, Louis, 'Demonic Elements in Anglo-Saxon Iconography', in Paul E. Szarmach (ed.), *Sources of Anglo-Saxon Culture*, Kalamazoo, 1986, pp. 283–318.

Joseph, Herbert S., 'Volsa Pattr: A Literary Remnant of a Phallic Cult', *Folklore*, 83, 1972, pp. 245–52.

Karras, Ruth Mazo, 'Pagan Survivals and Syncretism in the Conversion of Saxony', *Catholic Historical Review*, LXXII, (4), October 1986, pp. 553–72.

Katz, Steven T., 'Language, Epistemology and Mysticism', in S. Katz (ed.), *Mysticism and Philosophical Analysis*, New York, 1978, pp. 22–74.

Katz, Steven T., *Mysticism and Philosophical Analysis*, New York, 1978.

Kee, Alister, 'Review: Robin Lane Fox, *Pagans and Christians*', The *Scottish Journal of Religious Studies*, X, (2), pp. 151–2.

Keenan, Hugh T., '*Christ and Satan*: Some Vagaries of Old English Poetic Composition', *Studies in Medieval Culture*, V, 1975, pp. 25–32.

Kendrick, T. D., *A History of the Vikings*, London, 1968.

Kindrick, Robert L., 'Germanic Sapientia and the Heroic Ethos of *Beowulf*', *M&H*, n.s., 10, 1981, pp. 1–18.

Kirby, D. P., *The Making of Early England*, London, 1967.

Lacy, Alan F., 'Gothic *weihs, airkns* and the Germanic Notion of "Holy"', *JIS*, 7, (3)-(4), 1979, pp. 287–96.

Lasko, Peter, *The Kingdom of the Franks*, London, 1971.

Latouche, Robert, *Caesar to Charlemagne*, trans. Jennifer Nicholson, London, 1968.

Latourette, K. S., *A History of the Expansion of Christianity*, Vol. 1, London, 1944.

le Bras, Gabriel, 'The Sociology of the Church in the Early Middle Ages', in Sylvia Thrupp (ed.), *Early Medieval Society*, New York, 1967, pp. 47–57.

Lee, Alvin A., 'Heorot and the 'Guest Hall' of Eden', *MS*, 2, 1969, pp. 78–91.

Leeds, E. Thurlow, *The Archaeology of the Anglo-Saxon Settlements*, Oxford, 1913.

Lester, G. A., *The Anglo-Saxons*, London, 1976.

Levison, Wilhelm, *England and the Continent in the Eighth Century*, Oxford, 1946.

Linder, Amnon, *The Myth of Constantine the Great in the West*, Spoleto, 1987.

Lockwood, W. B., *Indo-European Philology*, London, 1969.

Loewen, Jacob A., 'Roles: Relating to an Alien Social Structure', *Missiology*, IV, (2), April 1976, pp. 217–42.

Loos, Noel, 'Concern and Contempt: Church and Missionary Attitudes towards Aborigines in North Queensland in the Nineteenth Century', in T. Swain and D. Bird Rose (eds), *Aboriginal Australians and Christian Missions*, AASR, 1988, pp. 100–20.

Lot, Ferdinand, *The End of the Ancient World and the Beginning of the Middle Ages*, New York, 1961.

Luckmann, Thomas, *The Invisible Religion*, New York, 1967.

Lukman, N., 'British and Danish Traditions: Some Contacts and Relations', *Classica et Medievalia*, VI, 1944, pp. 72–109.

Lund, Allen A., 'On the Meaning of a much-disputed passage in the *Germania* of Tacitus (26.1-2)', *Classica et Medievalia*, XXXI, 1970, pp. 124–31.

Luzbetak, Louis J., 'Unity in Diversity: Ethnotheological Sensitivity in Cross-Cultural Evangelism', *Missiology*, IV, (2), April 1976, pp. 207–16.

McCormick, Michael, *Eternal Victory*, Cambridge, 1986.

MacCulloch, J. A., *The Harrowing of Hell*, Edinburgh, 1930.

McGalliard, John C., '*Beowulf* and Bede' in Robert S. Hoyt (ed.), *Life and Thought in the Early Middle Ages*, University of Minnesota Press, 1967, pp. 101–21.

McKeon, Peter R., 'Archbishop Ebbo of Rheims (816–835): A Study in the Carolingian Empire and Church', *CH*, XLIII, 1974, pp. 437–47.

Mackey, James P. (ed.) *An Introduction to Celtic Christianity*, Edinburgh, 1989.

MacMullen, Ramsay, *Christianizing the Roman Empire (A.D. 100–400)*, New Haven, CT, 1984.

Markey, T. L., 'Nordic Niðvisur: An Instance of Ritual Inversion?', *Studies in Medieval Culture*, X, 1977, pp. 75–85.

Markus, R. A., 'The Chronology of the Gregorian Mission to England: Bede's Narrative and Gregory's Correspondence', *Journal of Ecclesiastical History*, XIV, 1963, pp. 16–30.

Markus, R. A., *Christianity in the Roman World*, London, 1974.

Martin, John S., 'Some Comments on the Perception of Heathen Religious Customs in the Sagas', *Parergon*, 6, August 1973, pp. 45–50.

Martin, John S., 'Some Aspects of Snorri Sturluson's View of Kingship', *Parergon*, 15, August 1976, pp. 43–55.

Mason, Arthur James, *The Mission of Saint Augustine to England*, Cambridge, 1897.

Mathisen, Ralph W., *Ecclesiastical Factionalism and Religious Controversy in Fifth Century Gaul*, Washington, 1989.

Mayr-Harting, Henry, *The Coming of Christianity to Anglo-Saxon England*, London, 1972.

Mayr-Harting, Henry, 'St. Wilfrid in Sussex', in M. J. Kitch (ed.), *Studies in Sussex Church History*, 1981, pp. 1–17.

Meaney, Audrey L., 'Æthelweard, Ælfric, the Norse Gods and North-umbria', *JRH*, 6, (2), pp. 105–32.

Meaney, Audrey L., 'Woden in England: A Reconsideration of the Evidence', *Folklore*, 77, Spring 1966, pp. 105–15.

Meaney, Audrey L., 'Bede and Anglo-Saxon Paganism', *Parergon*, n.s. 3, 1985, pp. 1–31.

Merivale, Charles, *The Conversion of the Northern Nations*, London, 1866.

Mitchell, Kathleen, 'Saints and Public Christianity in the *Historiae* of Gregory of Tours', in Thomas F. X. Noble and John J. Contreni (eds), *Religion, Culture and Society in the Early Middle Ages*, Kalamazoo, 1987, pp. 77–94.

Moisl, Hermann, 'Anglo-Saxon Royal Genealogies and Germanic Oral Tradition', *JMH*, 7, (3), September 1981, pp. 215–45.

Momigliano, A., 'Christianity and the Decline of the Roman Empire', in A. Momigliano (ed.), *The Conflict Between Paganism and Christianity in the Fourth Century*, Oxford, 1963, pp. 1–16.

Momigliano, A. (ed.), *The Conflict Between Paganism and Christianity in the Fourth Century*, Oxford, 1963.

Momigliano, A., 'Ancient Biography and the Study of Religion in the Roman Empire', in A. Momigliano, *On Pagans, Jews and Christians*, Wesleyan University Press, 1987, pp. 159–77.

Momigliano, A., *On Pagans, Jews, and Christians*, Wesleyan University Press, 1987.

Montford, Lawrence Walter, *Civilization in Seventh Century Gaul as Reflected in Saints' Vitae Composed in the Period*, University Microfilms, Ann Arbor, 1974.

Moorhead, John, 'Gregory of Tours on the Arian Kingdoms', *Studi Medievali*, serie terza, anno XXXVI, fasc. II, pp. 903–15.

Moorhead, John, 'Clovis' Motives for Becoming a Catholic Christian', *JRH*, 1985, pp. 329–39.

Morris, John, 'The Literary Evidence', in M. W. Barley and R. P. C. Hanson (eds), *Christianity in Britain 300–700*, Leicester, 1968, pp. 55–74.

Morris, Richard, 'Baptismal Places: 600–800', in I. Wood and N. Lund (eds), *Peoples and Places in Northern Europe 500–1600*, Woodbridge, 1991, pp. 15–24.

Murray, Alexander C., *Germanic Kinship Structure*, Toronto, 1983.

Musset, Lucien, *The Germanic Invasions*, trans. Edward and Columba James, London, 1975.

Neill, Stephen, *A History of Christian Missions*, Harmondsworth, 1964.

Nelson, Janet L., 'Rewriting the History of the Franks', *History*, 72, 1987, pp. 69–81.

Ní Chatháin, P. and Richter, M. (eds), *Irland und die Christenheit*, Stuttgart, 1987.

Nicholson, Lewis E., 'The Literal Meaning and Symbolic Structure of *Beowulf*, *Classica et Medievalia*, XXIV–XXV, 1963–4, pp. 151–201.

Nikkel, Marc R., 'Aspects of Contemporary Religious Change among the Dinka', *JRA*, XXII, (1), 1992, pp. 78–94.

Noble, Thomas F. X. and John J. Contreni (eds), *Religion, Culture, and Society in the Early Middle Ages*, Kalamazoo, 1987.

Nock, Arthur Darby, *Conversion*, Oxford, 1933.

Nock, Arthur Darby, 'Conversion and Adolescence', in A. D. Nock (ed.) *Essays on Religion and the Ancient World*, Oxford, 1972, Vol. I, pp. 469–80.

Nock, Arthur Darby, *Essays on Religion and the Ancient World*, Oxford, 1972.

Nurnberger, Klaus, 'Ethical Implications of Religious and Ideological Pluralism – A Missionary Perspective', *Missionalia*, 13, (3), November 1985, pp. 95–110.

Nyborg, Ebbe, *Fanden på væggen*, Wormianum, 1978.

Ó Croinin, Daibhi, 'Rath Melsigi, Willibrord, and the Earliest Echternach Manuscripts', *Peritia*, 3, 1984, pp. 17–49.

O'Dea, Thomas, *The Sociology of Religion*, Englewood Cliffs, NJ, 1966.

O'Donnell, James J., 'The Demise of Paganism', *Traditio*, XXXV, 1979, pp. 45–88.

Ó Fiaich, Tomas, *Columbanus in his Own Words*, Veritas Publications, 1974.

O'Loughlin, J. N. L., 'Sutton Hoo – The Evidence of the Documents', *Medieval Archaeology*, 8, 1964, pp. 1–19.

Olson, Lynette, 'The Conversion of the Visigoths and the Bulgarians Compared', in Lynette Olson (ed.), *Religious Change, Conversion and Culture*, Sydney Studies in Society and Culture, 12, 1996, pp. 22–32.

Olson, Lynette, (ed.), *Religious Change, Conversion and Culture*, Sydney Studies in Society and Culture, 12, 1996.

Opperman, C. J. A., *The English Missionaries in Sweden and Finland*, London, 1937.

Osheim, Duane J., 'Conversion, *Conversi*, and the Christian Life in Late Medieval Tuscany', *Speculum*, 58, April 1983, pp. 368–90.

Östvold, Torbjörg, 'The War of the Aesir and Vanir – a Myth of the Fall in Nordic Religion', *Temenos*, 5, 1969, pp. 169–202.

Owen, Gale R., *Rites and Religions of the Anglo-Saxons*, London, 1981.

Paasche, Fredrik, *Kristendom og Kvad*, Kristiania, 1914.

Paasche, Fredrik, *Møtet mellom hedendom og kristendom i Norden*, Oslo, 1958.

Palme, Sven Ulric, *Kristendomens genombrott i Sverige*, Stockholm, 1959.

Payne, Richard C., 'Formulaic Poetry in Old English and its Backgrounds', *Studies in Medieval Culture*, XI, 1977, pp. 41–50.

Pearce, Susan M. (ed.) *The Early Church in Western Britain and Ireland*, British Archaeological Reports, British Series 102, 1982.

Perowne, Stuart, *Caesars and Saints*, London, 1962.

Petersen, E. Ladewig, 'Preaching in Medieval Denmark', *MS*, 3, 1970, pp. 142–71.

Pickett, J. W., *Christian Mass Movements in India*, The Abingdon Press, 1933.

Pickett, J. W., *Christian Missions in Mid India*, Jubbulpore, 1938.

Puuhvel, Jan (ed.), *Myth and Law Among the Indo-Europeans*, Berkeley, CA, 1970.

Radford, C. A. Ralegh, 'Christian Origins in Britain', *Medieval Archaeology*, 15, 1971, pp. 1–12.

Rambo, Lewis, *Understanding Religious Conversion*, New Haven, CT, 1993.

Randsborg, Klaus, 'Barbarians, Classical Antiquity and the Rise of Western Europe', *P&P*, 137, 1992, pp. 8–24.

Reuter, Timothy, *The Greatest Englishman: Essays on St. Boniface and the Church at Crediton*, Exeter, 1980.

Reuter, Timothy, 'Saint Boniface and Europe', in Timothy Reuter (ed.), *The Greatest Englishman: Essays on St. Boniface and the Church at Crediton*, Exeter, 1980, pp. 69–94.

Reuter, Timothy, 'Saint Boniface the Monk', in T. Reuter (ed.), *The Greatest Englishman: Essays on St. Boniface and the Church at Crediton*, Exeter, 1980.

Riché, Pierre, *Education and Culture in the Barbarian West*, trans. John J. Contreni, Columbia, 1976.

Riché, Pierre, 'Columbanus, His Followers, and the Merovingian Church', in H. B. Clarke and Mary Brennan (eds), *Columbanus and Merovingian Monasticism*, British Archaeological Reports International Series 113, 1981, pp. 59–72.

Richter, Michael, 'Practical Aspects of the Conversion of the Anglo-Saxons', in Próinséas Ní Chatháin and Michael Richter (eds), *Irland und die Christenheit*, Stuttgart, 1987, pp. 362–76.

Ringgren, Helmer, 'The Problem of Fatalism', in H. Ringgren (ed.), *Fatalistic Beliefs*, Stockholm, 1967, pp. 7–18.

Robertson, Roland, 'The Sociology of Religion: Problems and Desiderata', *Religion*, 1, 1971, pp. 109–26.

Rothman, David J., 'Sociology and History', *P&P*, 52, August 1971, pp. 126–135.

Runciman, W. G., 'Accelerating Social Mobility: the Case of Anglo-Saxon England', *P&P*, 104, August 1984, pp. 3–31.

Russell, James C., *The Germanization of Early Medieval Christianity*, London, 1994.

Russell, Josiah Cox, 'The Problem of Saint Patrick the Missionary', *Traditio*, 12, 1956, pp. 393–8.

Salway, Peter, *The Oxford Illustrated History of Roman Britain*, Oxford, 1993.

Sauve, James L., 'The Divine Victim: Aspects of Human Sacrifice in Viking

Scandinavia and Vedic India', in J. Puuhvel (ed.), *Myth and Law Among the Indo-Europeans*, Berkeley, CA, 1970, pp. 173–92.

Sawyer, Birgit, Sawyer, Peter and Wood, Ian (eds), *The Christianization of Scandinavia*, Alingsås, 1987.

Sawyer, Peter, 'Ethelred II, Olaf Tryggvason, and the Conversion of Norway', *Scandinavian Studies*, 59, 1987, pp. 299–307.

Sawyer, P. and Wood, I. (eds), *Early Medieval Kingship*, Leeds, 1977.

Sawyer, P. H., *Kings and Vikings*, London, 1982.

Schoedel, William R., 'Christian "Atheism" and the Peace of the Roman Empire', *CH*, 42, (3), 1973, pp. 309–19.

Schreuder, D. and Oddie, G., 'What is "Conversion"? History, Christianity and Religious Change in Colonial Africa and South Asia', *JRH*, 15, (4), 1989, pp. 496–518.

Scullard, H. H., *From the Gracchi to Nero*, London, 1959.

Segal, Robert, *Religion and the Social Sciences*, Atlanta, 1989.

Seppänen, Paavo, 'Religious Solidarity as a Function of Social Structure and Socialization', *Temenos*, 2, 1966, pp. 112–37.

Sharpe, Eric J., 'Some Problems of Method in the Study of Religion', *Religion*, 1, 1971, pp. 1–14.

Sharpe, Eric J., 'Salvation, Germanic and Christian', in E. J. Sharpe and J. R. Hinnells (eds), *Man and His Salvation*, Manchester, 1973, pp. 243–62.

Sharpe, Eric J., *Comparative Religion*, London, 1975.

Sharpe, Eric J., 'The Old English Runic Paternoster', in H. Ellis Davidson (ed.), *Symbols of Power*, 1977, pp. 41–61.

Sharpe, Eric J., *Understanding Religion*, London, 1983.

Sharpe, Eric J., 'Reflections on Missionary Historiography', *International Bulletin of Missionary Research*, April 1989, pp. 76–81.

Sharpe, E. J. and Hinnells, J. R. (eds), *Man and His Salvation*, Manchester, 1973.

Simon, John, 'Snorri Sturluson: His Life and Times', *Parergon*, 15, August 1976, pp. 3–16.

Simpson, Jacqueline, 'Some Scandinavian Sacrifices', *Folklore*, 78, 1967, pp. 190–202.

Simpson, John, 'Comparative Structural Analysis of Three Ethical Questions in *Beowulf*, the *Niebelungenlied* and the *Chanson de Roland*', *JIS*, 3, (3), 1975, pp. 239–54.

Skovgaard-Peterson, I., 'The Coming of Urban Culture to Northern Europe: Vikings, Merchants and Kings', *Scandinavian Journal of History*, 3, 1978, pp. 1–19.

Sladden, John Cyril, *Boniface of Devon*, Exeter, 1980.

Smart, Ninian, *The Religious Experience of Mankind*, New York, 1969.

Smith, M. A., *The Church Under Siege*, Leicester, 1976.

Smith, R. C. and Lounibos, J. (eds), *Pagan and Christian Anxiety*, University Press of America, 1983.

Southern, R. W., *Western Society and the Church in the Middle Ages*, Harmondsworth, 1970.

Stafford, Pauline, *Queens, Concubines and Dowagers*, London, 1983.

Stancliffe, Clare, 'Kings and Conversions: Some Comparisons between the Roman Mission to England and Patrick's to Ireland', *Frühmittelalterliche Studien*, 14, 1980, pp. 59–94.

Stancliffe, Clare, *St. Martin and his Hagiographer*, Oxford, 1983.

Starr, Joshua, 'The Mass Conversion of Jews in Southern Italy (1290–1293)', *Speculum*, 21, (2), April 1946, pp. 203–11.

Stenton, Doris M., (ed.), *Preparatory to Anglo-Saxon England*, Oxford, 1970.

Stenton, Frank Merry, 'The East Anglian Kings of the Seventh Century', in Doris M. Stenton (ed.), *Preparatory to Anglo-Saxon England*, Oxford, 1970, pp. 394–402.

Stenton, Frank Merry, 'The English Element in Place-Names', in Doris M. Stenton (ed.), *Preparatory to Anglo-Saxon England*, Oxford, 1970, pp. 67–83.

Stenton, Frank Merry, 'The Historical Bearing of Place-Name Studies: Anglo-Saxon Heathenism', in Doris M. Stenton (ed.), *Preparatory to Anglo-Saxon England*, Oxford, 1970, pp. 281–97.

Stenton, Frank Merry, 'The Historical Bearing of Place-Name Studies: England in the Sixth Century', in Doris M. Stenton (ed.), *Preparatory to Anglo-Saxon England*, Oxford, 1970, pp. 253–65.

Stenton, Frank Merry, 'Lindsey and Its Kings', in Doris M. Stenton (ed.), *Preparatory to Anglo-Saxon England*, Oxford, 1970, pp. 127–35.

Stenton, Frank Merry, 'Medeshamstede and its Colonies', in Doris M. Stenton (ed.), *Preparatory to Anglo-Saxon England*, Oxford, 1970, pp. 179–92.

Stenton, Frank Merry, *Anglo-Saxon England*, Oxford, 1971.

Stephens, J. N., 'Bede's *Ecclesiastical History*', *History*, 62, 1977, pp. 1–14.

Stevens, C. E., *Sidonius Apollinaris and his Age*, Oxford, 1933.

Stevens, Lesley, 'Religious Change in a Haya Village, Tanzania', *JRA*, XXI, (1), 1991, pp. 2–25.

Straw, Carole, *Gregory the Great*, Berkeley, CA, 1988.

Ström, Åke V., 'Scandinavian Belief in Fate', in Helmer Ringgren (ed.), *Fatalistic Beliefs*, Stockholm, 1967, pp. 63–88.

Ström, Folke, *Den egna kraftens man*, Göteborg, 1948.

Strömbäck, Dag, *The Conversion of Iceland*, trans. Peter G. Foote, London, 1975.

Strutynski, Udo, 'Germanic Divinities in Weekday Names', *JIS*, 3, (4), 1975, pp. 363–84.

Sullivan, Richard E., 'The Carolingian Missionary and the Pagan', *Speculum*, 28, 1953, pp. 705–40.

Sullivan, Richard E., *Christian Missionary Activity in the Early Middle Ages*, Variorum, London, 1994.

Sullivan, Richard E., 'The Papacy and Missionary Activity in the Early Middle Ages', in Richard E. Sullivan, *Christian Missionary Activity in the Early Middle Ages*, III, Variorum, London, 1994.

Sundkler, Bengt, *The Christian Ministry in Africa*, London, 1962.

Sverdrup, Georg, *Da Norge ble Kristnet*, Oslo, 1942.

Swaan, Wim, *The Gothic Cathedral*, Paul Elek Productions Ltd., 1969.

Swain, Tony, *A Place for Strangers*, Cambridge, 1993.

Swain, Tony and Rose, Deborah Bird (eds), *Aboriginal Australians and Christian Missions*, AASR, 1988.

Szarmach, Paul E. (ed.) *Sources of Anglo-Saxon Culture*, Kalamazoo, 1986.

Tate, George S., 'The Cross as Ladder: *Geisli* 15-16 and *Liknarbraut* 34', *MS*, 11, 1978-9, pp. 258–64.

Taylor, Pegatha, 'Review of James C. Russell, *The Germanization of Early Medieval Christianity*', *M&H*, n.s. 23, p. 173.

Thelamon, Françoise, *Païens et Chrétiens au IVe Siècle*, Paris, 1981.

Thirsk, Joan (ed.), *Land, Church and People*, Reading, 1970.

Thomas, A. C., 'The Evidence from North Britain', in M. W. Barley and R. P. C. Hanson (eds), *Christianity in Britain 300–700*, Leicester, 1968, pp. 93–122.

Thomas, A. C., *Christianity in Roman Britain to 500 AD*, London, 1981.

Thompson, E. A., 'The *Passio S. Sabae* and Early Visigothic Society', *Historia*, IV, 1955, pp. 331–8.

Thompson, E. A., 'Christianity and the Northern Barbarians', *NMS*, 1, 1957, pp. 3–21.

Thompson, E. A., 'Early Germanic Warfare', *P&P*, 14, November 1958, pp. 2–30.

Thompson, E. A., 'The Conversion of the Visigoths to Catholicism', *NMS*, 4, 1960, pp. 4–35.

Thompson, E. A., 'The Visigoths in the Time of Ulfila', *NMS*, 5, 1961, pp. 3–32.

Thompson, E. A., 'The Visigoths from Fitigern to Euric', *Historia*, XII, 1963, pp. 105–26.

Thompson, E. A., *The Early Germans*, Oxford, 1965.

Thompson, E. A., *The Visigoths in the Time of Ulfila*, Oxford, 1966.

Thompson, E. A., *The Goths in Spain*, Oxford, 1969.

Thompson, E. A., 'Procopius on Brittia and Britannia', *Classical Quarterly*, n.s. XXX, 1980, pp. 498–507.

Thompson, E. A., *Romans and Barbarians*, University of Wisconsin Press 1982.

Thompson, E. A., *Who Was Saint Patrick?*, The Boydell Press, 1985.

Thrupp, Sylvia (ed.), *Early Medieval Society*, New York, 1967.

Tikhomirov, M. N., 'The Origins of Christianity in Russia', *History*, 44, 1959, pp. 199–211.

Todd, Malcolm, *The Northern Barbarians 100 BC–AD 300*, 2nd edn, Oxford, 1987.

Tolkien, J. R. R., *Beowulf, the Monsters and the Critics*, British Academy, XXII, 1936.

Toth, William, 'The Christianization of the Magyars', *CH*, XI, 1942, pp. 33–54.

Trevor-Roper, Hugh, *The Rise of Christian Europe*, London, 1965.

Trevor-Roper, Hugh, 'The Past and the Present: History and Sociology', *P&P*, 42, February 1969, pp. 3–18.

Trompf, Garry W., 'Salvation and Primal Religion', *Prudentia*, supp. no., 1988, pp. 207–31.

Trompf, Garry W., 'Macrohistory and Acculturation: Between Myth and History in Modern Melanesian Adjustments and Ancient Gnosticism', *Comparative Studies in Society and History*, 31, (4), October 1989, pp. 621–48.

Trompf, Garry W., 'The Church and Cultures: New Perspectives in Missiological Anthropology, Louis J. Luzbetak SVD, Orbis, NY, 1988', review article in *South Pacific Journal of Mission Studies*, 1, (2), January 1990, pp. 21–2.

Trompf, Garry W., *In Search of Origins*, London, 1990.

Trompf, Garry W., 'Rufinus and the Logic of Retribution in post-Eusebian Church Histories', *The Journal of Ecclesiastical History*, 43, (3), 1992, pp. 351–71.

Trompf, Garry W., Gough, J. and Otto, E., 'Western Folktales in Changing Melanesia', *Folklore*, 99 (ii), 1988, pp. 204–20.

Turville-Petre, E., *The Origins of Icelandic Literature*, Oxford, 1953.

Turville-Petre, E., *Scaldic Poetry*, Oxford, 1976.

Turville-Petre, G., *The Heroic Age of Scandinavia*, London, 1951.

Turville-Petre, G., *Nine Norse Studies*, London, 1972.

Ullmann, Walter, *The Carolingian Renaissance*, London, 1969.

Underwood, A. C., *Conversion: Christian and Non-Christian*, London, 1925.

Undset, Sigrid, *Saga of Saints*, trans. E. C. Ramsden, London, 1934.

van Andel, G. K., *The Christian Concept of History in the Chronicle of Sulpicius Severus*, Amsterdam, 1976.

van Dam, Raymond, *Leadership and Community in Late Antique Gaul*, University of California Press, 1985.

Verryn, Trevor, 'What is Communication? Searching for a Missiological Model', *Missionalia*, II, (1), April 1983, pp. 17–25.

Vlasto, A. P., *The Entry of the Slavs into Christendom*, Cambridge, 1970.

Wach, Joachim, *The Sociology of Religion*, London, 1947.

Wallace-Hadrill, J. M., *The Long-Haired Kings*, London, 1962.

Wallace-Hadrill, J. M., *Early Germanic Kingship*, Oxford, 1971.

Wallace-Hadrill, J. M., *Early Medieval History*, Oxford, 1975.

Wallace-Hadrill, J. M., *The Frankish Church*, Oxford, 1983.

Wallace-Hadrill, J. M., *The Barbarian West 400–1000*, London, 1985.

Wallace-Hadrill, J. M. and Davies, R. H. C. (eds), *The Writing of History in the Middle Ages*, Oxford, 1981.

Walzer, R., *Galen on Jews and Christians*, Oxford, 1949.

Wessels, Anton, *Europe: Was It Ever Really Christian?*, trans. John Bowden, SCM Press, 1994.

Whaley, Diana, *Heimskringla: An Introduction*, London, 1991.

Whitelock, Dorothy, *The Beginnings of English Society*, Harmondsworth, 1952.

Whitelock, Dorothy, 'The Pre-Viking Age Church in East Anglia', *A-SE*, I, 1972, pp. 1–22.

Whitelock, Dorothy, *From Bede to Alcuin*, London, 1980.

Whitlock, Ralph, *The Warrior Kings of Saxon England*, Bath, 1977.

Wilken, Robert L., *The Christians as the Romans Saw Them*, New Haven, CT, 1984.

Williams, Daniel H., 'The Anti-Arian Campaigns of Hilary of Poitiers and the *Liber Contra Auxentium*', *CH*, 61, (1), 1992, pp. 7–22.

Wilson, David M., *The Anglo-Saxons*, Harmondsworth, 1966.

Wilson, David M., *The Archaeology of Anglo-Saxon England*, Cambridge, 1976.

Wolfram, Herwig, *History of the Goths*, trans. Thomas J. Dunlap, University of California Press, 1988.

Wood, Ian, 'Gregory of Tours and Clovis', *Revue Belge de Philologie et d'Histoire*, LXIII, 2, pp. 249–72.

Wood, Ian, 'Pagans and Holy Men, 600–800', in Próinséas Ní Chatháin and Michael Richter (eds), *Irland und die Christenheit*, Stuttgart, 1987, pp. 347–61.

Wood, Ian, 'The Mission of Augustine of Canterbury to the English', *Speculum*, 69, (1), 1994, pp. 1–17.

Wood, I. and Lund, N. (eds), *People and Places in Northern Europe 500–1600*, The Boydell Press, 1991.

Woolf, Rosemary, 'The Ideal of Men Dying with their Lord in the *Germania* and in *The Battle of Maldon*', *A-SE*, 5, 1976, pp. 63–81.

Wormald, Patrick, '*Lex Scripta* and *Verbum Regis*: Legislation and Germanic Kingship, from Euric to Cnut', in P. Sawyer and I. Wood (eds), *Early Medieval Kingship*, Leeds, 1977, pp. 105–38.

Wormald, Patrick, 'Bede, *Beowulf* and the Conversion of the Anglo-Saxon Aristocracy', in Robert T. Farrell (ed.), *Bede and Anglo-Saxon England*, British Archaeological Reports, 46, 1978, pp. 32–95.

Wormald, Patrick, 'Bede, the *Bretwaldas*, and the Origins of the *Gens Anglorum*', in P. Wormald, D. Bullough and R. Collins (eds), *Ideal and Reality in Frankish and Anglo-Saxon Society*, Oxford, 1983, pp. 99–129.

Wormald, Patrick, 'Bede and the Conversion of England: the Charter Evidence', *Jarrow Lecture*, 1984.

Wormald, Patrick, 'Celtic and Anglo-Saxon Kingship: Some Further Thoughts', in Paul E. Szarmach (ed.), *Sources of Anglo-Saxon Culture*, Kalamazoo, 1986, pp. 151–84.

Wormald, P., *et al.*, *Ideal and Reality in Frankish and Anglo-Saxon Society*, Oxford, 1983.

Wright, Joseph, *Grammar of the Gothic Language*, Oxford, 1954.

Yarbrough, Anne, 'Christianization in the Fourth Century: The Example of Roman Women', *CH*, 45, (2), June 1976, pp. 149–65.

Yinger, J. Milton, *The Scientific Study of Religion*, New York, 1970.

Zenkovsky, Serge (ed. and trans.), *Medieval Russia's Epics, Chronicles and Tales*, New York, 1974.

Unpublished sources

Barlow, Jonathan, *The Success of the Franks: Regional Continuity in Northern Gaul in Late Antiquity*, doctoral thesis, University of Sydney, Department of History, 1993.

Bray, Daniel, 'Sacral Kingship in Indo-European Religion', fourth year Honours paper, University of Sydney, School of Studies in Religion, 1994.

Kennedy, John, *The Goðar*, unpublished doctoral thesis, University of Sydney, Department of English, 1985.

McCormick, Michael, 'Clovis at Tours: Byzantine Public Ritual and the Origins of Medieval Ruler Symbolism', unpublished typescript.

Mackey, James P., 'Primal Past and Christian Present: Religions of the Celts and the Koories', unpublished paper given at the *Australian Conference of Celtic Studies*, University of Sydney, July 1992.

Sharpe, Eric J., 'Seasons of Light and Darkness', unpublished typescript of drafts and plans for a book on religion in Britain.

Index

Ablasius 37

Adam of Bremen 135–6, 139–40, 142, 144, 147, 150–1, 160

Adda 107

Adrianople, battle of 43–7

Aegidius, king of the Franks 69–70, 73

Ælfheah, bishop 146

Aesculapius 173

Æthelberht, king of Kent 96–8, 100–2, 105–6, 177

Æthelburh 102, 105

Æthelfrid of Northumbria 106

Æthelred II, king of England 146–7

Æthelwahl, king 108

Æthelweard 146

Aetius, Flavius 66

Africa 9–14, 22, 34, 42, 48, 177

Agila, king of the Visigoths 51

Agilan 77

Agilulf, Lombard king 78

Aidan, bishop 107, 109, 119

Alamanni 66, 71, 73, 79

Alans 63

Alaric I, king of the Visigoths 47–8, 65

Alaric II, king of the Visigoths 67

Alban, St 88, 147

Albofled 73

Alchfled 107

Alcuin of York 110, 120–1

Aldgisl, king of the Frisians 120

Alfred the Great, king of Wessex 90

Althing, 999/1000 22, 148, 160–1, 164–7

Amanburch 125

Amand, St, bishop of Maastricht 79–80, 119, 123

Ammianus Marcellinus 37, 45, 68

Amoneburg 124

Anastasius, Byzantine emperor 72, 75

ancestors 74

Angles 89–90, 100

Anglo-Saxon Chronicle 90–1, 96, 99, 106, 146

Anglo-Saxons 66, 129, 152
  pre-Christian religion 36, 74, 76, 90–2
  conversion 88–111
    agency of rulers 20, 22, 74, 91
    apostasy 176
    Augustine's mission 98
    indigenization 110–11, 124
    pre-Augustinian Christianity 90, 93
    syncretism 76, 179
  missions to the continent 119–30

Anlaf, *see* Olaf

Anna, king of the East Angles 108

Anskar, St 124, 135–41

Anullinus, proconsul of Africa 34

Anund, king of Sweden 139

Aoric 42

Apollo 30

Apuleius, Lucius 5, 32

Aquitaine 63

Aquitania Secunda 47

Arbogast, Frankish count of Trier 67–8

Arcadius, eastern emperor 47

Ardgar 140

Ari the Learned 158–9, 161, 163–6

Ariacus, king 38

Arianism 39–40, 42, 44–51, 63–80, 130, 177

Arnulfing family 69, 123

Athanaric, Visigoth prince 38, 42, 44–6, 48, 101

Athanasius, St 39

Atharidus 42–3, 122

Athelstan of Wessex 143

Attila, king of the Huns 90

Aud the Deep-Minded 161

Audofled 73

Augustine, St, archbishop of Canterbury 33, 65, 93, 95–100, 105–6, 138, 178

Augustine of Hippo, St   89
Aurelian, emperor   68
Ausonius, Decius Magnus   65
Austrasia   78, 123
Autbert   136
Auxentius of Durosturum, bishop of
    Milan   39–40, 42, 49
Avars   128
Avitus of Vienne   79, 81

Bacchus   30
Balder   129, 142, 169
Basques   79
Bauto   68
Bavaria   123–4, 126, 128
Bede, Venerable   65, 77, 88–92, 94–7, 99,
    103–4, 106–8, 119–21, 123
Belgium   68
Beowulf   91, 110–11, 152, 169
Bernicia   106
Bertha of Kent   96–8, 178
Betti   107
Bible   6–7, 74, 168–9
    Gothic   33, 40–1, 46–7, 162
Birinus   108
Birka   137, 139–40, 144
Bischofsheim   124
Bithynia   31
Björn, king   137–8, 140
Bolli   148–9
Boniface, St   1, 123–7, 145
Bremen   139, 144
bretwalda (over-king)   74, 101, 107
    see also kingship; loyalty
Britain   88–90
    see also Anglo-Saxons; England; *named places*
Brunhild   78
Bugga, abbess   126
Burgundians   50, 65–7, 73, 101
burial   77, 108–9, 129

Cadwalla, British prince   106
Caesarius of Arles   67, 129
Canterbury   97
Capitulatio de Partibus Saxoniae
    (Charlemagne)   128
Carinthia   128
Carloman I   127
Carolingians   124, 127–9, 136, 139
Cassiodorus, Flavius Magnus Aurelius   37,
    50

Catholicism   46, 48, 50, 70
    Franks   51, 63–81, 94, 130
Cedd   106–7
Celsus   31–2
Celts   35–6, 63–4, 70
    Christianity   105, 107, 119, 177
Cenwalh, king of Wessex   108
Ceolwulf, king   95
Ceres   30
Černjachov   37
Charlemagne, king of the Franks,
    emperor   81, 124, 127–9, 135, 150,
    177
Charles the Bald   139
Charles Martel   124
Chester   106
Childebert I   77
Childeric, king of the Franks   69, 73, 77
Chlodio (Chlodion)   69
Chlotar II of Neustria   78
Chrotechildis, *see* Clotild
Chrysostom, John   63
Church Councils   127
Claudian   48
Claudius, emperor   88
Clotild (Chrotechildis)   70–2, 178
Clotsinda   80
Clovis   35, 67–81, 177
Codex Argenteus   50
Coifi   103–5, 145, 164
colonialism   1, 8–9, 13–14, 22
Columba, St   96
Columbanus, St   78–81, 125, 145
comitatus, see loyalty
communication   9–10, 100, 178
    see also language
Constantine, emperor   33–5, 48, 63, 69, 72,
    177
Constantinople   35, 39, 47, 70, 75
Constantius, emperor   33, 42
Constantius of Lyons   66, 89
conversion   8–11, 18–21, 42, 127, 173–8
    agents of   20, 23, 33, 71, 76, 102, 175, 178
    anthropological approaches   10–15, 17,
        177
    'bottom-up'   20, 39–40, 65, 161, 175,
        177
    individual   2–4, 6, 8, 16, 22, 93, 101–2,
        164, 167, 173–4, 176
    mass   3, 15–16, 22–3, 174, 176
    military contexts   22, 80, 123–4

political factors   2, 20, 22, 45–6, 51, 101–2,
    105, 107, 123–4, 139, 166, 174, 176
    see also 'top-down' *below*
psychological approaches   4–7
sociological approaches   2–4, 15, 46
'top-down'   18–20, 23, 167, 179
Corbie   135–6
Council of Antioch   39
Council of Nicaea, 325   34, 39
Cross Hills   161
cults   30, 128, 160–1
    see also mystery cults
culture   3, 9–11, 14, 19–22, 33, 41–2, 67,
    111, 174
Cuthbert, St   119
Cybele   5, 30
Cynegils, king of Wessex   108
Cyneheard   99
Cynewulf, king of Wessex   99
Cynthia (Hostia)   5, 32
Cyzicus   35

Dacia   38–40, 44, 46
Dagobert I   80
Dagobert II   120
Daniel, bishop of Winchester   126
Deira   106
Denmark   121–2, 135–6, 139–40, 144–6
Dettic   125
Devrulf   125
Diana   34
Diocletian, emperor   33
Diuma   107
divination   147, 166
Dokkum   123, 127
Donatists   34, 42

Eadbald   101, 105–6
Eanfled   105
Eanfrid, king of Bernicia   106
East Anglia   101–3, 107
East Saxons   91
Easter, date of   107
Eastern Empire   35, 94
Ebbo, bishop of Rheims   135, 139
Ecgfrith of Northumbria   120
Eddas   91, 93, 138, 142, 152, 160, 168
Eddi   119–20
Edict of Milan, 313   34, 63
Edict of Theodoric   50
education   78, 107, 141

Edwin of Northumbria   101–7, 164, 176–7
Egbert   119–20
Egil Skallagrímsson   159, 161–2
Egypt   30
Eidsivathing Law   163
Eigil, abbot of Fulda   127–8
Einhard the Frank   68–9
Eirik, king of the Swedes   148
Eirik Hákonarmál   148
Eligius, bishop of Tournai   119–20, 123
England   105, 107, 143, 147, 151
    see also Anglo-Saxons; Britain; *named places*
Eorpwald   103, 107
Eostre   91
Eparchius Avitus   66
Epicureanism   30
Erimbert   141
Ermoldus Nigellus   135
eschatology   104, 169
Essex   101, 104–6
Eugippius   49
Eulogius, bishop of Alexandria   98
Eunapius   37
Euric the Visigoth   67
Eusebius of Caesarea   33
Eusebius of Nicomedia   34, 39, 72
Eustasius   79
Eutyches   74
Eyvindr   143

family   22, 161–3, 167
Fates (Norns)   142
Felix, archbishop   107
Finan   107
Flemings   79
folk-beliefs   1, 179
Fosite   121
Frankfurt Declaration, 1970   8–9
Franks   22, 51, 63–81, 94, 98, 122, 130
    see also Clovis
Fredegar   80
Frederick, bishop of Saxony   163
Frey   36, 137, 142
Freya   36, 142, 163
Freyr   161
Frisians   119–24, 127–8
Fritigern   43–6, 48, 100
Fritzlar   124
Fro   129
Frösö   145
Fulda   124

Gaesmere   125
Galen   31
Gall   79
Gallo-Romans   64–5, 69, 75, 81
Gaul   38, 51, 63–6, 74, 119
Gautaz   36
Gauzbert, bishop   139, 141
Geiseric the Vandal   48–9, 66
Geneviève, St   72–3
Gepidae   46, 66
Germans
  conversion   39, 175–8
  culture   1, 20–1, 111, 175
  kingship   74, 98, 121, 129, 138
  pre-Christian religion   19, 35–6, 90–3, 175
  and Roman Empire   35–9
  society   162, 167, 175
Germanus, St, of Auxerre   65–6, 89
Gildas, St   89–90
Gimle   169
Giso, queen of the Rugi   49
Gizurr Teitsson (the White)   163–4, 166–7
Gnosticism   5, 14, 177
goðar   142, 160, 165
goðorðs   160–1, 167
Godric, king   135
gods   168
  African   12
  Christian   10, 32, 129
  Egyptian   5, 30, 32
  Norse   35–6, 81, 91–3, 129–30, 137–8, 142, 149–50, 161–3, 169
  Roman   5, 30, 32, 34–6, 92, 125, 173
  Saxon   36, 68, 79, 90–2, 125, 128
  see also named gods
Gorm   144
Gotafrid   135
Gothia (Dacia)   39, 42, 44
Goths   22, 43–5, 66–7, 73, 76
  Christianity   39–43, 98
    Bible translation   40–1, 46–7, 162
  culture   37, 50
  kingship   36, 38, 40, 91
  see also Ostrogoths; Visigoths
Les Grandes Chroniques   70
Gratian, emperor   45
Greeks   6, 30, 146, 173
Gregory the Great, pope   68, 102, 110, 126, 129, 178
  mission to Britain   88, 93–5, 98–100, 178
Gregory II, pope   126

Gregory IV, pope   139
Gregory Thaumaturgos   33
Gregory of Tours   64–5, 68–72, 74–5, 77–8, 80–1, 96
Grendel   91, 110
Greutungi-Ostrogothi   38
Grimkjell, bishop   151
Gudfast   145
Gundobad   70, 72
Gunther, archbishop of Cologne   139
Gwynedd   105

Hákon Haraldsson, king of Norway   143, 148
Halitgar, bishop of Cambrai   135
Hall the Godless   161
Hallfreðr Ottarsson Vandraeðskáld (the Troublesome Poet)   148–50, 161
Hallr Thorarinsson of Haukadalur   163
Hamburg-Bremen   135, 139, 144, 147
Harald Bluetooth (Gormsson)   144–6, 177
Harald Fairhair   147, 150, 160
Harald Graenske   147
Harald Klak, king   135–6, 139
Haukadalur   163
Hávamál   137, 168–9
Hedeby   140–1
Heimdall (Rig)   141
Helena, mother of Constantine   33
Helgi the Godless   161
Helgi the Lean   161
Heliand (Saxon Gospel)   129–30, 159
Heligoland   121
Hengest   90
Henry I (German)   144
Hercules   35–6
heresies, *see* Arianism; Eutyches; Pelagianism; Priscillianism; Sabellius
Herigar (Hergeir) of Birka   137, 139–40, 176
Herro   129
Hesse   123, 126
Hewald the Black   123
Hewald the White   123
Hilary of Poitiers   64
Hjalti Skeggjason   163–4, 166
Hlað   147
Holy Roman Empire   81
Holy Spirit   2, 173
Honorius I, pope   108
Honorius Flavius, western emperor   47
Horic I, king of Denmark   139–40

Horic the Younger, king of Denmark 140–1
Horsa 90
Hrothgar, Danish king 110
Huneric, king of the Vandals 49
Huns 45
Husaby 144
Hydatius, bishop 48

Ibn Fadlan 160
Iceland 1, 22, 138, 151, 158–69
  pre-Christian 160–1
  individual and family 161–3
  conversion 20–1, 148–9, 163–6
    consequences 166–9
  see also sagas
India 13, 15–16, 78
Indiculus Superstitionum et Paganiarum 128
indigenization 78–82, 108–11, 124, 129–30,
    150–1, 175
Indo-European religion 21, 36
Ing (Yngi) 137
Iona (Hii) 96, 99, 106
Ireland 65, 99, 107, 120, 161
Irmin 128
Irminsul 128
Isidore of Seville 50
Isis 5, 30, 32
Isle of Wight 108
Ísleif Guzursson, bishop of Skalholt 166–7
Íslendingabók 158
Isles of Scilly 146

Jämtland 145
Jarl 141
Jelling 145
Jerome, St 89
Jesus Christ 11, 30, 34, 74, 143, 149, 173
Jonas of Bobbio 78–80
Jordanes 37, 44, 46–7, 50, 91, 138
Judaism 4–5, 30–2
judges 38, 42, 44
Julian 'the Apostate', emperor 47
Julius Caesar 64, 88
Jupiter 30, 125
Justinian, emperor in the East 48, 50–1, 94
Justus, bishop of Rochester 106
Jutes 89–90

Kent 20, 91, 96–7, 101, 104, 106, 138, 178
Ketill, bishop 166
kingship 35–8, 49–50, 68, 129, 148–50, 164

pre-Christian 19
  role in conversion 13–14, 18, 20, 105,
    148–9, 175–6
  sacral 37, 40, 47, 68–9, 73–4, 91–2, 97,
    108–9, 121, 137, 141, 160, 177, 179
  see also bretwalda; loyalty
Kitzingen 124
Kjartan 148–9, 163
Konungr 141

Landnámabók (Book of the Settlements) 158,
    161
landvaettir 161
language 9, 41–2, 98–9, 124–5, 178
Lavoye burial, 319 77
law 50, 77, 101, 141, 160, 163–8
Lenteildis (Lantechild) 72–3
Leo III, pope 129
Leoba 126
Leuvigild, king of the Visigoths 51, 77
Lex Burgundionum 50
Lex Romana Visigothorum 50
Liber Historiae Francorum 71
Lincoln 37
Lindisfarne 107, 119
Lindsey 106
Liudhard, bishop 96–7
Lombardy 78
Lothar 139
Louis the German 139
Louis the Pious, emperor 135–6, 138–9
loyalty 19, 73, 98–9, 101, 129, 138, 160, 176
  see also bretwalda; kingship
Lull 127

magic 106, 147
Magnus I Olafsson 150
Maldon, battle of 146
Mars 35–6
Martin, bishop of Tours 63–4, 66, 80
Martin of Braga 94, 126
martyrdom 64, 109, 127
Maxentius, emperor 33
Maximinus 48
Mellitus, bishop of London 105–6, 110, 126,
    178
Mercia 101, 107
Mercury 35–6, 92
Merovech, Frankish ruler 68–9, 75, 91
Merovingians 68–9, 75, 78, 91, 123
Messiah 31

Milvian Bridge, battle of   33, 35, 72
miracles   64, 79–80, 108–9, 125, 143, 145
missionaries   3, 105, 124, 174, 177
   5th century   65–8
   10th century   143–6
   medieval   18–20, 23
   20th century   8–11
   see also named individuals and places
Mithraism   5, 30
Moesia   42, 45–6
monasticism   76, 78–9, 124, 126
Monophysitism   50–1
mystery cults   5–6, 30, 32
mysticism   7, 13
mythology   14, 36–7, 91, 142, 152

Nerthus   35–6
Nicetius of Trier   80
Nicholas, pope   139
Ninian, bishop   96
Nithard   139
Njál   158–9, 162, 165
Njord   36
Noricum   49
Norns (Fates)   142
Northumbria   101–7, 119
Norway   22, 137, 143, 146–8, 150, 160, 168

Ochsenfurt   124
Oddr Snorrason   146–7, 158, 164
Odin   36, 81, 91–3, 130, 137–8, 142,
   149–50, 161–2, 169
Odoacer   49
Ohrdruf   124
Olaf, Scandinavian king   140
Olaf Eriksson (Skötkonung, 'the Lapp
   king')   144, 151–2
Olaf Haraldsson (St Olaf)   143–4, 150–2
Olaf I Tryggvason   81, 144, 146–50, 152,
   163–6
Olaf the Swede   148
Olympiodorus   37
Ongendus, king of the Danes   122
Origen   31, 33, 88
Orléans   69
Orosius, Paulus   68
orthodoxy   63–4
Oseberg   69
Osric, king of Deira   106
Östersundsbro   145
Ostman   145

Ostrogoths   38, 45–6, 50
Oswald, St, king of Northumbria   105–6,
   108–9
Oswy of Northumbria   107
Otto of Bamberg   22
Otto the Great, emperor of Germany   144,
   146.

Pactus Legis Salicae (Lex Salica)   77
Paderborn   128
paganism   31–2, 35, 51, 68, 77, 80–1, 94,
   143, 177
Palladius   65
Pannonia   128
papacy   49, 81, 93–4, 124, 177
   see also named popes
Papianilla   66
Paris   73, 75
Patrick, St   65
Paul, St   5, 9, 30, 34, 159
Paulinus, bishop   102–4, 106, 164
Paulinus, St, of Nola   63
Peada   107
Pelagianism   66, 88–9, 93
Pelagius I   94
Penda, king of Mercia   106–7, 109
Pepin of Héristal   122
Pepin II   120, 122
Pepin III, 'the Short'   127
Peter, St   81
philosophy   5–6, 30
Philostorgios   37, 39–40, 49
Photius   39
Phrygia   30
Picts   66, 89–90, 96
Plato   5
Pliny 'the Younger'   31, 42
Plotinus   33
polygyny   77
polytheism   80
Pomerania   20, 22
Poppo   145
Porphyry   33
Priscillianism   48
Procopius   37, 95
Propertius   5, 32
Pythagoreanism   30

Radbod, king of Frisia   120–4, 145
Rædwald of East Anglia   77, 101–3, 107
Ragnarok   142, 169

Ravenna 49–50
Recared, king of Visigoths 50–1, 80
Remigius of Rheims, bishop–saint 72–3, 81
Restituta 48
Rhea 35
Rheims 80
Rhun 105
Ribe 141
Ricbert 107
Richomer 68
Rig (Heimdall) 141
Rigstula 141
Rimbert, bishop of Hamburg-Bremen 135–7,
    139–40, 143–4
Ripon 119
Robert, archbishop 150
Roman Empire 19, 21, 30–9, 50, 65–6, 88,
    177
    and Britain 90
    and Christianity 38, 47, 94, 108, 119
    and Goths 44–5
    pre-Christian religion 30, 64, 177
    see also Western Empire
Romania 39
Romano-British Church 66, 88, 93, 99–100,
    105, 107, 119
Rouen 150
Rufinus 47
Rugi 47, 49
Runic *futhark* 91
Russia 146, 160

Saba, St (the Goth) 40, 42–3, 122, 140, 176–7
Sabellius 74
Saberht of Essex 101, 105–6
sacred groves 64, 90, 142
sacrifice 36, 128, 178–9
    Iceland 159, 161, 168–9
    Scandinavia 137, 142–3, 149
Saemundr the Wise 166–7
sagas 135, 148, 158–63, 165, 168
saints 66, 80–1, 109
Salic law 77
salvation 2, 15, 20–1, 32, 142–3
Sarapis 5
Saxo Grammaticus 137–8
Saxons 22, 66, 89–90, 120, 124, 127–9
Scandinavia 1, 3, 22, 162
    pre-Christian religion 36, 91–2, 136, 138,
        141–3, 160
    early missions 122–3, 136–7, 139–40, 144

conversion 148–52
Scotland 88, 99
Seaxneat 36, 91–2
Selja 147
Sergius I, pope 120
Severin, St 49
Sicily 48
Sidonius, bishop of Auvergne 67
Sidonius Apollinaris 65–6, 69
Síðu-Hallr 163, 165
Sigbert, king of East Anglia 107
Sigbert, king of Essex 106
Sigfrid, bishop 143–4
Sigismund (Burgundian) 72
Sigurd, bishop 151
Sigurd, jarl of Hlað 143
Silvanus, king 68
Silverius, St, pope 94
Sîntana de Mures 37
skalds 143, 160
Skalholt 167
Skarðsárbók 159
slaves 19, 105
Slavs 79, 127–8, 139
Snorri Sturluson 91, 137–8, 143, 146–7,
    150–1, 158, 162, 164, 168
Socrates Scholasticus 44
Soissons 69, 127
Sol Invictus 34
Sozomen 37, 40, 44
Spain 38, 47, 50–1, 66
Stefni 164, 166
Stefnir Thorgilsson 163
Stiklestad, battle of 151
Stilicho 47
Stoicism 30
Sturm 127–8
Suevi 48, 66, 79
Sulpicius Severus 63–4
supernatural 3, 5, 19
Supreme Being 12–14, 23, 177
Sussex 101, 108, 120
Sutton Hoo 69
Svein I Haraldsson, 'Forkbeard' 145, 147–8
Svolder, battle of 148
Swabians 79
Sweden 136, 139–40, 144, 151
Syagrius 70
Sylvanus 34
syncretism 20–1, 67, 102, 126, 168–9, 178
Synod of Whitby 108, 119

Tacitus 19, 35–8, 43, 69, 90, 92
Teit Ísleifsson 163
Tertullian 88
Tervingi 38, 44–6
Teutons 124
Thanet 93, 96
Thangbrandr 158, 163–4
Theodora, wife of Justinian 50
Theodoret 63
Theodoric, king of the Ostrogoths 49–50, 70–3, 75
Theodoric II, king of the Visigoths 66
Theodoricus 158, 163
Theodosius I, emperor 45–6, 50
theology 22, 32–3, 143, 177
    see also salvation
Theophilus, bishop of the Goths 39
Therasia 63
Theudebert of Austrasia 78
Theuderic of Burgundy 78
Theudis, king 51
Thingvellir 160
Thor 36, 142–3, 149–50, 161, 163
Thorarin Loftunga 151
Thordis 167
Thorgeir 165–6, 168
Thorgils 163
Thorlakr, bishop 166
Thórmöðr 164
Thorvaldr 163
Thuringia 70, 123, 126
Thyri 145
Tiw 36
Tolbiac, battle of 72
Toulouse 66, 75
Tours 63, 71, 75
Trajan, emperor 31
Transylvania 37
Trier 63, 67
Trojan War 91, 138
Trondelag 143
Trondheim 148, 151
Truhtin 129
Trygve, king 147
Tyr 36

Ukraine 37
Ulfila (Wulfilas), bishop 39–2, 44, 46–7, 162
Úlfljót 160

Unni, archbishop 144
Uppsala 8, 142, 144, 148, 151, 160
Urien 105
Valdimarr, king of Russia 146
Valens, emperor in the East 42, 44–6
Valentinian II, emperor 68
Valentinian III, emperor 66
Valhalla 143
Vandals 42, 48–9, 66
Varasci 79
Västergötland 144
Victor of Vita 48–9
Vigilius, pope 94
Viken 147
vikings 139, 141
Virgil 71
Visigoths 42, 45–51, 63, 65–7, 75
Völuspá (The Sibyl's Prophecy) 142, 169
Vortigern, king 90
Vouille, battle of 67

Walcheren 122
Wales 95, 98–100, 105
Wansdyke 169
Water Newton 88
Wecta 90
Wessex 101, 108
Western Empire 42, 49, 51
Whithorn 96
Widsith 138
Widukind (Saxon chieftain) 128
Widukind of Corvei 145
Wihtberht 120
Wihtgils 90
Wilfrid of Hexham 108, 119–20, 123
Willeric, bishop of Bremen 135, 139
Willibald 123–5, 127
Willibrord, bishop of Utrecht 119–24
witan 103–4
Witmar 136–8
Witta 90
Wulfhere, king of Mercia 107–8
Wulframn, bishop of Sens 122
Wynfrith, see Boniface

Yahweh 74
Yeavering 145
Yngvi (Ing) 137

Zosimus 37